TEACHING FOR PEACE AND SOCIAL JUSTICE IN MYANMAR

Peace and Human Rights Education
edited by Monisha Bajaj and Maria Hantzopoulos

This book series brings together cutting-edge scholarship on peace and human rights education from leading scholars and practitioners in the field. It will provide a cross-section of scholarly research as well as conceptual perspectives on the challenges and possibilities of implementing both peace and human rights education in diverse global sites. The series will bring forth the voices of scholars of peace education and human rights education to address key questions for undergraduate- and Masters-level students seeking to deepen their understanding of the field.

Also Available in the Series:
Educating for Peace and Human Rights: An Introduction,
Maria Hantzopoulos and Monisha Bajaj

Advisory Board:

Loreta Castro, *Miriam College, Philippines*
Catalina Crespo Sancho, *Defensora de los Habitantes, Costa Rica*
Nancy Flowers, *Human Rights Educators USA, USA*
Asha Hans, *formerly Utkal University, India*
Andre Keet, *Nelson Mandela University, South Africa*
Margo Okazawa-Rey, *formerly Mills College, USA*
Betty Reardon, *International Institute on Peace Education, USA*
Hakim Williams, *Gettysburg College, USA*
Zeena Zakharia, *University of Massachusetts, USA*
Michalinos Zembylas, *Open University, Cyprus*

TEACHING FOR PEACE AND SOCIAL JUSTICE IN MYANMAR

Identity, Agency, and Critical Pedagogy

Edited by Mary Shepard Wong

BLOOMSBURY ACADEMIC
LONDON • NEW YORK • OXFORD • NEW DELHI • SYDNEY

BLOOMSBURY ACADEMIC
Bloomsbury Publishing Plc
50 Bedford Square, London, WC1B 3DP, UK
1385 Broadway, New York, NY 10018, USA
29 Earlsfort Terrace, Dublin 2, Ireland

BLOOMSBURY, BLOOMSBURY ACADEMIC and the Diana logo are
trademarks of Bloomsbury Publishing Plc

First published in Great Britain 2022
This paperback edition published 2024

Cover design: Charlotte James
Cover image © Fayek Tasneem Khan/Getty Images

A catalogue record for this book is available from the British Library.

A catalog record for this book is available from the Library of Congress.

Library of Congress Cataloging-in-Publication Data
Names: Wong, Mary Shepard, editor.
Title: Teaching for peace and social justice in Myanmar : identity, agency,
and critical pedagogy / edited by Mary Shepard Wong.
Description: London ; New York : Bloomsbury Academic, 2022. | Series: Peace and
human rights education | Includes bibliographical references and index.
Identifiers: LCCN 2022004438 (print) | LCCN 2022004439 (ebook) | ISBN
9781350184077 (hardback) | ISBN 9781350226975 (paperback) |
ISBN 9781350184084 (pdf) | ISBN 9781350184091 (epub)
Subjects: LCSH: Social justice and education–Burma. | Peace–Study and
teaching--Burma. | Critical pedagogy–Burma.
Classification: LCC LC191.98.B8 T43 2022 (print) | LCC LC191.98.B8 (ebook) |
DDC 370.11/5–dc23/eng/20220302
LC record available at https://lccn.loc.gov/2022004438
LC ebook record available at https://lccn.loc.gov/2022004439

ISBN: HB: 978-1-3501-8407-7
           PB: 978-1-3502-2697-5
           ePDF: 978-1-3501-8408-4
           eBook: 978-1-3501-8409-1

Series: Peace and Human Rights Education
Typeset by Integra Software Services Pvt. Ltd.

To find out more about our authors and books visit www.bloomsbury.com
and sign up for our newsletters.

This book is dedicated to the people of Myanmar who are bravely standing up against injustices in their struggle for human rights and peace. We stand with you.

CONTENTS

Part I
AGENCY

Part II
IDENTITY

Part III
CRITICAL PEDAGOGY

TABLES

CONTRIBUTORS

Radka Antalíková, PhD, is Lead Researcher of Thabyay Education Foundation, Myanmar, responsible for coordinating all of the foundation's research activities. From 2018 to 2020, she acted as Research Instructor/Mentor of the Peace Leadership & Research Institute (PLRI), one of the foundation's programs. Prior to working for Thabyay Education Foundation, Radka worked for a number of years as Teaching Assistant Professor at Aalborg University, Denmark, with which she is still affiliated today. In 2016, she took on the position of Academic Skills and Project Management Instructor at Global Border Studies, a university-level program for young refugees from Myanmar, located in Nu Poe Refugee Camp, Thailand. Radka holds a master's degree in Psychology from Comenius University, Slovakia, and a PhD in Cross-Cultural Psychology from Aalborg University, Denmark.

Naw Sah Blute is from the Ayeyarwady Region, Myanmar. She holds a bachelor's degree in English and a graduate diploma in Peace Leadership. She used to work as an English-language training coordinator as well as a freelance translator. After that, she joined Thabyay Education Foundation as Translator and Trainer, delivering teacher trainings and capacity development trainings for youth across the country. Currently, her position at Thabyay is the one of Senior Research Assistant for the Arts and Conflict Transformation project with St. Andrews University, UK. Naw Sah Blute strongly believes that education plays a major role in Myanmar's development as well as peacebuilding.

Erina Iwasaki is a PhD candidate in Comparative and International Education at Teachers College Columbia University, US and Curriculum Advisor to the Khayay International School in Yangon, Myanmar. Having lived in the Republic of Congo, Myanmar, and France for an extensive period of her childhood, her research focuses on multilingual education in West African and Southeast Asian countries. Her dissertation examines bi-multilingual education advocacy in Senegal. She is also a peace education trainer and regular consultant for multilingual education development in Myanmar. Erina holds a master's in Political and Moral Philosophy from the University of Paris-Sorbonne, France and a diploma in American Studies at Smith College, US. She speaks French, Japanese, English, Burmese, and Spanish.

Aung Khine is Civic Education Trainer for Mote Oo Education, Myanmar. He holds a bachelor's degree in Economics from the Institute of Economics Yangon, and Certificate as a Trainer for the Reading and Writing for Critical Thinking International Consortium. He was imprisoned for twelve and half years for involvement in Myanmar's democracy movements and then experienced nine years in exile. He is also a disabled person. Aung Khine has fifteen years of experience as a teacher and trainer of teachers, curriculum designer, researcher, negotiator, facilitator, translator, librarian, and consultant. He is the co-curriculum designer of *Histories of Burma: A Source-Based Approach to the History of Myanmar* (Mote Oo, 2013).

Soe Khine is a pseudonym for a teacher from Rakhine State, Myanmar. Soe Khine is studying for a bachelor's degree from Sittwe University, Myanmar. At the Institute for Political and Civic Engagement at Yangon's American Center, he studied civic education and undertook a training of trainer's course for civic educators. Soe Khine gained a diploma in social sciences in the first year of the program in Sittwe and went on to become a teacher in the second year. Soe Khine teaches subjects of civic education, gender, and human rights. (Soe Khine can be contacted through melwalker.myanmarconsulting@gmail.com.)

Joanne Lauterjung is a technical advisor, process designer, and curriculum specialist focusing on engaged pedagogy and locally driven, collaborative curriculum development. She has thirty years' experience in peacebuilding, communications, and organizational development working in the United States, Germany, Turkey, Fiji, Thailand, and, most recently, for ten years in Myanmar. Joanne is also an evaluator for peace programming and conducts ongoing research on the intersection of culture, arts, and peacebuilding. Joanne holds an MA in Conflict Transformation from Eastern Mennonite University's Center for Justice and Peacebuilding, US. She is a trained mediator and Strategies for Trauma Awareness and Resilience (STAR) practitioner. Joanne has authored two books: *The Community Dialogue* for Karuna Center for Peacebuilding and *Inclusive Peacebuilding: Online Training of Trainers for Gender-Sensitive Peacebuilding* for ChristianAid. She is currently working on a third book as co-author, *Strengthening Everyday Peace Formation through Arts-Based Workshops*, with Graceworks Myanmar. Joanne believes passionately in the power of arts and culture to engage, reflect, and learn in deeply divided societies.

Zoe Matthews is an instructional designer and researcher with almost twenty years of experience in teaching, training, research, and curriculum development. She has spent over ten years designing vulnerable population engagement strategies including targeted programming for migrants, refugee, and IDP adolescents and youth in developing/post-conflict/emerging market settings. She engages in projects that have an end game of normalizing relations and that create an enabling environment for social, political, and economic transformation. She has a Master of Education from the University of Wollongong, Australia. Her research expertise includes learner social identity, the intersection between English-language teaching, translanguaging, and civic and peace education, and the implications of this for teacher education.

Rosalie Metro is Assistant Teaching Professor in the College of Education at the University of Missouri-Columbia, US. In 2011, she earned a PhD in Learning,

Teaching, and Social Policy from Cornell University, US. Her dissertation was titled "History Curricula and the Reconciliation of Ethnic Conflict: A Collaborative Project with Burmese Migrants and Refugees in Thailand." She has been studying the education system in Burma/Myanmar since 2000, and her research interests include the conflicts that arise around history, language, and identity in the classroom. With Aung Khine, she is the co-author of *Histories of Burma: A Source-Based Approach to Myanmar's History*. A former high school social studies teacher, she currently trains teachers in the United States.

Grace Michel, MA, is Assistant Director of the Center for Intercultural Leadership at UC Berkeley, US, where she designs and facilitates experiential workshops and courses to build skills for working effectively across cultural differences. Grace holds an MA in Peace and Justice Studies from University of San Diego, US, and a BA in International Relations from Claremont McKenna College, US. Grace previously served as Assistant Director of the Center for Peace and Commerce, where she helped students launch social enterprises. Grace then went on to fulfill a lifelong goal of living and working in Burma/Myanmar, the country of her mother's origin, where she designed curricula to promote social cohesion and conducted education policy research. She has also volunteered with communities of refugees from Burma in the United States.

Ashley South has twenty years' experience as an independent author, researcher, and consultant. He has a PhD from the Australian National University, Australia, and an MSc from SOAS (University of London), UK, and is a Research Fellow at Chiang Mai University, Thailand. Main research interests: ethnic armed conflicts and peace processes in Burma/Myanmar and Mindanao (politics of legitimacy and governance); forced migration (refugees and internally displaced people); politics of language and education; climate change, resilience and (deep) adaptation; comparative philosophies of peacebuilding. Most of Ashley's published work in Myanmar is available at: www.AshleySouth.co.uk.

Ko Thant is a pseudonym for a teacher from Rakhine State, Myanmar. He has a bachelor's degree from Sittwe University, Myanmar and studied political science at the Institute for Political and Civic Engagement at the American Center in Yangon. He gained a diploma in social sciences in the first year of the program in Sittwe, where he went on to become a teacher in the second year. He teaches subjects of global issues and peace studies. He is also an independent peace trainer for local youth groups. (He can be contacted through melwalker.myanmarconsulting@gmail.com.)

Arkar Phyo Thant studied public health, political science, and philosophy. As a student, he became an activist and worked as a co-secretary, president, and advisor of the student Union in his university. Arkar is involved in supporting the political transition movement of Myanmar. Currently, he is working with People in Need as Project Manager for the social cohesion program in Mon, Kayin, and Rakhine.

Ardeth Maung Thawnghmung is Professor and Chair of political science at the University of Massachusetts Lowell, US, where she also serves as Interim Director of Peace and Conflict Studies. Her areas of research are on Myanmar/Southeast Asia, ethnic conflicts, and political economy. She is the author of several books, including *Behind the Teak Curtain: Authoritarianism, Agricultural Policies, and Political Legitimacy in Rural Burma* and *Everyday Economic Survival in Myanmar* (2019). She is also a co-author of a forthcoming book titled *Winning by Process: The State and Neutralization of Ethnic Minorities in Myanmar* (2022).

Kyawt Thuzar is an independent consultant (Education Policy, and Curriculum and Training) and works with different entities such as Westminster Foundation for Democracy, Institute for Political and Civic Engagement (iPACE), and Search for Common Ground. Her research areas are the sociology of education, educational policy, and education and politics. She holds a Master of Arts in Teaching English as a Second Language (Yangon Institute of Education, Myanmar), a Master of Education in Cultural and Educational Policy Studies (Loyola University Chicago, US), and is a Fulbright scholar.

Melanie Walker is a PhD researcher at the University of New South Wales, Australia, and Research Affiliate at the Regional Center for Social Science and Sustainable Development, Chiang Mai University, Thailand. Melanie's PhD research is on the everyday peacebuilding activities of youth in Rakhine State, Myanmar. Melanie is from the UK and has worked in Myanmar and its borderlands for over fifteen years in non-state education, nonformal education, youth civic empowerment, and civilian protection. Melanie has an MA in International and Development from Leeds University, UK, and has taught and delivered teacher training and civic education/peacebuilding training to young adults in Myanmar, Thailand, Bangladesh, and the UK. Melanie also writes on education on Myanmar's Karen border with Dr. Su-Ann Oh and PhD researcher Hayso Thako.

Tony Waters is Professor of Sociology at Payap University, Chiangmai, Thailand, where he has taught in the Peace Studies Department since 2016. He was also Professor of Sociology at California State University, Chico, US, from 1996 to 2021. Among his books are *Weber's Rationalism and Modern Society* (2015), *Schooling, Bureaucracy, and Childhood* (2012), *When Killing Is a Crime* (2007), and *Bureaucratizing the Good Samaritan* (2001). More recently, he published articles about Thai literature, the sociology of music, and international education. He is an occasional contributor to *The Irrawaddy* (Yangon).

Jasmine Tintut Williams is a multilingual education consultant and master's graduate from Teachers College, Columbia University, US, in International Educational Development. As an education consultant, she currently works in Kachin and Northern Shan developing curriculum and education materials. She has conducted multiple research projects in Myanmar, including her most recent work leading an ethnic-language-based multilingual education study across six

States in Myanmar to support the development of national languages-in-education programs. Her devotion to language rights and peace/human rights education in Myanmar stems from her upbringing as a half-Burmese/American woman in a family of educators.

Mary Shepard Wong is a three-time Fulbright scholar (Hong Kong 2012–13; Myanmar 2015–16; Taiwan 2022–3). She has authored or been the lead editor of four books and has written nineteen book chapters and numerous journal articles. Her research interests include language teacher education in Myanmar, language policy in education, social justice-oriented content and pedagogy, and the role of religion in language learning and teaching. She holds a doctorate in International Education (USC, US) and master degrees in East Asian Languages and Cultures (UCLA, US) and TESOL (APU, US). She is Professor at Azusa Pacific University in southern California, US, where she directs the field-based graduate TESOL program. She has taught English and been in teacher education for over three decades in the United States, China, Thailand, and Myanmar.

Kinsa San Yi is from Kachin State, Myanmar. She holds a bachelor's degree in chemistry and a graduate diploma in peace leadership. San Yi is a young researcher with a focus on peace education, conflict resolution, and economic governance. She has worked for different nongovernmental organizations, most recently for The Asia Foundation Myanmar and the Norwegian Refugee Council. Currently, she is working for the American Friends Service Committee as a Program Coordinator with the purpose of improving good governance and local economic development. San Yi's personal working goal is to enhance Myanmar's peacebuilding and sustainable economic development.

Kaung Zan works for Mote Oo Education, Myanmar, as a teacher/trainer, assisting the development of teachers in the adult education and postsecondary education sectors, mostly in the border areas of Myanmar. He travels throughout Myanmar as a teacher-trainer, working with education groups on teacher development, curriculum development, and quality evaluation. He is a freelance translator/ interpreter and dialogue facilitator.

Katie Zanoni holds an EdD in International and Multicultural Education from the University of San Francisco, US (2018), and is a lecturer at the University of San Diego, US. Katie is the co-founder of Education for Transformation, a consultancy group of scholar-practitioners advancing transformative approaches to education for peace and human rights. She has twenty years of experience in program design and management in the education and nonprofit sector. Katie works both locally and internationally and maintains a critical lens to examine issues of power, gender, race, and culture within her communities of practice to build trust and reciprocity.

PEACE AND HUMAN RIGHTS EDUCATION SERIES FOREWORD

By Maria Hantzopoulos and Monisha Bajaj

Over the past five decades, both Peace Education and Human Rights Education have emerged from the margins to become legitimate academic fields with a burgeoning and rich body of scholarship. We have seen both fields over time be influenced and framed by critical feminist thought, demilitarization and peace studies, movements for climate justice, decolonial and postcolonial engagement, and indigeneity, raising critical issues and reflection for future directions of the field. While there have been both a proliferation of books related to these fields and an exponential increase in journals dedicated to the topics (such as the *International Journal of Human Rights Education, the Human Rights Education Review, the Journal of Peace Education, In Factis Pax*, among others), this book series on Peace and Human Rights Education is the first of its kind. Encompassing two related fields that are in dialogue with each other—Peace Education & Human Rights Education—the contributions to the series need not cover both fields, but together will advance our understandings of their role in educational development and transformation.

This series highlights the central ideas, issues, debates, and questions surrounding peace and human rights education by bringing together cutting-edge scholarship on these fields, both separately and concurrently, from leading theorists, scholars, and practitioners in the field. The type of work in this series is robust—from the conceptual, to the reflective, to the empirical—as we aim to provide a cross-section of scholarly research that projects the dynamism of both fields as they have evolved over time. As a result, there are several overarching goals of the series, including (1) to highlight groundbreaking and rich studies and research on human rights and peace education around the globe; (2) to analyze limits and possibilities in the localization of peace education and human rights education in diverse contexts; (3) to analyze historical contexts that have shaped the directions of the fields; (4) to amplify marginalized voices and scholarship; and (5) to serve as the nexus for key debates, questions, and issues in the field.

We launched the series with our own book, *Educating for Peace and Human Rights: An Introduction*, to lay the groundwork of the foundations of each field and explore the fertile terrain that lies at their intersection, conceptualized through the heuristic of a banyan tree nourished by the shared soil of core concepts such as dignity and transformative agency. One of the unique features of banyan trees is their capacity to drop down new roots (which, over time, conjoin with the primary trunk). We argue that these new drop-down roots are the renewals of the field, some which branch out in new directions, others that coalesce with the trunk and become central components of the tree. We envision each subsequent book in this series as a branch or drop-down root that offers new insights in distinct contexts and deepens our understanding of how liberatory education—namely efforts toward peace, human rights, and social justice education—is enacted, contested, and advanced in different local, transnational, and global settings.

Our series advisory board, who are leaders in the fields, provide sound guidance, expertise, and perspective on frameworks developed and future directions of the fields. While some advisory board members are rooted more centrally in peace education, and others more firmly in human rights education, we have many members whose work also rests at the intersections of those fields. We hope that collectively this series provides space for scholars, students, and practitioners to pursue new pathways for the fields, recognizing that multiple realities and worlds (human, natural, and spiritual) coexist (Mignolo, 2018), as this series maps the multiple and possible trajectories. We aim to allow room for learning from and across other fields, and for meaningful engagement with feminist, decolonial, and other critical approaches that interrogate taken-for-granted or normative assumptions that undergird the fields. We are excited that this series will encourage more robust conceptual considerations, innovative methodological approaches, and rigorous empirical work, yielding new insights as we continue to respond to the contemporary challenges we face locally, transnationally, and globally.

Mary Shepard Wong's edited book, *Teaching for Peace and Social Justice in Myanmar*, takes up these challenges and considers how to teach peace when peace itself is politicized and authoritarian violence is looming. Drawing from practitioners and peace educators active on the ground in diverse regions of Myanmar, as well as from those outside of Myanmar that work alongside local actors, the contributions represent the linguistic, ethnic, and religious diversity that exists within Myanmar and amplifies local voices, experiences, and knowledges. Across multiple chapters, Wong asks contributors to consider "How are various actors in Myanmar raising awareness, fostering attitudes, and teaching skills that are needed to bring about more peaceful communities and a more just state? And how might what they are doing be adapted for use in other contexts?" Given the subsequent post-February 2021 coup, these questions are even more relevant as the work of local actors may also contribute "to the current Civil Disobedience Movement (CDM) in Myanmar, in which people are bravely standing up against injustice even at the risk of their lives (p. 11, this volume)." By framing the book into sections on agency, identity, and critical pedagogy, Wong and the authors disentangle the ways in which peace and peace education might manifest in their particular context, amidst large-scale state-sanctioned and authoritarian violence. This edited volume deepens our understandings of education and peacebuilding localized in one national context in contested and diverse ways. Yet, it also simultaneously provides practitioners and scholars beyond Myanmar rich, illustrative examples of peacebuilding that can transcend that particular context. We are excited for others to grapple and engage with this dynamic text that we have also found so instructive and generative for our own practice and scholarship in peace and human rights education.

FOREWORD

Ardeth Maung Thawnghmung

Myanmar's military coup has destroyed lives, dreams, and the economy. It has been emotionally and physically devastating not just for the country's youth, who grew up in a relatively freer political environment than earlier generations, but also for those like myself, who grew up under an earlier junta in the 1970s and 1980s, briefly interrupted by nationwide democracy demonstrations in 1988 before they were repressed by security forces who imposed another round of repressive military rule. We welcomed and embraced a series of political reforms over the last decade, despite their imperfections, and believed we had finally seen the light at the end of the tunnel after decades of lost opportunities. Many of our "88 Generation" have returned to Myanmar to participate in rebuilding the country in whatever way we can or had planned to make these contributions in the future. Our dreams were destroyed as we helplessly watched the history of 1988 repeating itself in 2021. But to some extent, the February coup has occurred in a drastically different context from the events of that fateful year. This time around, there is a sizeable Myanmar diaspora in Asia, Europe, Australia, and North America who support the anti-coup movement, the targeted assassination of alleged "collaborators" and explosions in urban areas, and the widespread availability of internet helps the opposition movement share information and coordinate their activities. It is nonetheless still a déjà vu moment, characterized as in 1988 by the fleeing of young people to border areas controlled by non-state armed groups, attempts by the exile government to draft another federal constitution, and divisions within the anti-coup opposition that has allowed the military to divide and rule.

I was a product of the 1988 pro-democracy movement which was crushed by Senior General Than Shwe's military dictatorship. I left the country in search of better educational opportunities in 1990. Mary Wong was the instructor of the very first class in America I took in the summer of that year at Pasadena City College. She taught non-English speakers and helped give them a smooth transition into other subjects. I remembered her as a very lively, passionate, and captivating teacher who was firm but helpful, generous, and dedicated. She talked a lot about China, so at first I did not feel like I shared many common academic interests with her. I was also struggling financially and emotionally, hardly participated in class discussion, and barely kept up with the class assignments. So when I bumped into her at the college's cafeteria the following semester, she looked at me in disbelief, asking: "Aren't you supposed to repeat the class?" I replied to her that I got a B in her class, which qualified me to move on to the next class, and moved quickly away from her before she even said another word. That was the end of our conversation until we reconnected in 2016 and accidentally and surprisingly rediscovered the brief past we once shared. Never in a million years would I have imagined that I would one day reunite with my first teacher, let alone seeing her in Myanmar as a person with avid personal and academic interest in the country I call home. That was the reason why we did not recognize each other when she was introduced as a Fulbright scholar in Myanmar by some mutual friends in 2010. She also looked even younger, and more vibrant and energetic, than she was twenty years ago.

Many things had happened in the decades since we first met. I completed my undergraduate degree and went on to do my master's and PhD. I cautiously conducted my PhD field research in 1999 under Than Shwe's dictatorship and went back to the country almost every summer, never knowing whether my visa would be rejected, or my stay revoked. My first sense of freedom in Myanmar was in 2011 at Yangon International Airport when I was greeted by unusually friendly immigration and customs officers who no longer subjected me to lengthy interrogations or meticulously rifled through my luggage like their predecessors did. My colleague, who was hounded by special intelligence officers just a year prior, was summoned to meet with Thein Sein, the new president, and eventually became his advisor. Thein Sein's government implemented democratic reforms that allowed people to express themselves more openly, introduced checks and balances against various centers of political power, offered economic opportunities, and facilitated top-level peace negotiations. It also welcomed nongovernment organizations to engage in activities that attempted to heal deeply polarized and wounded communities. Unfortunately, a grassroots approach to peacebuilding, and the teaching of the values of diversity and tolerance in schools and the community, was neglected in favor of top-level negotiations such as the Nationwide Ceasefire Agreement.

It is my pleasure to introduce you to this very timely and important volume edited by Dr. Mary Wong, which focuses on a topic that has received insufficient scholarly attention so far. The book discusses a variety of approaches toward an inclusive educational curriculum to build trust, establish mutual understanding, and be more sensitive to the needs of women, minorities, and people with disabilities, in order to set a foundation for peace among different ethnic and religious groups in Myanmar. It focuses on peace promotion in the classroom, a crucial venue of learning and socialization, in addition to the realm of the family, communities, and religious institutions. Dr. Wong has gathered outstanding contributors from a diverse range of disciplines and professions, across different ethnic, religious, and nationality backgrounds, who each share their experiences in various parts of Myanmar. Their myriad backgrounds, approaches, and orientations on an understudied subject make this volume truly outstanding and remarkable. Most chapters are situated within specific and relevant political and social contexts and begin with an introduction of each author's background, and how it helped shape their reflections and critical evaluations of Myanmar's existing education system, teaching methods, and curriculum. They each offer new approaches to promote social justice, equality, and empathy.

Numerous community leaders and members of nongovernment organizations, including authors in this volume, have joined the civil disobedience movement opposing the coup, and supported in varying capacities or participated in a parallel government now known as the National Unity Government (NUG). Despite many challenges and limitations, the NUG has quickly adopted policies that are more inclusive and sensitive to the needs of minorities. This development may have partly resulted from the scale and brutality of recent military repression, allowing the country's ethnic Bamar majority to better understand the minority who have historically suffered disproportionately from military atrocities. But there is no doubt that increased awareness of and exposure to human rights, federalism, and tolerance for differences, through a series of workshops, pilot projects, and media coverage during Myanmar's brief democratic era, have prepared civil society groups to push for more drastic reforms in the aftermath of the coup. This edited volume sheds light on some aspects of those grassroots efforts to promote peace, justice, and equality that have been incubated over the past decade and will help guide the nature and direction of opposition to authoritarian rule in the future.

ACKNOWLEDGEMENTS

I would like to express my deep appreciation for the contributors in this volume who work tirelessly as peace workers in Myanmar, often in difficult conditions without the acknowledgement and support they deserve. To ask these peace workers to carve out extra time to write a chapter for an academic text in English, which in many cases is not their first language, is a demanding request. When the pandemic hit in early 2020 disrupting their work and access to the people and resources needed for this project, their challenges were exacerbated. When the February 1, 2021, coup took place in Myanmar, everything changed. Some of the authors had to leave Myanmar, and some who stayed relocated to safety. The local authors and their students were demonstrating to the world how to stand up to injustice. To have twenty-one contributors produce chapters for this volume in spite of these difficulties is extraordinary, especially for those inside Myanmar.

Earlier in the process, when a few contributors asked for a group Zoom call for encouragement, I jumped at the idea. For the first time, we came together virtually, joining from numerous countries and time zones as we shared how we were finding ways to collaborate from a distance during a pandemic. Most chapters have Myanmar-based nationals as co-authors paired with authors who were working in Myanmar. The call rallied us and we were back on track. I have learned so much from these peace workers/authors. Due to the pandemic, my sabbatical, which would have taken me to Myanmar to engage in peacebuilding research while working on this book, had to be postponed. The delay was hard to accept, but as I read the insights and passion of each chapter I received, I was renewed with a sense of purpose. Thank you! This book was written to celebrate you and your work.

I also want to thank Mark Richardson of Bloomsbury for his support of the book and the co-editors of the series, Maria Hantzopoulos and Monisha Bajaj. I approached them at the Comparative and International Education Society (CIES) conference in San Francisco with my idea of a volume that highlighted the voices of local peace workers in Myanmar, and they embraced the idea. I had read their edited volume *Peace Education: International Perspectives*, and knew I wanted to work with them and Bloomsbury. The timing for their call for books in their Peace and Human Rights Education series was fortuitous.

Thanks also goes to the Provost's office at Azusa Pacific University, which provided two small grants through the Office of Research and Grants to enable me to work on the book. Specifically, release time from two courses over two terms to meet with a small group of scholars with whom I could discuss the work and receive critical feedback that led to this volume. In addition, a summer Malibu writers' retreat offered through the Provost's office provided uninterrupted time to pull the final manuscript together.

I would not have gotten into this work or been able to continue it without several small grants that I received, first from Fulbright in 2015, and then The United Board for Christian Higher Education in Asia in 2016. World Learning and the US Department of State provided funding for the Pedagogies of Peace Workshops at the Jefferson Center in Mandalay in 2018. The UB funded workshop in January of 2020 through Payap University enabling us to travel to Mandalay University who hosted our week-long Peacebuilding across the Curriculum Workshops for university faculty. My heartfelt thanks for these small grants that provided access to the peacebuilding community in Myanmar and served as the impetus for this book.

Finally, I would like to thank my husband, Sam, who was born in Rangoon (now Yangon). He has supported me in our many trips to Myanmar from 1998 to 2020 in my efforts to support peace education. After many of the workshops, he would keep in touch with participants and arrange for us to reunite in tea houses on our return visits, which I am looking forward to doing again as soon as conditions permit.

ACRONYMS

AFPFL	Anti-Fascist People's Freedom League
ARSA	Arakan Rohingya Salvation Army
ASEAN	Association of Southeast Asian Nations
CBO(s)	Community-Based Organizations
CESD	Center for Economic and Social Development
CDC	Child Development Center
CDM	Civil Disobedience Movement
CIES	Comparative and International Education Society
CLS	City Life Survey
CPE	Cultural Political Economy
CSO(s)	Civil Society Organization
DKBA	Democratic Karen Buddhist Army
DRL	Department of Human Rights and Labor
EAO(s)	Ethnic Armed Organization
EBEP(s)	Ethnic Based Education Provider
ELB-MLE	Ethnic Language-Based Multilingual Education
EPWG	Education for Peace Working Group
ICCS	International Civic and Citizenship Education Study
ICT	Information and Communications Technology
IDP(s)	Internally Displaced People
INEB	International Network of Engaged Buddhism
INGO(s)	International Non-Governmental Organization
iPACE	Institute for Political and Civic Engagement
IWP	International Women's Parternership for Peace and Justice
JPF	Joint Peace Fund
KCO	The Karen Central Organization
KCP	Karuna Center for Peacebuilding
KECD	Karen Education and Culture Department
KIA	Kachin Independence Army
KNDO	Karen National Defense Organization
KNLA	Karen National Liberation Army
KNU	Karen National Union

L1-based MLE	First Language-Based Multilingual Education
L1/L2	First/Second Language
LGBTQ	Lesbian, gay, bisexual, transgender and queer or questioning
LST	Learn and Share Together
MNEC	Mon National Education Committee
MNLA	Mon National Liberation Army
MoE	Ministry of Education
MTBE/MTB	Mother Tongue-Based Education
MTB-MLE	Mother Tongue-Based Multilingual Education
NCA	Nationwide Ceasefire Agreement
NESP	National Education Strategic Plan
NGO(s)	Non-Governmental Organization
NLD	National League for Democracy
NUG	National Unity Government
PIN	People in Need
PBC	Peace-Building Champions
PLRI	Peace Leadership & Research Institute
RFP(s)	Requests for Proposals
SDG(s)	Sustainable Development Goals
SLORC	State Law and Order Restoration Council
SPDC	State Peace and Development Council
STARS	Strategies for Trauma Awareness and Resilience
STEM	Strengthening pre-service Teacher Education in Myanmar
TC	Teachers College, Columbia University
TESOL	Teaching English to Speakers of Other Languages
TTT	Train the Trainer
UN	United Nations
UNESCO	United Nations Educational, Scientific and Cultural Organization
WEIRD	Western, Educated, Industrial, Rich, and Democratic

MAP

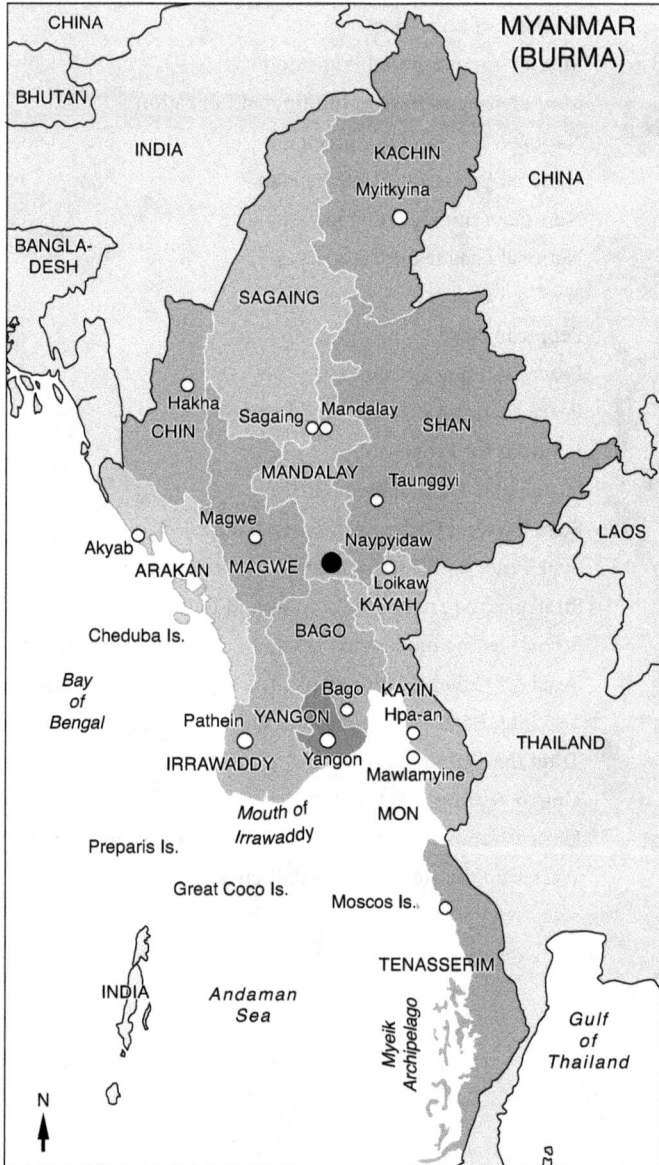

CHINA

MYANMAR
(BURMA)

BHUTAN

INDIA

KACHIN

Myitkyina

CHINA

BANGLA-
DESH

SAGAING

Hakha
Sagaing   Mandalay
CHIN

SHAN

MANDALAY

Taunggyi

Magwe

Naypyidaw

LAOS

Akyab

ARAKAN   MAGWE

Loikaw
KAYAH

Cheduba Is.

BAGO

Bay
of
Bengal

Bago   KAYIN

Pathein   YANGON   Hpa-an

THAILAND

IRRAWADDY   Yangon
Mawlamyine

Mouth of
Irrawaddy   MON

Preparis Is.

Great Coco Is.   Moscos Is.

TENASSERIM

INDIA   Andaman
Sea

Myeik
Archipelago

Gulf
of
Thailand

N

Map 1 Map of Burma/Myanmar.

Introduction

TEACHING FOR PEACE IN MYANMAR: WHAT'S AT STAKE

Mary Shepard Wong

Introduction

This volume focuses on the praxis of teaching for peace on the local level and seeks to answer the questions posed by Bajaj and Hantzopoulos (2016), "How are various actors designing and implementing peace education endeavors [and] how are educators and learners making meaning of such peace education efforts?" (p. 6). While the concept of seeking wisdom and insights on peacebuilding from local practitioners is not new, a volume with almost half of its authors from Myanmar, a country with the notorious distinction of having one of the longest civil wars in history, is unique. To contextualize and humanize the process of teaching for peace, most chapters are launched with personal narratives. In keeping with this practice, I start this introduction with my story of how I found my way into this field and to this book on peacebuilding in Myanmar, and the question of what is at stake if we fail to teach for peace.

A Rude Awakening and a Late-Life Crisis

In the early 1990s, I had just received my master's degree in Teaching English to Speakers of Other Languages (TESOL) and landed a full-time position at a community college not far from South Central Los Angeles. Having passed my comprehensive TESOL exams as well as the interview for one of the few full-time ESL positions available at the community college level in the area, I felt prepared for anything. Apparently, I was not ready for the 1992 LA Uprising, a six-day "race riot" as some referred to it, that took place not far from our college, resulting in sixty-three deaths and thousands of injuries and arrests and a wakeup call that not all was well in the heart of Los Angeles. I had not been taught how to respond to post-conflict scenarios in which Black students were being targeted by those sworn to protect them, and Korean shop owners, including my students, had taken up guns to defend their stores from looters. I had students on both sides of the conflict in my classes that spring of 1992. Do we just continue with the past progressive, or do we talk about what happened, and was still happening, and if so, how? Simply saying "Please note the use of the past progressive in your response to the question, what were you doing last night when the fighting, looting and fires broke out?" did not seem like an adequate response.

About a decade later, it was déjà vu. There I was, this time with a freshly minted PhD in International Education from the University of Southern California. It was the first weeks of my full-time position at this university, but I was so confident in my abilities that I had agreed to allow a Chinese delegation of about a half dozen people to sit in the back of my ESL class to observe. They ended up coming back to observe another day because all planes were grounded and they could not return to China. It was September 11, 2001. The visitors got to see firsthand how I would handle a class of students from all over the world, including the Middle East, respond to this event. Perhaps the guests emboldened me, but I told the students to return their textbooks to the bookstore and I created a new syllabus. The focus of our writing class would be 9/11 and their analysis of the event and its aftermath. We established ground rules for the course and civil open discourse. They would work in small groups to find, read, discuss, summarize, and synthesize related articles, and draft a paper that the students would be writing, editing, and sharing throughout the course. This time, we dealt with what was happening head on, and came together to try to understand it through group reading and writing projects.

Fast-forward about two decades, and I am still at that same university, now a professor who researches and writes about intercultural communication, religious identity, and educational language policy in Myanmar—but also peacebuilding. It may seem odd for a language teacher educator to focus on peacebuilding. Perhaps it is a kind of late-life crisis, but the more I engage in research, the question of why we teach languages looms larger than how it is done. There is a convenient overlap of social justice and peace between the fields of language and culture learning. Learning about and respecting the Other is key to intercultural communication. English, on the other hand, seems to have a more sinister history as English has played no small part in the colonization and oppression of peoples in many parts of the world, sometimes leading to the death of languages and cultures when English replaced nondominant languages at the early primary levels of education. As one ages, one tends to think about legacy, and what one has done to make the world a better place. Producing better English speakers is not as compelling a raison d'être compared to advancing social justice and world peace. Thus, peacebuilding is now the focus of my scholarship, research, and teaching.

After this chapter draft was completed, Covid-19 broke out, and soon after that the George Floyd arrest recording was made public showing a police officer holding Mr. Floyd down in a choke hold that resulted in his death in spite of his continued cries of "I can't breathe." This enraged not only people of color, but all people of conscience. This injustice, and those that preceded it, sparked some of the largest protests we have witnessed in decades in the United States. It reminded me of the LA Uprising of 1992, but this one was different. It felt like it was everywhere and impacted everyone. Systemic racism and white supremacy were not topics limited to our classes. The nation was being schooled, and these topics were being discussed while we "sheltered at home" watching protests on our screens and on the streets, or joining protests with masks and social distancing. If good came of this, it was that more of us were finally getting it. I wondered what previous students who had questioned whether systemic racism "was a thing" (their words) in former Intercultural Communication courses were thinking now. The nation was having a crash course in injustice and our complicity in it. An awakening was taking place but not just for me, as this one was on a national scale. A spate of webinars took place to inform faculty how to change their curriculum and pedagogy to be antiracist. Academic organizations provided links to a host of antiracist educational resources. In addition, conferences addressing these issues became available, including one that I chaired.

In saying I am now concerned with more than just teaching English, I do not mean to convey that helping people learn to speak additional languages is not important. It is! In fact, the language classroom can be a place where students interact with people they might never have met otherwise and thus it has great potential for learning with and from the Other (the contact hypothesis). The language classroom is also where students can acquire not only an additional language, but a new identity and an expanded worldview. Language students can hone their communication skills needed for peacebuilding such as deep listening, speaking with respect, showing concern, and inviting others to talk when they practice these skills while engaging in small groups and task-based learning, often used in language classrooms. Students can learn to apply a critical lens to critique oppressive systems through topics that focus on current events and issues of social justice, sometimes found in English-language texts, and I assume other foreign language textbooks. I have invested forty years in the field of language education, and see great value in it. My point here is that my focus in teacher education has shifted from merely teaching others to improve the English of their students, to enlarging their students understandings of the "peace dividend" (Wong, 2019) that learning and valuing other languages, cultures, and peoples can have. It is exciting to see how new trends, such as translanguaging, are being explored to support this more inclusive, anti-hegemonic view of language learning and teaching.

Education is both powerful and dangerous. As Paulo Freire noted, education can either indoctrinate or liberate; it can be a tool for conformity or transformation. Metro (2019) reminds us that education can have other results by stagnating in the "meh" middle, avoiding either extreme but resulting in mixed results and the loss of the full transformative potential that peace education can have. I contend that education is crucial to peacebuilding, but it needs to be a critical education which interrogates inequalities, examines power structures, and acknowledges and unleashes agency to teachers and students.

Since international education was my training, and Southeast Asia where I often worked and researched, I made Myanmar, the country where my husband was born, my focus. Myanmar has experienced rapid change. After six decades of civil war, international isolation, and neglect of the education sector, the past decade witnessed a gradual opening up and lessening of restrictions, with the emergence of a limited democracy. This ended abruptly on February 1, 2021, with the military coup and the violence the junta unleashed on their own people. Even before the coup and people's impressive united and sustained protest, Myanmar was a rich context to learn of the possibilities of teaching for peace and responding to social injustices. Through leading three study abroad trips on the Thai/Burma border, engaging in a Fulbright at Yangon University, and speaking at several conferences in Myanmar spanning over a decade, I have had the opportunity to hear dozens of stories for the struggle for peace and I wanted those stories to be shared. That is how this book came about.

This is my fourth edited volume, and as the editor I see my role as creating a space where something creative and transformative can take place by bringing together people who have common passions. It is a space where we share our stories, learn from each other, and encourage and inspire those who join. We speak of circles of communities of practice, but we should consider our scholarly circles to be more like horseshoes, creating a space for others to join. For those of us in power, who have access to publishing, an antiracist practice is to welcome and support indigenous voices that have not been heard. This book, with almost half of the authors from Myanmar, is an attempt to do that. So welcome to our open community. We don't have all the answers or agree on all the ones we have, but we are open to being informed and influenced by one another.

Why the Focus on Identity, Agency, and Critical Pedagogy?

I woke up in Mandalay in 2018, the morning I was to deliver a lecture with five words in my head that encapsulated what I was trying to convey on the topic "pedagogies of peace." The five words form three questions: *Who's missing? Why? What next?* This seems to be the core of what educators who are concerned about social justice and peacebuilding are asking. Who is missing in our classrooms, textbooks, graduation ceremonies, school administration, media, movies and soap operas, businesses, leadership positions, government representatives? And as a consequence of their absence, whose languages and cultures are being ignored and excluded?

The subtitle of this volume is *Identity, Agency, and Critical Pedagogy*. This first question of who is missing addresses identity, while the next question, why are they missing, addresses the critical aspect of this book. Why do some groups not have the same access to quality education and do not enjoy the same graduation rates and outcomes that the dominant group has? The critical view taken in this book interrogates the power structures in place that prevent some groups from achieving as much as other groups can. A critical peace education lens examines identity-based violence and entrenched structural and cultural violence as causes of their invisibility and obstacles that certain groups may encounter more than others.

The final question what next? addresses agency and pedagogy. What can we do about this, and more specifically, what can teachers do? Teachers are everywhere, in every providence, city, town, and village, and have abundant access to the country's most valuable resource, its young people. Teachers can and are changing the world, although they may not all be totally aware of their agency to do so.

These stories will hopefully encourage them and embolden them in their work. But before we turn to the stories of Myanmar's peace entrepreneurs, I will provide some definitions of key terms, a sample analytical framework, a brief background on Burma/Myanmar, the book's purpose and format, and conclude with the chapter summaries.

Definition of Key Terms

Peace and Peace Education

Verma (2017) states that peace is undefined, but notes this ambiguity is a double-edged sword as it empowers students to "continually define and redefine peace in meaningful and engaged dialogue and hence create radical openings" (p. 8). This is akin to Freire's thoughts on critical pedagogy which he said must be constantly made and remade. It also resonates with Bajaj and Hantzopoulos' (2016) claim that the diversity of local meanings of peace is a strength (p. 234). Peace is often defined not just by the absence of violence (negative peace), but by the presence of just and equitable nonviolent means to address conflict and injustice (positive peace). Moreover, comprehensive peace addresses structural and indirect violence, such as racism and sexism, and when access to resources such as food, health, employment, or educational opportunities is diverted to the wealthy or privileged groups such as the military in some contexts. Comprehensive peace also addresses cultural violence, which are aspects of culture, including language, ideology, religion, and science used to justify structural violence, making it seem natural or normal. My understanding of peace requires ongoing work in at least three dimensions: the protection of human rights (legal/political dimensions), the understanding of the causes of conflict and the importance of diversity (intellectual/educational dimensions), and the development of human compassion (spiritual/religious/social dimensions).

Comprehensive peace education helps people acquire and apply the knowledge, attitudes, and skills needed for peacebuilding in order to transform the world to be more just, understanding, and compassionate in every discipline including law, politics, business, art, economics, communication, media/film, education, religion, science, and health. Although education is often a place of indoctrination rather than transformation, educators can play a key role in peacebuilding with an education-for-peace approach to their pedagogy and scholarship. Reardon defines peace education as "educational policy, planning, pedagogy, and practice that can provide learners—in any setting—with the skills and values to work towards comprehensive peace" (as cited in Bajaj, 2008, p. 1). Just as wars begin with thoughts that take root in our minds and hearts, so too does peace begin in our imagination, or what Lederach (2005) calls "the moral imagination." Thus, peace can be fostered and taught. Educating for peace is no easy task since learners come with memories of injustices that need to be voiced, misinformation that needs to be unlearned, and hurtful ways of interacting that need to be challenged and changed. For transformation to take place, educators from pre-kindergarten classrooms to postdoctorate research teams, to community-based workers, need to be aware of what is at stake if we neglect to foster human compassion in students and fail to prioritize the teaching and research of issues that impede human flourishing. What is at stake if education for peace is neglected is not only the quality of life, but the ability for some to live their lives at all.

Social Justice and Social Justice-Oriented Teaching

Pope Paul VI (among others) has stated, "if you want peace, work for justice," speaking to the connection between peace and justice, and more specifically to social justice, which is concerned with providing all people access to the resources (food, health, transportation, education, meaning work) that allows them to thrive, regardless of their social class, cultural background, religious beliefs, or other ascribed or avowed identities. When educators seek to apply a social justice approach to their teaching and to teacher education, this, according to Zeichner (2011), "goes beyond a celebration of diversity to attempt to prepare teachers who are willing and able to work within and outside of their classrooms to change the inequities that exist in both schooling and the wider society" (p. 10). A social justice-oriented teaching framework is not just teaching about social justice, it is using social justice as a lens to guide the curriculum, pedagogy, and assessment and applying and engaging in social justice not just in the classroom, but in society and the world.

Identity, Agency, and Intersectionality

Identity and agency are foundational to peace education since they contribute to why and how peace educators engage in their work. Identities, both ascribed and avowed, are complex, multiple, dynamic, and fluid, and interact in ways that both provide and deny privilege. Intersectionality, defined as "the interconnected nature of social categorizations such as race, class, and gender, regarded as creating overlapping and interdependent systems of discrimination or disadvantage" (Oxford Dictionary), is important to peace work. Overlapping identity markers can cause a complex convergence of oppression. For example, if someone is from the non-dominant religious group, does not speak the dominant language, and is perceived as not coming from the dominant ethnic group, that person faces multiple interwoven and compounded prejudices and barriers. While just one of these identities alone would likely cause barriers to receiving a high-quality education, work, and housing conditions, the additional overlapping identities intensify the oppression.

Hantzopoulos and Bajaj (2021) discuss the importance of human dignity and transformative agency to both human rights education and peace education, which they see as intertwined. They demonstrate that by focusing on the local learners and their understandings of peace in their contexts, we can view peace education as a prism refracted in multiple ways rather than a top-down Western notion applied to all contexts in a monolithic, normalized, universal way. Dignity and agency are foundational to envisioning and bringing about a more just world based on the Freirean tenants of pedagogy that equalizes teacher and student roles in the co-construction of knowledge, the understanding that knowledge is never neutral, and a problem-posing approach to education that requires critical reflection on the world and actions taken to transform it.

Critical Pedagogy, Critical Theory, and Critical Peace Education

Critical pedagogy/theory, based on Paulo Freire's notion of "conscientization," encourages learners to follow the power, to pose problems and challenge their social conditions, to question and analyze their historical realities, and to work toward a more democratic society. Critical Peace Education, according to Bajaj (2008), pays attention to structural inequalities, local understandings, and transformative agency. The goal of peace education, according to Bajaj (2008), is the "transformation of educational content, structure, and pedagogy to address direct and structural forms of violence at all levels" (p. 135). Bajaj argues for a "politicization approach" that goes beyond the idealistic, intellectual, and ideological approaches as described by Haavelsrud (1996). It calls for investigation into local realities and action for social justice. Hantzopoulos and Bajaj (2021) note that peace and human rights education can be both formal and informal as well as both explicit and implicit. They state that some of the most radical forms of peace education may not happen in classrooms, but in community-based projects, and in spaces where teaching may need to be implicit rather than explicit due to the backlash or undermining what may happen if terms like "human rights" were used directly, or used in more formal educational contexts. Thus, critical peace education is not conscribed to classrooms or a set of terms.

The 4R Peace and Social Justice Analytical Framework

Chapter authors of this book were encouraged to include a theoretical framework that informed the creation, implementation, and evaluation of their educational peace initiatives. One social justice-oriented framework that can be used to analyze teachers' role as peace agents in Myanmar is the 4Rs Framework (Redistribution, Recognition, Representation, Reconciliation). It provides a holistic approach to understand the full potential teachers can have in peace education, acknowledging that transformation of enduring and systemic unjust structures is necessary in addition to educational and teacher-led efforts (Lopes Cardozo & Maber, 2019). Novelli and Sayed's (2016) table of teacher agency outlines how the 4R framework can be used as a tool to assess the extent that education is or is not supporting the peace process. It helps to determine what inequalities are addressed in the redistribution of resources, the recognition of difference, the representation and participation of teachers in education and peace process, and in the reconciliation process, referring to dealing with past wrongs and injustices. In Wong (2019), I added an additional column to highlight how language policies and practices in particular were supporting peacebuilding in Myanmar (see the last column in Table 0.1, "Potential indicators that language policies and practices support peacebuilding").

Table 0.1 Analyzing Teacher Agency through the 4Rs with Special Consideration of Language-in-Education Policies and Practices

	Potential indicators that education is supporting teacher agency for peacebuilding	Potential indicators that language policies and practices are supporting peacebuilding
Redistribution (addressing inequalities)	• Equitable resource distribution as well as vocational and developmental opportunities for teachers from diverse identity groups • Targeted deployment and recruitment to redress inequities • Capacity development to effectively address inequalities in the classroom, and the school	• Equitable language resource distribution as well as vocational and developmental for teachers from diverse language groups • Targeted deployment and recruitment to redress inequities in language use • Capacity development to effectively address inequalities in the classroom, and school in terms of language use
Recognition (respecting difference)	• Diversification of the teaching work force • Empowering teachers to recognize and respect differences • Empowering teachers to communicate differences empathically and conflict-sensitively	• Diversification of the teaching work force in terms of their language use • Empowering teachers to recognize and respect linguistic differences • Empowering teachers to communicate language differences empathically and conflict-sensitively
Representation (encouraging participation)	• Ensuring opportunities of participation and representation of teachers in education structures, across backgrounds and identity groups • The right to join trade unions • Participatory school culture and administration • Enabling teachers to foster active participation in the classroom	• Ensuring opportunities of participation and representation of teachers in education structures, across linguistic backgrounds and identity groups • The right to join language rights groups • Multilingual school culture and administration • Enabling teachers to foster active participation in the language classroom
Reconciliation (dealing with past, present, and future injustices)	• Teaching the past, present, and future • Understanding one's own positionality when teaching the past, present, and future • Healing and "understanding that humanizes" • Teaching multiple narratives and histories	• Teaching Myanmar's language policies' past, present, and future • Understanding one's own positionality when teaching the past, present, and future of Myanmar's language policies • Healing and "understanding that humanizes" those who speak different languages • Teaching multiple narratives and histories in different languages and about different language groups

Note: Table 0.1 was first adapted from Novelli & Sayed, 2016, p. 19 and was used in Wong, 2019, an open source journal.

Overview of the Peace Process in Current Day Myanmar

For readers less familiar with Burma/Myanmar, a brief overview is provided here to contextualize the volume. More nuanced, personalized histories are provided by the authors in each chapter, who also provide additional background of the regions and peoples they discuss. The largest of the mainland Southeast Asian states, Myanmar (referred to as Burma pre-1989) is south of China, sandwiched between India on its Western border and Thailand to the East. Myanmar also shares over 100 miles of border with Bangladesh and Laos. Myanmar has fourteen provinces made up of seven divisions and seven states, the latter named for the major ethnic groups residing there (Mon, Kayin, Rakhine, Kayah, Shan, Chin, and Kachin States). Myanmar is rich with linguistic, cultural, and natural resources, but is perhaps better known for having one of the longest civil wars in history. The people, especially ethnic minorities, have suffered for decades from neglect and oppression under military rule. Buddhism is the majority religion of Myanmar (just under 90 percent) and is supported by the state in various ways. Christianity is the majority religion among the Chin and Kachin, and Islam is the majority religion of the Rohingya. Animists and Hindus are also present, although each makes up less than 1 percent of the nation's roughly 54 million people.

While there have been brief periods of civilian rule, such as after independence from the British in 1948 following two decades of colonial rule, and the emerging democracy taking shape from 2011 to 2021, these periods ended with the military taking back control. The gains made over the last ten years with the emerging democracy in Myanmar were brought to an abrupt end on February 1, 2021, when the military junta staged a coup. In the weeks and months that followed the coup, the junta arrested legally elected officials, detained thousands of people, and killed hundreds of people who were protesting on the streets. By February 2022, a year after the coup, over 12,000 Myanmar citizens had been detained and over 1,500 killed by military junta (AAPP, 2022). Myanmar has been a member of the Association of Southeast Asian Nations (ASEAN) since 1997. At the time of writing, it remains to be seen what influence ASEAN can have on the strategically located, but politically troubled state of Myanmar, and how the junta will respond to the recommendations ASEAN has laid down to support the people of Myanmar.

Reconciliation among ethnic groups is a major challenge facing Myanmar, which has been engaged in armed conflicts for the past six decades. Injustices in Myanmar include the internationally criticized human rights violations committed against the Muslim Rohingya, including the forced relocation of over 700,000 Rohingya, and the 2017 Rohingya massacre (Wa Lone et al., 2018). However, violence against other ethnic/religious groups also takes place. The Karen and Kachin ethnic groups have been engaged in a decades-long armed resistance struggle with the Burman-dominated Central State. Their respective Ethnic Armed Organizations (EAO) have been leading the struggle for social justice. In November 2015, Aung San Suu Kyi's National League for Democracy (NLD) swept the national elections, ushering in Myanmar's first civilian government since 1962. However, the ethnic peoples' hopes for peace under the new NLD-led government were not realized, and the armed conflict escalated in some regions. Escalation of violence against the people of Myanmar of all backgrounds became evident after the February 1, 2021, military coup, which will shape peacebuilding for years to come.

There are a number of publications examining peacebuilding in education in Myanmar (Higgins et al., 2016; Lo Bianco, 2016; Lopes Cardozo & Maber, 2019; Novelli, Lopes Cardozo, & Smith, 2015; Novelli & Sayed, 2016; South & Lall, 2016). However, more investigations into the role of education in the peace process in Myanmar are needed responding to what Higgins et al. (2016) stated was "a stark divide between the national peace process and education reform" (p. 10). Lopes Cardozo and Maber's (2019) comprehensive edited volume provides compelling evidence of the role educators can have in contributing to the peace process but also exposes the challenges and complexities of the process. This current volume seeks to continue and build upon this body of work, and demonstrate what local practitioners are doing to advance peace and social justice.

The Purpose of the Book and Chapter Format

Purpose

This book provides a space to highlight the peace workers of Myanmar. It contains the personal stories that launched the actors into peace work, an analysis of their local contexts and the unique challenges they face, and examples of breakthroughs they have experienced so that others within and outside of Myanmar can be inspired by and learn from these agents of peace. The book intentionally includes young local educators in classrooms from diverse regions of Myanmar, who represent a variety of languages, religions, and group affiliations. It also includes those outside of Myanmar, such as scholars and peace workers who work alongside local practitioners. Whenever possible, chapters are written by or with local practitioners, offering a platform to amplify marginal voices and provide the academy access to their local knowledge and insights.

The volume is based on the premise that in order to reduce armed conflicts and promote a more just and equitable nation, diversity must be valued and social justice made a priority. This means that new ways of thinking about interacting with those who differ from one's own cultural, linguistic, or religious group need to be developed. Peacebuilding skills are not innate, and respect for others is not the default, but these skills and attitudes can be fostered. State-run schools have traditionally been places where peace is undermined, diversity ignored or undervalued, and resistance curtailed. But even in government schools, there are places in the margins of the curriculum where teachers can draw from their identities, evoke agency, and engage in critical pedagogy to engage in, rephrasing Apple (2013), bearing witness to inequalities, illuminating spaces to challenge reality, and imagining workable alternatives. This volume addresses the following questions: How are various actors in Myanmar raising awareness, fostering attitudes, and teaching skills that are needed to bring about more peaceful communities and a more just state? And how might what they are doing be adapted for use in other contexts? In hindsight, speaking from the position of post-February 2021 coup, we might also ask, how has their work contributed to the current Civil Disobedience Movement (CDM) in Myanmar, in which people are bravely standing up against injustice even at the risk of their lives.

Chapter Format

Authors were encouraged to share their own stories of what launched their desire to engage in social justice-oriented content and pedagogy that advances peacebuilding. Each chapter provides a description of the context, so readers get a sense of the conditions, constraints, and challenges faced by students and teachers in their school and communities. They provide a specific activity, task, or approach of how they foster and teach the attitudes, knowledge, and skills needed for peacebuilding, with enough detail so that readers can adapt it in other contexts and assess its impact. Finally, the authors provide suggestions for practitioners in other contexts or with other students, addressing how their activity might be adapted, for example, for a younger or older group, a larger or smaller group, a more diverse group, in a shorter time span, or a context with limited resources. We turn now to the chapter summaries.

Chapter Summaries

The volume is bookend with a foreword and afterword by invited noteworthy authors, as well as an introduction and conclusion by the editor. The main chapters are presented in three sections with three chapters each. The first focuses on agency, the second on identity, and third on critical pedagogy, although aspects of all three of these concepts are found in most chapters.

Forward and Introduction

A foreword by Ardeth Maung Thawnghmung launches the book. In her foreword, she reminds us of the personal, social, and economic toll of social injustice in Myanmar. She describes her story of being a product of the 1988 pro-democracy movement in Burma (now Myanmar) and brings us up to date describing the impact of the February 1, 2021, coup. She notes that the topic of peacebuilding and social justice in Myanmar has received insufficient scholarly attention to date and applauds the effort of bridging together such a diverse group of authors and perspectives. In the midst of such tragic destruction of "lives, dreams, and the economy" as she puts it, she ends with a glimmer of hope, describing the people-led parallel government that is beginning to form. She attributes this to the grassroots efforts of peacebuilding and social justice that the authors in this book describe.

Permit me to share my take on the personal anecdote Ardeth wrote about us, which will serve as a segue to the next chapter on ESL teachers as agents of social change. After meeting Ardeth briefly during her Fulbright in 2010 in Yangon and later reading her book *The Other Karen,* I became her fan (not knowing at that time that I had once been her teacher). Later I learned of her career as chair of the Political Science department and current Director of Peace and Conflict Studies at University of Massachusetts, which only intensified my interest. Knowing that she would be the Keynote speaker at the conference I was going to in Mandalay in 2016, I wanted to ask her to sign her book for me. I asked a colleague of mine to introduce us at the pre-conference banquet, and nervously asked if she would autograph her book. Her response stunned me. "Do you speak Chinese?" she asked. It was odd that she would know this fact about me. I am Caucasian, so it is not evident that I speak Mandarin. When she followed up with, "Did you teach English at Pasadena City College in 1990?" I was wondering where this was going. "You were my first teacher in the US!" she said with excitement. It was hard to believe at first, but when she retold some of my class jokes, it was hard to deny. (Also, how did she remember my jokes?) I knew so little about Burma and peace education when I taught this young Karen student who had just arrived in the United States, some thirty years ago now. When we had met in Yangon in 2010, we had not made our student/teacher connection from a decade earlier, but I was glad in 2016 that we finally had. My years of teaching ESL suddenly took on greater significance. So that is how our mutual fan club started, with me her first US teacher, and her, an accomplished author, Burma expert, and political scientist I followed and now have the honor of being in a book with. The next chapter discusses the connection of ESL teachers and peace educators, a connection that I am fortunate to have made, which is the first chapter in Part I, "Agency."

Part I: Agency

Part I focuses on promoting agency in peace education in Myanmar. It contains three chapters. The first, "Promoting Inclusion with Pro-Social Capital: From English Language Teachers to Agents of Social Change in Myanmar," is co-authored by two educators/peace workers, one based in Myanmar, Kyawt Thuzar, and her colleague, Zoe Matthews, co-founder of Mote Oo, a publishing company in Myanmar committed to social justice and peacebuilding. The authors in this chapter contend that one of the biggest challenges that Myanmar faces is multi-ethnic identity politics. Marginalized by their lack of access to higher education opportunities and limited social mobility, teacher trainers who they investigated chose a path less politicized and more readily accessible at the community level, that is, English-language teacher training. This chapter documents the journey of sixteen key informants aged between twenty-four and thirty-seven, nine of whom formerly worked in formal education and seven in the non-formal education sector in Myanmar. Their journey reflects their transformation from English-language teachers to agents of social change. The data reveal detailed professional and behavioral histories of the participants including what motivated them, and the context, conditions, and challenges faced on their journey.

The two other chapters in this section, authored by Kaung Zan and Joanne Lauterjung, focus on dialogue. In Chapter 2, "Lessons Learned Facilitating Dialogue to Bridge Divides within and between Diverse Communities in Myanmar," Kaung Zan is the lead author. In this chapter, the authors, who provide both insider and outsider perspectives gleaned from years of collaborative work on peacebuilding in Myanmar, describe stories of communities finding their way to self-determination and collaboration to bridge ethnic and religious divides. The authors contend that people in Myanmar can gain more agency when they are taught *how* to learn and learn to take full advantage of the influx of new tools, ideas, and concepts. Helping participants develop a mindset of inquiry and empathetic listening is key to their work. After a section on dialogue in Myanmar and challenges for education for peace in Myanmar, they discuss the constraints of working with Non-Governmental Organizations NGOs (also discussed in more detail in Chapter 9 in this volume). Working within these constraints, they describe opportunities for change and innovation, with a number of recommendations. They describe how they have prepared, facilitated, and evaluated their workshops that employ creative and experiential practices promoting peacebuilding in Myanmar.

In Chapter 3, the authors continue their description of peace work in Myanmar, this time with Joanne Lauterjung as lead author, looking into specific case studies. In this chapter, "Case Studies in Using Creative Dialogue Structures to Foster Reflective Learning in Myanmar," they discuss the use of creative dialogue structures to help stimulate people's natural curiosity, recognize there are multiple learning styles, and begin to develop and appreciate lifelong learning. The authors contend that dialogue structures are needed in societies that do not have a cultural norm of dialogue that uses give-and-take conversations for learning. In a strongly hierarchical society, speaking is power, and the longer you speak, the more power you gain. Learning to value listening as a necessary tool takes practice, and structures allow a sense of safety and predictability with which to practice speaking and listening. This chapter demonstrates that using engaged pedagogy through two specific arts-based activities, "Five Steps to Change" and "Collage." In these activities, students can begin to shift from the "banking model" of education to a student-centered approach that values indigenous knowledge, and helps people develop peripheral vision to see beyond what is to what can be.

Part II: Identity

In Part II, Identity, three chapters provide insights on how identity informs education and peace work. In Chapter 4, "Changing Narratives and Transforming Conflict through Non-formal Education for Youth in Rakhine State," Melanie Walker and two Rakhine teachers, Soe Khine and Ko Thant, discuss how they are seeking to build sustainable peace at their school for youth in Sittwe, Rakhine State. Their chapter outlines the ongoing tensions in the regions, notably toward the Rohingya and the effects of the apartheid-like conditions there, in which negative attitudes toward the Other persist. The two Rakhine teachers, who were former students of the program, discuss how they apply their newly developed identity as peacebuilders to foster and teach the attitudes, knowledge, and skills needed for peacebuilding through a global education curriculum of civic education, human rights, global issues, and conflict and peace studies. The local-to-global methodology of the curriculum assists students to perceive the broader dynamics behind the conflicts in their region and to increase their awareness of the processes of Othering, specifically through analysis of the Rwandan genocide and the identification of commonalities across world religions. The learning is then actualized through experiential learning visits and service learning opportunities.

In Chapter 5, "Reframing Policy and Practice: Languages in Education as Resources for Peace in Myanmar," Erina Iwasaki and Jasmine Tintut Williams, two graduate students with family ties to Myanmar completing degrees at Teachers College Columbia University, describe two multilingual education projects in Myanmar. Their project is a revision of a multilingual literature curriculum for a private school in Yangon and technical support for a multilingual education project for an ethnolinguistic group in Kachin State. While these two contexts differ in the ethnolinguistic and socioeconomic backgrounds of the students, languages, and communities they serve, both are trying to address Myanmar's proclaimed democratization, its commitment to educational equity, and its transition to a market-based economy. The authors contend that while the national curriculum continues to undergo reform, it does not currently represent the linguistic and cultural diversity of the country, nor does it discuss current social phenomena. In a country with this outdated, teacher-centered curriculum that relies on rote learning, plurality of views and critical discussions are rarely encouraged in classrooms. The work they do uses multiple languages to provide an innovative, learner-centered pedagogical environment for students to engage in critical thinking and to problematize essentializing and dominant discourses that are present in both the Myanmar national curriculum and imported international school curricula. The two programs have addressed this by incorporating linguistic and cultural relevance in their educational approaches, and by creating spaces for nondominant and more cosmopolitan discourses to emerge.

Chapter 6, "Designing Peace Education for Community-Based Action within Myanmar: Reflections of a Collaborative Approach," has three co-authors, Grace Michel, a Karen-American peace educator, Arkar Phyo Thant, a peacebuilding practitioner from Myanmar, and Katie Zanoni, a peace educator from the United States. They discuss how their personal stories inform their involvement in the Learn and Share Together (LST) Project they developed and piloted in Kayin State in 2017–18. The LST program is part of a social cohesion initiative led by a nongovernmental organization, People in Need (PIN), which sought to involve students and teachers as well as community members. They highlight key principles learned through a process of collective reflection, namely, the need to contextualize the curriculum, offer experiential learning activities, adapt the curricula, and allow sufficient time to develop curricula collaboratively.

Part III: Critical Pedagogy

Part III contains three chapters that explore critical questions about peace work and research in Myanmar. In Chapter 7, "Peace Education in Myanmar's Middle School Curriculum: A Qualitative Study of Educator and Expert Perspectives," the three authors, Kinsa San Yi, Naw Sah Blute, and Radka Antalíková, argue that the current educational reforms should work to include peace content in the curriculum. In 2018, the authors worked with the Peace Leadership & Research Institute (PLRI), a newly launched initiative by Thabyay Education Foundation, to conduct evidence-based research on the presence of peace education contents in the national middle school curriculum. For this purpose, the first two authors conducted three focus group discussions with thirteen middle school teachers in total as well as three individual interviews with education experts. The results showed that the current Myanmar national curriculum in secondary school has not yet integrated the concept of peace education. Specifically, the findings indicated that the current learning contents and objectives are not promoting students to learn about human rights, respect for diversity, collaboration, problem-solving skills, or social harmony.

Rosalie Metro, an academic from the United States, and Aung Khine, an author and educator in Myanmar, team up in Chapter 8, "Putting Down Our Weapons When We Talk about History: Using Primary Source Documents to Teach Multiple Perspectives on Burma's Past." They discuss their failed attempt in 2009 to help teachers from many of Burma's ethnic groups on the Thai-Burma border to "put down their weapons" and create history textbooks that promoted peace and were acceptable to all. They came up with a new approach that built a common base of knowledge while illustrating multiple perspectives. Instead of creating a traditional textbook, they gathered primary source documents from Burma's history and design activities that would allow students to build the historians' skills needed to form their own interpretations. The result of this process was the impetus of the book, *Histories of Burma: A Source-Based Approach to Myanmar's History*, published by Mote Oo Education. Today it is used by private post-secondary schools both inside and outside Myanmar. The authors contend that an honest reckoning with history is necessary in order to build lasting peace, and *Histories of Burma* is an attempt to contribute to this healing and promote national reconciliation. When students examine documents carefully, simplistic narratives that fuel conflict are disrupted, and the divisions between "us vs. them" start to break down.

The last chapter of this section, "Researching Peacebuilding in Myanmar: Framing Research Questions with Our Grandparents' Moral Imagination," is written by Tony Waters. This chapter addresses two main topics. First, there is the nature of peace research and the "moral imagination" inherited from grandparents, whose values influence emotions about war and peace. Second is the donor-centric research system in Myanmar that emerged in 2012 and draws on Western peace traditions, rather than those of Myanmar. The author begins by pointing out that researching peacebuilding is inherently difficult, especially in Myanmar where research is funded almost extensively by foreign donors who frame the research questions rooted in pre-existing assumptions about peace, war, and society from outside Myanmar. Drawing from John Paul Lederach's (2005) work, he contends that a "moral imagination" is needed for researchers and peace workers to explore what is outside the box, what is serendipitous and complex, rather than pre-planned, prescribed, and measurable within a research contract's terms of reference. He provides examples from some of his seventeen doctoral students' work in peace education, the majority of whom are from Myanmar, to illustrate Lederach (2005) and Boulding's ideas of regarding the historical narratives needed to develop cultures of peace. Ultimately, he believes that the ability to use a moral imagination in peace work and research in Myanmar is hampered by the insistence of foreign donors on framing research questions on the basis of Western grandparents' values, rather than those of Myanmar's peoples.

Final Chapters

In the conclusion chapter, I revisit the purpose of the volume and how authors from both outside and inside Myanmar have come together to draw from their identities, evoked their agency, and applied critical pedagogy to struggle for social justice and advance peace in their classrooms and communities. I explore the power of vision and use it to describe an analytical framework that helps to critique peace endeavors that fail to address the larger more systemic drivers of conflict. Reference to the possibility tree task (Hantzopoulos and Bajaj, 2021) is made and applied to the ongoing effort of the people of Myanmar to envision and establish an alternative, more socially just educational system. Finally, a list of discussion questions is provided to help readers reflect on the volume and apply the insights in other contexts.

In the Afterword, noted author of Myanmar studies, Ashley South, provides an insider's perspective of the political context of Myanmar in the past decade, as well as the incomplete peace efforts and disappointing leadership that led up to the coup. He provides a concise account of the unique contribution of each chapter, providing a useful summary and account of what can be gleaned from each author's contributions. He concludes that this important collection of essays helps us better to understand some of the underlying drivers of conflict, and how these can be addressed and transformed through the techniques and values of peace education.

Works Cited

AAPP (2022). The Assistance Association for Political Prisoners (Burma), retrieved from https://aappb.org/.

Apple, M. W. (2013). *Can education change society*. New York: Routledge.

Bajaj, M. (Ed.). (2008). *Encyclopedia of peace education*. Charlotte, NC: Information Age Publishing.

Bajaj, M., & Hantzopoulos, M. (Eds.). (2016). *Peace education: International perspectives*. London: Bloomsbury Academic.

Haavelsrud, M. (1996). *Education in developments*. Norway: Area Publishers.

Hantzopoulos, M., & Bajaj, M. (2021). *Educating for peace and human rights: An introduction*. London: Bloomsbury Academic.

Higgins, S., Maber, E., Lopez Cardozo, M. T. A., & Shah, R. (2016). *Selections of a research report on education and peacebuilding in Myanmar*. Research Consortium

Education and Peacebuilding, University of Amsterdam. Retrieved from: https://educationanddevelopment.wordpress.com/rp/outputs-research-consortium/

Higgins, S., & Novelli, M. (2020). Rethinking peace education: A cultural political economy approach. *Comparative Education Review, 64*(1), 1–20.

Lederach, J. P. (2005). *The moral imagination.* Oxford, UK: Oxford University Press.

Lo Bianco, J. (2016). *Myanmar country report language, education and social cohesion (LESC) initiative.* UNICEF, EAPRO, Bangkok, Thailand. Retrieved from https://www.researchgate.net/publication/296334128_Myanmar_Country_Report_Language_Education_and_Social_Cohesion_LESC_Initiative

Lopes Cardozo, M. T. A., & Maber, E. J. T. (Eds.). (2019). *Sustainable peacebuilding and social justice in times of transition: Findings on the role of education in Myanmar.* Singapore: Springer Nature.

Metro, R. (2019). The third face of education: Moving beyond the good/bad binary in conflict and post-conflict societies. *Compare: A Journal of Comparative and International Education,* Retrieved from https://doi.org/10.1080/03057925.2019.1657317

Novelli, M., Lopes Cardozo, M., & Smith, A. (2015). *A theoretical framework for analyzing the contribution of education to sustainable peacebuilding: 4Rs in conflict-affected contexts.* Available online at: https://www.eccnetwork.net/sites/default/files/media/file/theoretical-framework-jan15.pdf.

Novelli, M., & Sayed, Y. (2016). Teachers as agents of sustainable peace, social cohesion and development: Theory, practice & evidence. *Education as Change, 20*(3), 15–37.

Reardon, B. (1988). *Comprehensive peace education: Education for global responsibility.* New York, NY: Teachers College Columbia Press.

South, A., & Lall, M. (2016). Language, education and the peace process in Myanmar. *Contemporary Southeast Asia, 38*(1), 128–53. DOI: 10.1355/cs38-1f.

Thawnghmung, A. M. (2012). *The "Other" Karen in Myanmar: Ethnic minorities and the struggle without arms.* New York: Lexington Books.

Verma, R. (2017). *Critical peace education and global citizenship: Narratives from the unofficial curriculum.* New York, NY: Routledge.

Wa Lone, Kyaw Soe Oo, Lewis, S., Slodkowski, A. (2018). Massacre in Myanmar. Reuters Special Report. Retrieved from: https://www.reuters.com/investigates/special-report/myanmar-rakhine-events/

Wong, M. S. (2019). The peace dividend of valuing non-dominant languages in language-in-education policies in Myanmar. *The Forum for International Research in Education, 5*(3), 49–68. https://fire-ojs-ttu.tdl.org/fire/index.php/FIRE/article/view/143/64

Zeichner, K. (2011). Teacher education for social justice. In M. Hawkins (Ed.), *Social justice language teacher education* (pp. 7–22). Bristol, UK: Multilingual Matters.

Part I

AGENCY

Chapter 1

PROMOTING INCLUSION WITH PRO-SOCIAL CAPITAL: FROM ENGLISH-LANGUAGE TEACHERS TO AGENTS OF SOCIAL CHANGE IN MYANMAR

Kyawt Thuzar and Zoe Matthews

Introduction

Kyawt

From 2004 until 2017, I worked as the youngest female teacher at two grassroots-level community-based organizations (CBOs) which offered informal low-cost language classes, basic Information and Communications Technology (ICT) training, and bookkeeping programs. These CBOs were led by English-language teachers whose age ranges spanned two generations and whose race and religions were as diverse as their class participants. These organizations resisted the ruling military regime's[1] tactics of intimidation, harassment, and arrests following the 2007 Saffron Revolution crackdown by continuing to cautiously open classes. Those were the times when classes were under surveillance by military intelligence personnel in plainclothes. Teachers' names and class schedules were to be reported to the township administration office, and the founders faced constraints like needing permission to open up large-size (50+) classes.

At the time, it was mandatory for schools to sign formal agreements promising that they would not be involved in any kind of political activities or make any mention of human rights in and outside the classroom. My working experiences at these CBOs granted me first hand experience in how dialogic and dialectic pedagogies (Freire, 1970) could be used creatively with large-size classes. It also taught me how grassroots and civilian-led education initiatives were being suppressed and how learners and educators could find loopholes in the regime's tactics and initiate discussions about social justice.

These community-based social and political movements flourished later as Civil Society Organization (CSO)-led activities after 2011 with the technical support of

---

1. https://www.sciencespo.fr/mass-violence-war-massacre-resistance/en/document/repression-august-8-12-1988-8-8-88-uprising-burmamyanmar.html.

international organizations such as the Institute for Political and Civic Engagement (iPACE), World Learning. My tenure as an iPACE trainer was from 2014 to 2017. I provided six-week intensive training for members of political parties, and CSOs like ethnic rights-based organizations, training-based organizations for Internally Displaced People (IDP), student and worker unions, and Lesbian, gay, bisexual, transgender and queer or questioning (LGBTQ) rights-based organizations. Through engagement with these participants, I have come to understand that multiple realities exist in multiple contexts. These could be the everyday realities of different ethnic groups, socio economically marginalized groups, and sidelined political parties. All these realities have been dictated by twenty-five years under one-party totalitarian political ideology, twenty years of dictatorship, and the world's longest civil war between ethnic groups and the Burmese military, the Tatmadaw.

With these personal and professional experiences as a backdrop, as part of the research project for my MEd in Cultural and Educational Policy Studies at Loyola University as a Fulbright scholar (2017–19), I chose to focus on refugees in Chicago. All these positionalities as a researcher and a writer in the field of education have resulted in my exploration of topics like nonacademic support for secondary school girls living as refugees in Chicago, and the interplay between state and non-state education providers and their implications for peace in Myanmar in collaboration with Zoe, my co-author.

Zoe

Cyclone Nargis, the worst natural disaster in Myanmar's recorded history, hit the Irrawaddy Delta in May 2008, leaving 140,000 dead and millions affected by the devastation.[2] I was volunteering at a small education project in Bangkok for migrants from Myanmar at that time so I witnessed firsthand the galvanizing of my students toward organizing donations and coordinating relief efforts to help their communities. I started working for Thabyay Education Foundation in the Thai-Myanmar border town of Mae Sot not long after. There I was responsible for providing curriculum and teacher training for the postsecondary schools operating out of the seven refugee camps along the border between Thailand and Myanmar. What I found were the everyday realities of living in the midst of an ongoing struggle over governance and identity (Oh et al., 2019). These were everyday people caught between a "rock and hard place": the reluctant hosts, the Thai state, and their oppressors across the border. The local "behind the scenes advocacy" (South, 2010) to build systems of resiliency against structural injustices was inspiring.

As I continued to implement teacher training workshops in our affiliated schools, I witnessed the organization and self-determination of non-state education regimes like the Karen and Karenni Education Departments on the border to promote well-being and sustainable futures for their communities. These structures for protection and resilience were part of a "Third Force," a network of individuals and groups who "sought change through engaging the junta or created

2. http://postconflict.unep.ch/publications/nargis_case_study.pdf.

opportunities where the state was failing" (Mullen, 2016, p. 9). Education-wise, because of this network, the context along the Thai-Myanmar border was alive with initiatives to address the realities of a failed state for both migrants from Myanmar on the border and the refugee camp residents.

It was within that Third Force community that I had my first interactions with the types of teachers and trainers on whom this chapter is based. These teachers and trainers were the embodiment of Freire's dialogic practitioners (Freire, 1970). They were the ones who had broken ranks with the army of teacher-centered "banking educators" or teachers who relied purely on rote memorization to implement their curriculum. Instead, these dialogic teachers and trainers expertly wielded their own repertoire of teaching tools to facilitate dialogue in their classrooms using participatory, learner-centered methodology. One result of this expertise is a safe zone, where all students feel a sense of agency, their voices are heard, and their values such as respect, empathy, trust, humility, and integrity being practiced every day. The other outcome is a new generation of individuals equipped with the tools they need to transform their current realities to their preferred futures. Twelve years later, I am still having regular interactions with the Third Force in Myanmar, now faced with the challenge of struggling free of the clutches of pre-transition regime mentalities. With the evidence we present from our research in this chapter, and in future studies, Kyawt and I hope to shed light on the lessons for peacebuilding that can be learned from the change agents still very much in action in the present day.

Our Lens and Context

As mentioned in the Introduction of this book, the 4R (Redistribution, Recognition, Representation, and Reconciliation) framework provides a way for us to capitalize on the interconnectedness between education and peacebuilding (Lopes Cardozo & Maber, 2019). The 4R framework is directly applicable to the Myanmar context (Novelli & Sayed, 2016). A number of other authors have examined the role of education in sustainable peacebuilding, including Lo Bianco (2016), South and Lall (2016), and Salem-Gervais and Raynaud (2020). We will endeavor to look at the matter through the lens of notable classroom pedagogies and inclusive practices in education.

There are two contexts in which the intrinsic meaning of all-inclusive education for unity and peace can be interpreted by education providers in Myanmar (South & Lall, 2016). An education provider can sometimes serve as a proxy for accumulating sociocultural capital: in other words, it is a way to establish their power and legitimacy. This is the danger of education in the eyes of John Dewey (Hopkins, 2018) as the focus is taken away from the needs of the child and placed on the needs of the governing power. If only certain social groups are included or there is only an emphasis on one social group obtaining more sociocultural capital at the expense of another social group, education becomes a divider rather than a connector. The result is that one social group has more power than the other(s).

This is the narrative of identity politics introduced by the regime government, the State Law and Order Restoration Council (SLORC), in 1988. They created the narrative that there are in total 135 national races/ethnic nationalities. Of the 135 "national races," there are 120 living ethno-linguistic groups (Salem-Gervais & Raynaud, 2020). This narrative is reflected in the grievances listed by ethnic groups. Realization of unity between ethnic groups in Myanmar thus becomes difficult. Disputes over the number of ethnic groups by other actors perpetuates the basic worldview that education, regardless of who provides it, is only intended to "oppress" or marginalize which introduces two contexts in which to think about "inclusion."

The first context is to think about what and whose narratives of content to include in the curricula for promoting inclusion and peace in a diverse Myanmar where differing narratives for what "unity" is has implications for sustainable peace (Thuzar & Matthews, 2020). The effort and practices in constructing genuine "unity" through education require Myanmar as a whole to recognize the importance of a shift in an individual's mindset and culture in classrooms and beyond. Educators need to develop a mindset that breaks free of the fragilities left behind by pre-transition era regimes and overcomes the all-pervasive "us vs. them" narrative. This means to nurture a culture that embraces diverse sets of perspectives and life experiences in education curricula, in pedagogies, and in approaches. This is an integral part of having effective and meaningful "all-inclusive education."

A second context is to understand the presence of different educational providers who position themselves in three domains. Within the first domain are the education providers in the formal state education sector. Within the second domain are the education authorities in ethnic regions, or in other words, the Ethnic Based Education Providers (EBEPs) or non-state ethnic education systems (South & Lall, 2016). Civil society becomes the third domain for the implementation of educational processes. In each domain exists a multitude of challenges: from geographic to administrative and from political to linguistic.

The First Domain—State Education

Notable challenges in this domain are, first, the language diversity and population dispersion of a total of over nine million school children in formal education representing different ethno-linguistic groups. Many contend that it is not feasible for state schools to deliver all state curricula in line with the Mother Tongue-Based Multilingual Education (MTB-MLE, or Mother Tongue-Based Education, MTBE or MTB, in short) system to satisfy all language speakers when 46,000 schools are in linguistically heterogeneous communities (Salem-Gervais & Raynaud, 2020). In addition, for nearly two decades, the educators in this domain are the legacy of the "banking education" system from the colonial and following authoritarian regimes (1948–2011). In this domain, training educators to use dialogic and democratic pedagogies is a fundamental solution to breaking down the hierarchy that exists between the learners and educators (Dewey, 2001; Freire, 1970). However, the majority of state educators are not yet fully trained to feel confident in using learner-centered approaches which demand uprooting the teacher-centered pedagogies instilled in communities.

On the one hand, with its recent education reforms, the state was attempting to extinguish the "us vs. them" fire or the fire between all ethnic groups, including the Bamar (Burman) majority, as well as their respective ethnic subgroups. This fire was lit, politicized, and started in colonial classifications of ethnic groups in Myanmar (Clarke et al., 2019). The flames of this fire were fanned by the 1960s' language-in-education policy appropriation (International Crisis Group, 2003). Under the semi-civilian government in late 2011, the attempts included the formulation of a comprehensive Nationwide Ceasefire Agreement (NCA) which brought preliminary ceasefires with some Ethnic Armed Organizations (EAOs). Nevertheless, the major issues such as security sector reform, power distribution in the public administration sector, and lack of ethnic minority voices in the Comprehensive Education Sector Review[3] (Jolliffe & Speers-Mears, 2016) for education reform were not resolved, and consequently, the "Ethnic-Bamar" fire is still burning.

After the 2015 election, other attempts include the acknowledgement in the National Education Strategic Plan 2016–21 (NESP) that language barriers for ethnic minority students need to be addressed to reduce the number of school dropouts. Next is the recognition of EBEPs and their MTBE system. In this context, children start primary education with their mother tongue as a medium of instruction followed by a gradual shift toward the national language as they progress through the education system. Finally, with technical support from international actors like United Nations Educational, Scientific and Cultural Organization (UNESCO), for example, by way of the "Strengthening Pre-service Teacher Education in Myanmar (STEM)" (UNESCO, 2020) project, the state was looking for ways to reform its teacher education system. These reforms aimed to equip teacher educators with professional skills such as creative and reflective thinking skills, ICT, leadership, and problem-solving skills required for delivering subjects like Morality and Civic Education. Such skills are necessary for an individual to constructively engage with the processes that are affecting their community, and contribute to transformation of the conflicts around them.

The Second Domain—Ethnic-Based Education

As mentioned at the beginning of this section, education is a way of accumulating sociocultural capital for an education provider. Bourdieu contends that educational qualifications can produce "a form of cultural capital which has a relative autonomy vis-a-vis its bearer and even vis-a-vis the cultural capital s/he effectively possesses at a given moment in time" (as cited in Sadovnik & Coughlan, 2016). However, there has also long been a competition in the politics of education due primarily to language policy and use in education and public administration since the 1960s (International Crisis Group, 2003). Among the so-named 135 national

---

3. http://www.cesrmm.org/documents.

races/ethnic nationalities, there are those referred to as ethnic nationality elites. These refer to the major ethnic group, that is, Jinghpaw as compared to Lisu in Kachin state, or Rakhine as compared to Mro.

Language rights have therefore been framed as the main discourse for autonomy by these ethnic nationality elites. These rights construct a narrative of identity and accumulation of social and cultural capital through education. To gain autonomy and sociocultural capital, some EBEPs have resorted to taking a harder stance with reference to language rights and use only the mother tongue at the primary schooling system and in public administration (South & Lall, 2016). Others have taken a softer approach and teach both the nondominant languages in addition to the dominate language of Burmese, and later an international language such as English. Whichever stance they take, some critical questions are awaiting the EBEPs. One question is which ethnic language and which narrative will be reflected in the curricula and in local governance. The most poignant question is how linguistic and political inclusion in that curricula amount to a unanimous sense of unity between all ethnic groups both within and beyond classroom walls. There are questions which need to be answered by the "120 living ethno-linguistic groups" in the second domain.

The spatial distribution of the 120 ethno-linguistic groups' language and population dispersion constructs seemingly insurmountable challenges to language-in-education policy and administration policy. Each ethnic group, by way of policy, pursues the accumulation of socio economic capital and political gain. Having experienced oppressive political regimes throughout the colonial era, post-Independence and successive military dictatorships, the providers adopted an "attitude of adhesion to the oppressor" (Freire, 1970, p. 45). This means they adopted the same attitudes as their oppressor, which is then reflected in their educational curricula, pedagogy, and approaches. This has remained the case even as the National League for Democracy (NLD) government was sworn into power in 2015.

It is understandable that the fire of "us vs. them" is burning among the 120 ethno-linguistic groups amidst a discussion about the language rights of "elite" and "non-elite" groups. Within the many layers of the education provision, attitudes might range from more separatist to more "pro-union" (South & Lall, 2016). In the words of Salem-Gervais and Raynaud (2020, p. 43), they approach curricular, pedagogy, and education generally according to "a spectrum going from assimilation, to integration and accommodation." Their attitudes speak to the trade-offs that need to be made in terms of one of the 4Rs, Recognition (Lopes Cardozo & Maber, 2019). Decision-making in education policy needs to incorporate the voices of all, whether they are the so-called elite or non-elite groups.

The Third Domain—Civil Society

While the other two domains are disharmonic in narrative and discourse about language-in-education and administration policy, a third type of provider has emerged together with global civil society. This emergence started within a climate of change in the 1980s to the 1990s, where the role of global civil society movements in public affairs aimed to increase the accountability of the government. Globally, liberals hailed civil society as democracy in action while Marxists cherish the challenge to the dominant order (Marchetti, 2017). In the case of Myanmar, education has been a key sector in which civil society has been able to challenge the status quo imposed by the government. Civil society activity in Myanmar reached a peak in the 1988 pro-democracy revolution, the 2007 Saffron revolution, and following Cyclone Nargis in 2008, and of course most recently in the Civil Disobedience Movement (CDM) following the February 2021 military coup. These events exposed the government's crude accountability deficits and human rights violations on the global political stage. Prior to the 2021 coup, it was in education that everyday people could stand up to challenge the legitimacy of the military government from the "bottom up."

After Cyclone Nargis in April 2008, financial aid and technical support were provided to CSOs specifically for humanitarian aid and educational projects. This included support for the setting up of English-language programs (British Council, 2016). While a challenge is posed by the diversity in ethnic languages for State curricula and for the curricula of EBEPs, English language became a major source for knowledge building within the confines of ruthless suppression by the ruling regime at that time. This reflects "the capacity to imagine something rooted in the challenges of the real world yet capable of giving birth to that which doesn't yet exist" (Lederach, 2005, p. 29). In the context of using English to drive knowledge building, educators have accepted the challenge of their suppression and given birth to the idea of addressing universal human rights through other means.

In this section, we have talked about education as a means of accumulating sociocultural capital. We would go one step further to say that education can be the medium for building "pro-social capital," a phrase coined by Birch (2009, p. 21), who recognized that rather than coming from the outside-in or top-down, sustainable peace must be built "bottom-up and inside-out" by communities of pro-social capitalists at the grassroots. These are "followers" of social justice, who cooperate to create a dense intercommunal network with the aim of transforming violence into dialogue. English-language teachers through their vast alumni create their own community. This is the potential space within civil society where an army of social justice advocates within that alumni can be created. English-language teachers in the Myanmar context thus have a similar capacity to become social change agents who can accumulate pro-social capital for the imagined "unity" beyond the classroom.

Myanmar's Social Change Agents in the Third Domain: English-Language Teachers Turned Educators for Social Justice and Peace

While both the peace process and education reform in Myanmar have started, time will be needed for elite-level discussions around the management of ethnic diversity and recognition of the roles of each domain in education governance.

The ongoing conflicts in and the perpetuation of racial and religious stereotyping in Rakhine and beyond remind us that these pro-social capitalists are still needed to lay the groundwork for peace negotiations to bear fruit.

Our Study

Our small-scale research project, on which this chapter is based, is an earnest effort to document the journey of sixteen key informants (seven males and nine females) aged in their twenties and thirties with one older, retired teacher. The participants were from a variety of social and ethno-linguistic backgrounds and were employed as educators for social justice and peace. Following a purposive sampling process, semi-structured in-depth interviews were conducted to gather information about these trainers in Myanmar. Snowball sampling was then utilized in order to locate alumni of the research participants who themselves have developed the agency or "pro-social capital" (Birch, 2009) necessary to participate in community development, democratization, and peacebuilding. Nine of the participants formerly trained and worked in the first domain of state education and seven in the second and third domains of education in Myanmar, EBEPs and civil society. Note that they all attended English-language teacher training or worked as English-language instructors. See Table 1.1 for an overview of the participants.

Table 1.1 Profiles of Research Participants

	Background/school type	Ethnicity	Languages spoken
A	Formally trained at an unnamed Education College, now freelance civic education trainer	Mon	Myanmar (mother tongue), English (upper-intermediate)
B	BEd in Secondary Education from overseas, now working as a peace educator	Kayah	Myanmar (mother tongue), English (upper-intermediate)
C	Retired (worked at Education College), then as civic education trainer for Dhamma school	Bamar	Myanmar (mother tongue), English (intermediate)
D	BEd from Yangon University of Education specializing in ELT, now trainer for INGO	Shan/ Pa-O	Pa-Oh (mother tongue, Myanmar (fluent), English (upper-intermediate)
E	BEd from Yangon University of Education, now freelance civic educator	Bamar	Myanmar (mother tongue), English (intermediate)
F	BEd from Yangon University of Education, worked for government school, now civic educator trainer	Rakhine	Rakhine (mother tongue), Myanmar (fluent), English (pre-intermediate)
G	BEd from Yangon University of Education (mathematics, physics, and bio), now peace educator for INGO	Kayin	Myanmar (mother tongue), English (intermediate)

	Background/school type	Ethnicity	Languages spoken
H	BA in English, worked for government-affiliated school, now working for a postsecondary school as civic educator	Kachin/Jinghpaw	Jinghpaw (mother tongue), Myanmar (fluent), English (upper-intermediate)
I	BEd from Yangon University of Education, studying for his MEd overseas, was working for an EBEP as an English and civic educator	Mon	Mon (mother tongue), Myanmar (fluent), English (upper-intermediate)
J	Bachelor in Law from H University, now working for post-secondary school as a civic education trainer	Kayin	S'gaw Kayin (mother tongue), Myanmar (fluent), English (intermediate)
K	Did not attend university, worked as an English and Civic Education trainer for a postsecondary school, now working as a peace educator	Kachin/Jinghpaw	Jinghpaw (mother tongue), Myanmar (fluent), English (upper-intermediate)
L	BA in History from Yangon University, Diploma in Social Work, civic educator for NGO	Bamar	Myanmar (mother tongue), English (intermediate)
M	Diploma in English, master's in Political Science, now a civic educator for an NGO	Kaman	Kaman (mother tongue), Rakhine (fluent), Myanmar (fluent), English (upper-intermediate)
N	Still in the final year of distance education, but attended a free community development and leadership program in Yangon, and worked for Yangon Bakehouse and YWCA as a civic educator	Kayin	S'Gaw Kayin (mother tongue), Myanmar (fluent), English (intermediate)
O	Bachelor of Economics from Monywa University of Education, now a freelance civic educator	Bamar	Myanmar (mother tongue), English (upper-intermediate)
P	Master of English from the University of Yangon, teaches English and civic education at a monastery-affiliated nonformal education program	Bamar/Kayin	Myanmar (mother tongue), English (upper-intermediate), Japanese (pre-intermediate)

In order to identify what motivated our trainers and the context, conditions, and challenges faced on their journey, data from these interviews were analyzed using the Antecedents, Processes and Cognitive/Behavioral Outcomes framework from the International Civic and Citizenship Education Study (ICCS) (Schulz et al., 2016). This reveals a rich landscape of professional and behavioral histories between the participants and provides individual overviews of their evolution toward becoming educators for social justice and peace. In the same way that the ICCS assesses what influences outcomes of civic knowledge and engagement in young people over time, our own study aims to assess what has influenced the outcome of our participants in their journey to becoming pro-social capitalists. The first step is to establish what were the contextual variables or the "antecedents and processes" (Schulz et al., 2016) that lead to the way the study participant now thinks and behaves. For example, these could be the wider community around the participant: the education system, and the history and culture where the participant lives or works.

In Myanmar, as we have mentioned, narratives may differ depending on the domain of education and identity politics has a direct consequence for how one thinks and behaves. Influences like the school or classroom where the participant studied could also be an antecedent. Likewise, the home and peer environment, such as the family social grouping, or the home/peer language(s) can be an influence. While antecedents describe the teacher or trainer's characteristics or origins, processes are both influenced by the antecedents and characterized by the socialization of the trainer toward community and societal well-being. This is the cognitive and behavioral outcome of those antecedents and processes: that the teacher or trainer displays civic disposition, and a care for the processes of social justice in their community.

Participant J grew up in a context of Kayin- or Karen-centric spiritual, moral, social, and cultural perspectives on the periphery of clashes between Karen armed groups and the Tatmadaw. (See Table 1.2 for a list of the antecedents, processes, and outcomes for Participant J.) J graduated with a Bachelor in Law from a University and became a freelance English teacher. In Birch's (2009) words, J was working toward creating a "glocal" community where J's network of students appropriated the English language J taught and made it their own. In other words, they used the social capital of English as a global language in order to get ahead in their own community, establish their own schools, or become English teachers themselves. J then moved on to a job at a postsecondary school, in which a community of educators and students strived toward the values of respect, responsibility, and equality for example. There, J began a transformation to an expanded worldview, away from a single narrative about history, politics, and social justice issues to an

Table 1.2 Antecedents, Processes, and Outcomes of Participant J

Antecedents (leading to teacher characteristics)	Processes (teacher socialization and learning)	Cognitive and affective behavioral outcomes
• **Wider community:** Ethnocentricity in Karen state, emphasis on SMSC rights and responsibilities from Karen perspective • **School/classroom:** H University (low resource, large class sizes), freelance English teacher • **Home and peer environment:** Trilingual, working toward a glocal community in Hpaan	• **Wider community:** Community postsecondary school network • **School/classroom:** Values of the school (respect, responsibility, participation, cooperation, equality), multiple teaching resources and training • **Home and peer environment:** Alumni, likeminded educators	• Need to expand worldview away from local historical/political demands • Equal focus on rights and responsibilities of all

interest in diverse narratives. J then applied an awareness of diverse narratives, about who were the champions of Burmese independence efforts, or of the Panglong Agreement, for example, to build the awareness of J's students to also recognize that there are other voices as well as the ones they know well. This is with a view to expanding the worldview of others as well, and cherishing pluralism and diversity as a way to understand the world around us.

As another example, Participant I grew up in the context of Mon-centric spiritual, moral, social, and cultural perspectives. I's hometown is in an area on the periphery of skirmishes between Mon National Liberation Army (MNLA) and the Burmese armed forces. (See Table 1.3 for a list of the antecedents, processes, and outcomes for Participant I.) Having attended basic education in Mon state, I then moved to Yangon to study to become a teacher at the Yangon Institute of Education (now called the University of Education). After gaining a Bachelor's in Education, I returned to Mon state to work as an English teacher for Mon National Education Committee (MNEC), a nonprofit organization under the education department of the New Mon State Party. I's disposition was always toward a passion for teaching and educating others. Instead of remaining firmly within I's home context, I endeavored to be exposed to new experiences and ideas by applying for a job elsewhere. By way of the processes of working for MNEC, honing I's trade and then later developing into a teacher trainer with a nongovernmental organization in Yangon, I was able to reconcile the needs of different ethnic/linguistic groups from around the country. I's awareness of these shared realities meant that I's future work as a program manager for MNEC and civic education trainer would then be driven by the principles of equity, rather than singularly advocating for the language and cultural rights of I's own people.

Table 1.3 Antecedents, Processes, and Outcomes of Participant I

Antecedents (leading to teacher characteristics)	Processes (teacher socialization and learning)	Cognitive and affective behavioral outcomes
• **Wider community:** Yangon University of Education • **School/classroom:** Learned to teach government curriculum but retained interest in the teaching of ethnic language, in addition to Burmese and English • **Home and peer environment:** Trilingual, educators, education-invested	• **Wider community:** Work in an MTB-based education system (EBEP) and work in the nonprofit/civil society sector, exposure to regional realities • **School/classroom:** Varied, trainings around the country with a new job at a nongovernment organization and with various ethnic and linguistic affiliated schools • **Home and peer environment:** Yangon-based, regionally based training alumni and peers	• Need to expand worldview away from local historical/political demands • Advocate for linguistic and cultural minorities or those who have difficulty in raising their voice, making sure that their voices are heard at every level of society

As shown by these two examples, teachers or trainers go through specific social and civic processes, starting from where and when they were born, to be able to cherish the idea of living together with others in a diverse democratic society with shared values and attitudes. Their experiences demanded them to "transcend the borders of affiliation and identity" (Birch, 2009, p. 111). Both Participants I and J could have easily led their lives striving for the rights of their own cultural, ethnic, and language identities. They could have succumbed to becoming a cog in the wheel of identity politics and "us vs. them" narratives. Instead they used their experiences of working and studying in the different domains of education to deliberately cultivate "pro-social capitalist" attitudes. They used their teaching skills and their civic knowledge and skills developed over time by way of these experiences to advocate for social justice and equity across ethnic divides. The result was a perpetuation of pro-social attitudes rather than just teaching simply for the improved sociocultural capital of individual students.

The Approaches of the Research Participants

This section will focus on approaches in teaching for learning and assessment for learning, as used by the participants in order to perpetuate pro-social capital as a way to bring sustainable peace to Myanmar. The approaches of the participants of our study have been analyzed using the theories of three pioneer education theorists, which can be applied in the context of education for peacebuilding: Paulo Freire, John Dewey, and Jack Mezirow.

Teaching for Learning: Problem-posing and Reflection

Problem-posing, or conscientizing (Freire, 1970), where the outcome is meant to be agency, is different from problem-solving, where the outcome is some kind of answer. It helps people become conscious of the contributions that their culture or local knowledge makes to their regard for the world around them. Prior to understanding that they are critical parts of their communities, an individual might be apathetic or as mentioned previously confused by multiple narratives about the realities relating to social injustice and violence that surround them. Learners first need to step outside of their comfort zones and explore the realities of the society they live in before they can connect their own lives to the world around them. As Participant P said:

Civic education is a bridge to positive change: only the people who have the knowledge and the skills to make their future better can go over this bridge and can blossom. Those who don't, don't know the dangers and don't know how to prepare themselves for problems that arise in society. The students just know their own comfort zones, they only know how to eat and sleep, go about their daily lives, but they never think about the bigger picture. The first step is to promote self-awareness, civic education helps you do that.

(Participant P)

Problem-posing requires confrontation with the complex past and present and with uncertainty and ambiguity (Birch, 2009, p. 65). Sustainable peace requires a shared sense of unity/goals, but in Myanmar, "us vs. them" narratives from previous generations are preventing young people from realizing their common ground (Thuzar & Matthews, 2020). These "us vs. them" narratives can be problematized when the teacher generates an open-ended question about a story where conflict between two parties has occurred. This placing of an exploratory lens over divisive narratives then serves to reduce their legitimacy, and therefore the fervor with which they are spread. Learners are then able to imagine other preferred futures. An example of this can be seen in Participant B's activity plan provided here.

Two Villages

Objective: Learners will be able to practice applying the knowledge, skills, and values necessary to transform intergroup conflict.

Materials: Story of two villages—printed and given to the students.

Activity (1 hour):

1. Divide learners into groups of three. Groups read the story of the coconut trees newly bearing fruit on the border between two communities: the A Shay Ywar and the A Naunt Ywar. Each of the two communities wants the trees for their own purposes. Each group discusses what is happening in the story and the reasons why the two communities are fighting over the coconut trees.
2. Combine two groups of three to make groups of six. Tell the learners that we will now be engaging in a role play. Three of the learners are members of the A Shay Ywar community and three of the learners are members of the A Naunt Ywar community. Each of the members has a reason why they really want to have access to the trees for their own purposes (e.g., one of them is a herbalist who wants to use the coconuts to make traditional medicine, one is a farmer who wants to achieve his parents dream of having acres of fruit-bearing coconut trees, another is a business woman who wants to sell the coconuts and make a profit, another has had a bad experience of the opposing community "stealing" their trees in the past and wants revenge).
3. Learners prepare to act out their role plays between U Maung Shwe, Daw Nwe Nee, and Saya Tin Oo from the A Shay Ywar community and Ma Pont, Daw Ngwe Toe and ko Tun Lwin from the A Naunt Ywar community in their groups.
4. Learners do their role plays.
5. Learners analyze the situation: Distribute the diagram and introduce the concepts of polarization and uneven distribution of power.

6. Have learners reflect back on their role plays and identify features of polarization and power imbalance and where/when they might have experienced those concepts before.
7. Pose dilemma questions about the individual needs of members in each community for group discussion:
   a. How can U Maung Shwe from A Shay Ywar offer the coconuts at the monasteries *and at the same time,* how can Ma Pont from A Naunt Ywar make snacks for the community?
   b. How can Daw Nwe Nee from A Shay Ywar satisfy her goal of making medicine *and at the same time,* how can Daw Ngwe Toe from A Naunt Ywar meet her goal of making profit for future investment?
   c. How can Saya Tin Oo from A Shay Ywar overcome honoring his community's identity and homeland *and at the same time,* how can ko Tun Lwin from A Naunt Ywar plant the coconut trees for his business?
   d. What would a mutually satisfactory *relationship* look like if each party could meet their own interests?
8. Plenary discussion and then debrief with the key takeaways:
   a. How a dilemma can become a shared challenge for conflict parties to overcome constructively together.
   b. How the skillful practice of reframing a conflict by looking at the basic needs of the players can help the parties re-examine the power dynamics.

As can be seen from this lesson plan summary, a story is used as the basis for an experience—it is the problem being posed. This then provides a springboard into a study of conflict dynamics and how the process of transformation can begin. The idea of problem-posing indicates that dialogue is taking place, an essential prerequisite for coexistence with others (UNESCO-IICBA, 2017). Through dialogue, a learner who may have previously made fixed assumptions about that scenario will then be more able to reflect and open to changing those perspectives (Mezirow, 2003). In Democracy and Education (2001[1916]), John Dewey explains that dialogue requires communication, and communication is in itself educative because we are able to talk about our experiences:

> The experience has to be formulated in order to be communicated. To formulate requires getting outside of it, seeing it as another would see it, considering what points of contact it has with the life of another so that it may be got into such form that he can appreciate its meaning.
>
> (Dewey, 2001, p. 10)

As in Participant B's situation, the experience here could be the learner(s) reading a story about intercommunal conflict and then in a role play, taking on the roles of individuals in the context of that conflict. The teacher creates the "point of contact with the life of another" or a "concrete experience" (Kolb, 1984), which the learner can then reflect on and learn from. It allows the practice of empathy and the harnessing of imagination (English, 2016) using dilemma questions: in other words, asking questions in a way that the learners can imagine alternative endings to the story beyond conflict.

Participant G provides another example of how a concrete experience or a point of contact can be provided between learners and the characters of a potential conflict situation as seen in this lesson plan.

Who Gets the Oranges?

Objective: Learners will be able to identify the invisible dynamics in a simulated conflict situation and apply the idea of visible and invisible dynamics to other conflict situations.

Materials: Role-play scenario cards, one card for each group.

Activity (30 minutes):

1. Divide the learners into three groups and each group takes on the role of a character: the vendor, the hospital owner, the perfume company owner.
2. Each group reads their allocated scenario cards:
   a. Hospital owner: Your hospital needs the orange juice to save the lives of the patients. You need 70 oranges but you only have 1,200 kyats.
   b. Perfume Company owner: You are almost bankrupt and to save your company, you can introduce a new orange perfume formula to potential investors. To make the new perfume, you need the skin of 70 oranges but you only have 1,500 kyats.
   c. The vendor: You are the only vendor in the market selling oranges. However, you are worried that if you don't sell your oranges, then you won't be able to pay for your child's tuition and the oranges will go bad tomorrow. You bought the oranges for 80 kyats each and your selling price is 100 kyats per orange.
3. Learners in their groups plan a strategy for how they will negotiate with the other characters in the story to get what they want/need and then carry out their strategy. They carry out the role play whereby each character tries to negotiate and get what they want without saying what they really need or why they want it.

---

4. After the simulation problem-solving activity, learners analyze what the character assigned to other groups wanted and what they think their fundamental underlying needs were. They then compare what they imagined with other groups to confirm whether they were correct.

What did they want? What strategies did they use? What basic needs do you think they were trying to satisfy?

Example reflection questions:
a. How did the hospital owner try to negotiate? What strategies did they use?
b. What did they say they wanted? What basic needs do you think they were trying to satisfy?
c. Did the negotiation between characters end in a win-win solution for all? How might the characters be able to find a win-win solution to their problems?

In this lesson, Participant G encouraged the learners to assume the roles of the characters in a potential conflict. The root of the potential conflict is a scarcity in resources, so the characters have to put themselves in the shoes of the characters in order to negotiate within the constraints of that scarcity. While the learners are actually negotiating as the hospital owner, company owner, or vendor, the key takeaway (that each actor in a conflict has their own underlying wants and needs) is not immediately internalized. It is only when the reflection questions are asked that learners begin to acknowledge that what they were negotiating for was the satisfaction of their basic needs for survival. In this way the experience and the reflection serve as a powerful point of reference for learners to imagine alternative futures for other conflicts they may be affected by.

Teacher Positioning

Dewey and Freire agree that during dialogue, a teacher shares power with their learners in the learning process and becomes a learner themselves. They use the opportunity of being situated on the same level as their learners to find out what activities and techniques facilitate more dialogue and learning. The teacher uses their authority to be the facilitator of discussion. They represent the interests of the class as a whole (Hopkins, 2018) by ensuring that each and every learner is able to have a voice. When asked what skills a trainer needs in order to do to be able to facilitate dialogue, Participant B provides an example of how a teacher needs to be able to position themselves in the classroom and represent the interests of all learners here:

Showing that you are neutral, that you don't take sides, that you are open to all opinions, open to grey areas, setting ground rules in order to resolve unexpected arguments or tensions, encouraging all to talk by giving a chance for everybody to participate through activities, classroom management techniques including different grouping techniques, games that require everyone to talk.

(Participant B)

When the teacher positions themselves as the facilitator who is there to create opportunities for dialogue by introducing a scenario and asking questions about that scenario, both learner and teacher are responsible for "a process in which [they] all grow." The formulation of Dewey's prescribed "experience" where learners have contact with the lives of others and how the teacher positions themselves to lay the groundwork for learners to be able to transform their perspectives is resonant in Participant K's activity plan on student protest here:

Student Protest

Objective: Learners will be able to analyze a specific conflict through different "lenses" and begin to explore the importance of understanding others' points of view.

Materials: P. 66, Conflict and Peace: Understanding Conflict, Mote Oo Education, https://www.youtube.com/watch?v=ZpbRIZGFElo.

Activity (50 minutes):

1. Show a picture of students protesting. Facilitates using questions to establish the context; e.g., What is happening in this picture? Do you remember which news story this picture might relate to? What do you know/remember about this news story?
2. Learners discuss the questions in pairs and then share as a class.
3. Facilitator shows a short video clip from YouTube of news from the protest.
4. Facilitator poses questions and students discuss these in groups: Why did the students protest? Do you think that the government treated them justly? What are the needs of the government? What are the needs of the students? Do the students and the government have different lenses for looking at the conflict? How do you know?

In this example, the teacher is not imposing any of his own narratives for the student protests on the learners. Participant K is asking questions which encourage the learners to reflect on the conflict through both the eyes of the students and those of the government. In the same way that learners are given a point of contact with another in a conflict scenario by Participant B's story and role play, Participant K helps the learner to begin developing a sense of the "Other." He asks questions in such a way that learners start to understand that each side of a conflict has its own needs. Similarly, Participant B asks learners questions to help them examine the conflict between two communities fighting over resources from the perspectives of the individuals on both sides of the conflict. The worldview of the learner then expands from their own frame of reference to an awareness of alternative narratives or viewpoints, and in contexts chosen by the facilitator by their familiarity to the learner. As Christie et al. (2015) state:

> Mezirow claimed that individuals have difficulty changing because their worldviews become unconscious frames of reference constructed of habits of the mind. He argues that particular points of view can become so ingrained that it takes a powerful human catalyst, a forceful argument or what he calls a disorienting dilemma to shake them.
>
> (p. 11)

Both participants B and K pose a dilemma to the learners and then help them to understand the situation. In Participant B's case, a role play is used to "shake" the learner, forcing them to "put themselves in the shoes" of a particular community member in the context of intercommunal conflict. In Participant K's case, K starts by connecting the lesson to the background knowledge of the learner before using multimedia to build more detailed information onto that prior knowledge: the facts that learners already know about the student protests. This use of an alternative resource built on background knowledge of the topic provides the catalyst for a "shake up" in the learner. K then discusses the dilemma with the learners, asking questions that encourage them to analyze and evaluate the actions of both parties in the conflict.

Obviously, these ideas may be simplistic when acknowledging the presence of such deeply ingrained hurt or traumas that might exist in post-conflict or current conflict-affected areas of Myanmar. In the case of Participant E, one training E had delivered was to adolescents (between twelve and sixteen years) originally from Maung Daw, where thousands were displaced during the military offensive and humanitarian crisis in August 2017.[4] Within this group of primarily Rakhine Buddhist adolescents, there was a great deal of interpersonal conflict so the way he positioned himself was integral to how his learners would eventually develop a rapport with each other.

4. https://reliefweb.int/map/myanmar/satellite-imagery-and-analysis-reveals-myanmar-s-scorched-earth-campaign-against.

A Football Match

Objective: Students will be able to explain the meaning of teamwork using their experiences in the activity.

Materials: Football, football ground, or some space which can be turned into temporary football ground, whistle.

Activity (2.5 hours):

1. Explain to the students that we are going to play a football game. Randomly assign numbers 1 and 2 to students so that they are divided into two teams.
2. Explain and demonstrate the rules of the game, providing time for practice of the key skills like passing, dribbling, and ball control.
3. Conduct a quiz on the rules of the game with the students still in their teams.
4. Students play a game and the teacher takes the role of both the referee and coach.
5. After the game, ask the students to share their feelings about the game and why they feel that way.
6. Debrief on the benefits and drawbacks of working alone versus working with others to achieve a goal, using their experiences in the game to guide the discussion. Questions include
   a. Do you feel more or less tired when you are trying to achieve a goal alone? What about when you try to achieve it as a team?
   b. When you have a team of players or a team of people working toward one goal, do they all have the same skills and personalities? How can you use this to your advantage when trying to achieve a goal?
   c. How can you define "teamwork"?

In this training, Participant E laid the foundations for transformation in a challenging context by using a team sport. In this case, he used football as an instrument to help the students move away temporarily from the harsh realities of daily life[5] and focus only on how and why we work together with others. E strategically is positioned as a referee to make sure the ground rules of the game are followed and to prevent other conflicts caused by rule breaches. This positioning

5. UNESCO (n.d.) *Sport for Peace and Development.* Retrieved from: http://isca-web. org/files/United%20Nations/UNESCO%20Activities%20for%20sport%20peace%20 and%20developemnt.pdf.

as a coach means that the power from his role in the teacher–student relationship is removed (Sammut, 2014). This then allows the focus to be on the collaboration of coach and player toward working as a team and scoring goals.

In effect, the students look beyond their interpersonal conflicts stirred up by the warring narratives about ethnicity and religion that surround them. Respect and trust begin to cement in working together as a football team, players, and coach included. The players' experience in the game is the jumping off point for Participant E as the teacher to ask about the benefits of working together and working through personal differences. Within the context of the team sport are opportunities for satisfying the basic needs of the student—a building of self-esteem and a sense of belonging (Taormina & Gao, 2013). Building on that positive experience, the teacher (or coach) poses a question related to the learning objective. As in Freire's dialogic model for teaching, "answers are not end points (for learning) but a stimulus for further questions in a long chain of dialogue" (Wegerif, 2006). Participant E processes lessons from the game by asking questions to get students thinking about the relationship between diversity and teamwork. This is first posed to the larger group, but then beyond the "classroom," students can appropriate this strategy and apply it to other situations made fraught by diversity in their lives.

In reference to Participant E, an alumnus and co-volunteer teacher with him, remarked on E's ability to show neutrality and create training plans like the above through his understanding of the "spirit of Ubuntu" or "humanity toward others" (UNESCO-IICBA, 2017):

> *We have to plan lessons together and think of outcomes that we (and the learners) need to have. Through discussion, we have learned about (what it means to be an) active citizen and the "spirit of Ubuntu."*
>
> (Alumni of Participant E and co-teacher, 22 years old, Rakhine, now training to become a government school teacher)

The words of his alumni and co-teacher paint a picture of how the experiences of lesson planning as a volunteer teacher in Rakhine and learning about Ubuntu and active citizenship have shaped Participant E's approach to educating for peace. In this case, using a football game to remind students of their inextricable connection to and need for each other as humans.

Using Multiple Resources

The dialogic or democratic pedagogy explored by Freire and Dewey and other theorists involves not only teachers and learners but also contributions from other thinkers outside of the classroom. A teacher can select material from not just their textbooks but also alternative resources, such as case studies, news reports, or YouTube videos discussing social issues. The idea is again to expose the learner to multiple narratives on one topic so that they are able to compare their own worldview with the worldview of others. Wegerif (2006) called this the "dialogic switch in perspective." Even though we sometimes don't understand the worldview of others presented either by a person or virtually by means of an online resource, we can work to reconstruct it in a way that we do understand it. That "inhabitation" in the other's viewpoint doesn't mean that we lose our own worldview. It just means that we are able to understand that there are different perspectives that exist, albeit in tension.

The teacher considers the language needs and social backgrounds of their students and chooses relevant material that would facilitate an understanding of an alternative perspective to their own on a social issue. This adds to the "significance" of the teaching and learning process (Reickmann, 2018), whereby Mezirow's transformation can take place. An example is presented again in a training plan by Participant E, a former government school teacher:

Our Constitution

Objective: Students will be able to describe the rights laid out in the Myanmar constitution and the factors that may lead to violation of rights.

Materials: Grade—9/10 history textbooks, Political Spectrum picture (https://miro.medium.com/max/800/1*vh33g6fmpP9Xz5zMZjgHFg.jpeg), preambles of different countries constitutions, Myanmar Constitution 2008 app (https://play.google.com/store/apps/details?id=mms.net.mmconstitution&hl=en), news reports of rights violations in Myanmar related to the assigned Constitution articles.

Activity (45 minutes):

1. Warm-up activity—asking students to think about what is "left wing" and "right wing" as written in their history textbooks and discuss within their group.
2. Refer them to the "Political Spectrum Picture" and the relationship between each level of the spectrum and citizens' rights.
3. Ask the students to discuss in their groups the meaning of "constitution" written in their history textbooks, and discuss where/how/when they have come across this word and what it means for a citizen.
4. Post the preambles of different countries' constitutions around the room. Ask students to record which rights are addressed in each and which level of the spectrum they might be.
5. Elicit where in the spectrum Myanmar might lie and then refer students to the "Constitution of Myanmar, 2008" (Chapter 1, Article 21 a, b, c, d; Article 28 a and b; Article 34).
6. Students compare rights and protections afforded by each selected article of the constitution and current news reports of rights violations.

In this example, Participant E is teaching 15–16-year-old (Year 9 and 10) students from different ethnic groups and religions in a government school in Yangon. E builds on the students' basic knowledge of rights to introduce how they might feature in a country's constitution using visual aids and tools which the students can find online and use as additional resources for self-learning outside of the classroom. Within this lesson again is a question posed by the trainer to challenge the status quo—in this case, conscientization of the fact that the rights protections written into a constitution might not be reflected in reality.

If the teacher was to use only the grade 9/10 history textbook, there is a danger that this specific resource may only contain a single narrative—that of the state. The same rule applies if the teacher were only to use a textbook from a non-state education provider. If there is only one narrative conveyed in that resource, however subtle, it can be divisive and continue to perpetuate the mentality (Metro, 2019). For example, the representation of historical and cultural figures, and even the names and skin color of the characters in the illustrations of a textbook, can be used to serve only one worldview, that is, portraying that only one ethnic group exists in some cases. In Participant J's case, the variety of resources used builds the students' awareness of communities without borders in today's society not just in her own teaching and learning materials, but also in empowering the students to find their own resources to research their assigned community:

Our Communities

Objectives:

- Students will be able to identify the similarities and differences between different types of communities in both local and global society.
- Students will be able to build on their awareness of communities that are not bound by geography only, by conducting research on their assigned communities.

Materials: Active Citizenship (Chapter 2, pp. 24–8), Mote Oo Education https://www.moteoo.org/en/products/active-citizen-teacher-book-english-version; three case study cards (one paragraph each, e.g., education community, football community, Facebook community); "Modern community" on three cards (Urban Communities, Online Communities, Diaspora Communities).

Activity (1 hour):

1. Write down the word "Community" on the whiteboard. Elicit what this word means to the students. Write down all the ideas from the students on the board. Elicit the characteristics of a community.

2. Divide the students into three groups. Give each group a case study about a community. The students read the case study and discuss and brainstorm the common values/characteristics in the community they have read about/received.
3. Students share their case study with the class.
4. Students think for one minute about the communities they belong to and the common values between people in those communities. Students then work in pairs and share what they have thought about with their partner. Teacher asks volunteers to share their communities with the class and facilitates a discussion about the similarities and differences between the communities we belong to (focusing on how each community shares common values and how those values differ between communities).
5. Explain that the communities we have looked at so far can be defined as "modern communities." Each group is given a card with one type of modern community. Students read the card and discuss the key characteristics of their assigned community.
6. Students in groups conduct research online to find three examples of their assigned community from both Myanmar and around the world and present their findings.
7. Wrap up the lesson by asking students, "How have transport and communication changed the way we understand community?" Elicit/guide students to the idea that communities are no longer bound by geography, there are communities with shared values that span over the entire globe.

Here, Participant J translates classroom instruction to notions of conscientization and transformation by encouraging the learners to personalize the text—that is, "I am a member of these communities, therefore this is relevant to me." From the starting point of making the lesson objective significant to the learner in this way, the learners are then positioned to critically reflect on their assumptions (Mezirow, 2003) about what a community is. They may have previously assumed that a community is bounded by geographical, ethnic, or religious borders for example. By paving the way to independent research by the students, Participant J gives them a chance to build on that assumption using other virtual voices. The lesson outcome is not only that the students explore how communities of shared values can transcend traditional "borders," but also becomes the stimulus for future questions and dialogue (Freire, 1970). They might in future lessons, for example, start to think about the implications of online or diaspora communities for identity or inclusion.

Classroom Language Use

As mentioned previously in this chapter, the debate over language rights and identity politics continues to inflame and perpetuate "us vs. them" narratives. It is also difficult to achieve transformation as imagined by Mezirow because both teachers and learners have been trained by conventional schooling for most of their lives to believe that the teacher's voice is the most important in the classroom (Lall, 2010). Our study participants show that within this context the teacher can use their authority to encourage dialogue in the language of their learners' choice, at least at the group work level. In fact, in reporting on the role and operations of EBEPs in Basic Education in eastern Myanmar, Jollife and Speers-Mears (2016) note that a door has recently been opened at policy level for teachers to feel more comfortable doing so:

> A 2015 amendment to the National Education Law provides that, "if there is a need, an ethnic language can be used alongside Myanmar as a language of instruction at the basic education level". In some areas, at least, this merely recognizes the status quo. In one school visited for this study, for example, government teachers said they had long used the Mon language in class, and that they had always had permission to do so. Nonetheless, the change in the law has likely helped in some schools where teachers who could speak the languages of their ethnic students may have lacked confidence to do so in class.
>
> (p. 37)

While in Mon state, this amendment does not bear any significance to those who have already been using diverse "classroom languages" (Salem-Gervais & Raynaud, 2020); this is an acknowledgement of the need to use language as a tool for learning. According to Chandrasan (2015), these different classroom languages become the learners' multiple identities. For example, the learner could be a person from Mon state who speaks Mon. They could be a Mon first language (L1) speaker who learnt English and therefore can also function in English. Additionally, they can also be a Mon first language speaker who completed his/ her Basic Education and therefore can also function as a Burmese speaker. In addition to these identities are the learners' other identities, including, say, their occupation, their musical preferences, their enjoyment of online gaming, to list just a few. Dialogic practitioners or democratic classroom practitioners adapt their teaching methodology to the learner's social and linguistic backgrounds to build interest in a lesson topic. In Chandrasan's (2015) words, both teacher and learner can learn to manipulate a flexible system of identities in order to create meaning.

In the case of a Yangon-based alumnus of Participant B, the language of the materials compiled to take this alumnus and classmates through the steps of developing a community engagement project was in English. Meanwhile, the processing of what the learners took away from the community mapping activity— the questions asked to help them reflect on what they learned—was in Burmese. The activity was therefore able to "shake up" the learner because they could reflect on what they were learning about their community in their first language.

Particularly the community mapping activity really blew me away—her explanations were really clear and the way she facilitated the session, asking the right questions and making sure that you have time to reflect. This was the most productive activity I remember!

(Participant B)

A follow-up on this is that an alumni of Participant B now conducts online trainings for a CSO providing training and consultancy services to development organizations. This example provides a snapshot of the multilingual approach in action. Participant L provides two more snapshots, this time where the trainer uses Burmese as the language of instruction as well as English as a classroom language. In another case, Participant L uses the learners' mother tongue as a tool for navigating meaning.

It's important to use the trainees' mother tongue because their understanding of the concepts will be much clearer. Sometimes in English is better. For example, at Sagaing university we were talking about social contract theory but they didn't understand the concept when we talked about it in Burmese even though it was the trainees' mother tongue, so we ended up using English which they found much easier. In Shan, they found it much easier to use their mothertongue Ta-ang for discussions—they were ok if I used Burmese as my language of instruction though. In Mon state, they preferred Mon or English rather than Burmese.

(Participant L)

Participant L pinpoints clarity of concepts as the target situation for trainings. The outcome is two fold: understanding makes learning possible but it also gives the learner motivation to voice what they think about the concept. This has implications for both civic and peace education. Vinterek (2010) explored the ways in which learners can "live a democracy" in their classroom: They need to be willing to express their thoughts, willing to listen, willing to respect and tolerate each other, and finally they need to be able to trust in their own ability. If they are obligated to use a language that they are not completely confident in using, the willingness to communicate is removed, as is the self-esteem of the learner. This is regardless of whether learners are willing to respect and tolerate each other.

When placing a conflict transformation lens over the use of classroom languages in discussions, language could be assumed as an instrument for increasing the capacity of learners to express a clear sense of themselves and their place in life. According to Lederach (2003, p. 56), increasing this capacity for self-awareness is important to accomplish at the same time as lowering the level of "reactivity" and blame in the middle of a conflict. So in Participant L's case, in addition to acknowledging the multiple identities of her learners, L's decisions to use their mother tongue, or even English, helps them to build their self-awareness. It also builds their willingness and capacity to communicate with respect and tolerance.

Competency-Based Assessment for Learning

What we have detailed so far are specific moments where our research participants employ teaching for learning approaches toward an outcome of peacebuilding. These approaches develop the learners' ability to engage in learning experiences and participate in a joint process of meaning making through dialogue to help them adapt to their social and physical environment. The participants' teaching approaches when framed by each lesson outcome become holistic. Their attention is paid to multiple teaching and learning processes from how they pose "problems," to how they position themselves, to how they use classroom languages as a tool for communication, etc. Just as teaching and learning approaches need to be holistic to be effective, assessment for peacebuilding also needs to be holistic (UNESCO-IIBA, 2017). Holistic approaches benefit both learner and teacher. While teachers are able to track the progress of their learners, the learners themselves are also able to understand their own changes in behavior, relationships, attitudes, and competencies. Each of the participants mentioned have situated their teaching and learning objectives in a competency framework: one that describes which knowledge, skills, and attitudes are to be practiced by learners in an activity. This is captured in Table 1.4.

Table 1.4 Deconstructing Lesson Objectives: KSA/V Competencies

	Lesson topic/objective	Example knowledge/skills/attitudes addressed by participants' curriculum
	Problem-posing and reflection approach	
B	**Two villages** Learners will be able to practice applying the knowledge, skills, and values necessary to transform intergroup conflict.	K: The concepts of polarization and uneven distribution of power. S: Identify key factors in individual and collective identities, explore values and where they come from, recognize constructive and destructive strategies in a conflict A: The importance of understanding motivations, needs, and fears
L	**Who gets the oranges?** Learners will be able to identify the invisible dynamics in a simulated conflict situation and apply the idea of visible and invisible dynamics to other conflict situations.	K: Identify the visible and invisible dynamics of conflict, goals of actors in a conflict S: Recognize underlying reasons for actors' goals, analyze different points of view A: The importance of understanding motivations, needs, and fears
	Problem-posing, reflection, and teacher positioning approach	
K	**Student protest** Learners will be able to analyze a specific conflict through different "lenses" and begin to explore the importance of understanding others' points of view.	K: Needs of the government and the needs of the students during the student protests—needs as a source of conflict S: To use different lenses to analyze a conflict A: The importance of understanding others' points of view

	Lesson topic/objective	Example knowledge/skills/attitudes addressed by participants' curriculum
E	**A football match** Students will be able to explain the meaning of teamwork using their experiences in the activity.	K: That we as humans are interconnected in our diversity, how this can be applied in the context of teamwork S: Teamwork, spatial and physical coordination, problem-solving skills, cooperation A: Empathy, unity, solidarity with other players and the coach
	Multiple resources/narratives	
E	**Our constitution** Students will be able to describe the rights laid out in the Myanmar constitution, and the factors that may lead to violation of rights.	K: The intersection between history and the constitution S: Critical thinking—evaluation of the human rights protections afforded in the constitution A: Appreciate the underlying core values of each right
J	**Our communities** –Students will be able to identify the similarities and differences between different types of communities in both local and global society. –Students will be able to build on their awareness of communities that are not bound by geography only, by conducting research on their assigned communities.	K: The relationship between community and values, relationship between values and rights S: Explore similarities and differences between different communities A: Belonging, inclusion, community, changing values, and the reasons for change

Caveats for Other Contexts

The teaching for learning and assessment for learning approaches employed by our research participants are used in response to the ongoing fragmentation of the country in the midst of intercommunal conflicts and a lack of attention to what "all-inclusive education" actually means. The availability of teaching resources for teachers and trainers varies between the commercial center of Yangon, capitals of each state and their periphery. At the same time, depending on the context where they work, our participants' student numbers can also range fifteen to eighty in a class. Nevertheless, we have endeavored to imagine how the activity plans of the participants can be adapted to other contexts, as laid out in Table 1.5

A Concluding Note for Educators with Similar Backgrounds to Our Research Participants

As a final note and as a way to bridge the more peace education-specific chapters that will follow, it is hoped that there will be readers who can see some of their own identities, motivations, and classroom behaviors mirrored in those of our research participants. It is hoped that in the same way that these participants realized their agency in using their teaching skills to promote inclusion and peace, others can be shown just how possible it is to make their own transformations to gaining pro-social capital for peace.

Table 1.5 Adaptations for Alternative Contexts/Participants

Context (students, classroom, resources, etc.)	Adapted methodology/alternative context
Two villages	**What if you have more students?**
Used in: Yangon/Loikaw	For thirty or more learners
Venue: Training room based	– Divide learners into groups of six.
Number of learners: 15–20	– Instead of three members from each
Age group: Youth	community, provide learners with role cards for six members from each community, each with their own individual needs.
Materials/grouping arrangements: Story of two villages—printed and given to the learners, combine two groups of three to make groups of six: three of the learners are members of the A Shay Ywar community and three of the learners are members of the A Naunt Ywar community.	– When the role play starts, six members will be from the A Shay Yway community and six members from the A Naunt Ywar community.
Activity duration: 1 hour	
Who gets the oranges?	**What if you have younger learners?**
Used in: Various locations in Rakhine State, Shan state, and Yangon	– Give them actual oranges rather than a description of the number of oranges.
Venue: Low-resource training space, sometimes without electricity	– Have learners spend time getting to know their assigned characters, for example, by getting them to create their setting and props with classroom stationery for the role play: e.g., the hospital owner can create a stethoscope to put around their necks and have a white a coat to wear during their role plays.
Number of learners: 15–20	
Age group: Youth, 30+ years	
Materials: Role-Play Scenario Cards, one role for each group	
Activity duration: 30 minutes	
Student protest	**What if you don't have a laptop or projector?**
Used in: Sittwe, Yangon, Taunggyi	– Have learners connect to their background knowledge of the student protests and read the related news articles.
Venue: Training room with projector and laptop	
Number of learners: 20	– Use a "Fish Bowl" activity to encourage the learners to take on the role of the government or the students. As they imagine themselves in those roles, they need to listen to the experiences and perspective of others while practicing withholding the judgment.
Age group: Youth	
Materials: P. 66, Conflict and Peace: Understanding Conflict, Mote Oo Education, https://www.youtube.com/watch?v=ZpbRIZGFElo	
Activity duration: 50 minutes	
A football match	**What if you have no space to move?**
Used in: Sittwe	– Instead of a football game, conduct any game or activity that brings out sportsmanship and teamwork spirit.
Venue: Football field	
Number of learners: 20 learners whose dialect and first language is different from the teacher	For language differences:
Age group: Youth	– Ensure that there is a thorough reflection session after the game/match to assist with translation issues or confusion.
Materials: None	
Activity duration: 2 and a half hours	– Have an assistant teacher or translator who speaks the language of the learners.

Context (students, classroom, resources, etc.)	Adapted methodology/alternative context
Our constitution	**What about low-resource contexts?**
Used in: OkKen	Draw "Political Spectrum" on a board
Venue: Classroom in government school	– Preamble flash cards can be passed around between pairs and 2 minutes allowed for each pair/group to record the addressed rights.
Number of learners: 40+	
Age group: Youth	For learners new to politics:
Materials: blackboard, "Constitution of Myanmar, 2008" (Chapter 1, Article 21 a, b, c, d; Article 28 a and b; Article 34)	– Pitch the language used for instruction, focus on gist (i.e., rights and responsibilities) rather than specific terminology.
(apps on learner's phones)	
Activity duration: 45 minutes	
Our communities	**What about lower literacy among students?**
Used in: Hpaan	– Class is divided into three/four groups representing each community.
Venue: Training room based with projector and laptop	– In groups, ask students to take on the roles of different communities, and in a role play ask questions to inquire about the values of the other groups' community.
Number of learners: 20	
Age group: Youth	
Materials: Active Citizenship (Chapter 2, pp. 24–8), Mote Oo Education https://www.moteoo. org/en/products/active-citizen-teacher-book-english-version; three case study cards (one paragraph each, e.g., education community, football community, Facebook community); "Modern community" on three cards (Urban Communities, Online Communities, Diaspora Communities)	– Groups analyze the values of different communities using a visual organizer, i.e., they compare the similarities and differences between each community using tables.
	– Teacher builds awareness of the common identities within traditional communities, e.g., ethnic group, religion.
Activity duration: 1 hour	– Teacher presents the three modern communities. Learners brainstorm the values of these communities from their background experience.
	– Teacher debriefs asking about ethnic groups, religions, geographical locations of each community. Learners compare traditional communities with modern communities.

Works Cited

Birch, B. (2009). *The English language teacher in global civil society*. New York, NY: Taylor & Francis.

British Council. (2016). *Life stories: Past, present and future*. Retrieved from https://www. britishcouncil.org.mm/sites/default/files/bc1601_exhibitionbooklet_4.0_withcover.p

Chandrasan, N. (2015). Monolingualism, bilingualism and multilingualism: The human rights perspective. In H. Coleman (Ed.), *Language and Social Cohesion in the Developing World* (pp. 15–21). Sri Lanka: British Council & Deutsche Gesellscha für Internationale Zusammenarbeit (GIZ) Retrieved from: https://www.academia. edu/21648655/Language_and_Social_Cohesion_in_the_Developing_World

Christie, M., Carey, M., Robertson, A., & Grainger, P. (2015). Putting transformative learning into practice. *Australian Journal of Adult Learning, 55*(1), 9–30. Retrieved from: https://files.eric.ed.gov/fulltext/EJ1059138.pdf

Clarke, S. L., Myint, S. A. S., & Siwa, Z. Y. (2019). *Re-examining ethnic identity in Myanmar.* Centre for Peace and Conflict Studies (CPCS). Retrieved from: https://reliefweb.int/sites/reliefweb.int/files/resources/Ethnic-Identity-in-Myanmar.pdf

Dewey, J. (2001[1916]). *Democracy and education.* Hazleton, PA: Pennsylvania State University. Retrieved from: https://nsee.memberclicks.net/assets/docs/KnowledgeCenter/BuildingExpEduc/BooksReports/10.%20democracy%20and%20education%20by%20dewey.pdf

English, A. R. (2016). John Dewey and the role of the teacher in a globalized world: Imagination, empathy, and "third voice". *Educational Philosophy and Theory, 48*(10), 1046–64. Retrieved from: https://www.tandfonline.com/doi/abs/10.1080/00131857.2016.1202806

Freire, P. (1970). *Pedagogy of the oppressed: 30th anniversary edition.* New York, NY: The Continuum International Publishing Group Inc.

Hopkins, N. (2018). Dewey, democracy and education, and the school curriculum. *Education 3–13, 46*(4), 1–8. DOI: 10.1080/03004279.2018.1445477

International Crisis Group. (2003). *Myanmar backgrounder: Ethnic minority politics.* Retrieved from: https://www.files.ethz.ch/isn/28615/052_myanmar_ethnic_minority_politics.pdf

Joliffe, K., & Speers-Mears, E. (2016). *Strength in diversity: Towards universal education in Myanmar's ethnic areas.* Asia Foundation. Retrieved from: https://asiafoundation.org/wp-content/uploads/2016/10/Strength-in-Diversity-Toward-Universal-Education-Myanmar-Ethnic-Area.pdf

Kolb, D. (1984). *Experiential learning: Experience as the source of learning and development. Prentice Hall.* Retrieved from: https://www.researchgate.net/publication/235701029_Experiential_Learning_Experience_As_The_Source_Of_Learning_And_Development

Lall, M. (2010). Pushing the child centered approach in Myanmar: The role of cross national policy networks and the effects in the classroom. *Critical Studies in Education, 52*(3), 219–33. Retrieved from: https://www.tandfonline.com/doi/abs/10.1080/17508487.2011.604072#:~:text=In%20Myanmar%20schools%2C%20rote%20learning,form%20of%20teaching%20and%20learning.&text=Focus%20groups%20were%20also%20held,or%20grandparents%20across%20four%20schools.

Lederach, J. P. (2003). *The little book of conflict transformation.* New York, NY: Good Books.

Lederach, J. P. (2005). *The moral imagination.* Oxford, UK: Oxford University Press.

Lo Bianco, J. (2016). *Myanmar country report language, education and social cohesion (LESC) initiative.* Bangkok, Thailand: UNICEF, EAPRO. Retrieved from https://www.researchgate.net/publication/296334128_Myanmar_Country_Report_Language_Education_and_Social_Cohesion_LESC_Initiative

Lopes Cardozo, M. T. A., & Maber, E. J. T. (Eds.). (2019). *Sustainable peacebuilding and social justice in times of transition: Findings on the role of education in Myanmar.* Singapore: Springer Nature.

Marchetti, R. (2017). Global civil society. In S. McGlinchey (Ed.), *International Relations* (pp. 78–96). Bristol, England: E-International Relations Publishing. Retrieved from: https://iris.luiss.it/retrieve/handle/11385/171242/46436/2016%20E-IR-GloCivSoc.pdf

Metro, R. (2019, November 12). A missed opportunity for schoolroom reform. *Frontier Magazine*. Retrieved from: https://www.frontiermyanmar.net/en/a-missed-opportunity-for-schoolroom-reform/

Mezirow, J. (2003, January). Transformative learning as discourse. *Journal of Transformative Education, 1*(1), 58–63. DOI: 10.1177/1541344603252172.

Mullen, M. (2016). *Pathways that changed Myanmar*. London, England: Zed Books, Ltd. Retrieved from: https://www.academia.edu/30633226/Pathways_that_Changed_Myanmar

NESP. (2016). The Government of the Republic of the Union of Myanmar. (2016). Myanmar National Education Strategic Plan 2016–2021. Ministry of Education. Retrieved from: http://www.moe-st.gov.mm/wp-content/uploads/2018/01/NESP_20Summary_20-_20English_20-_20Final_20-_20Feb_2023.pdf

Novelli, M., & Sayed, Y. (2016). Teachers as agents of sustainable peace, social cohesion and development: Theory, practice & evidence. *Education as Change, 20*(3), 15–37.

Oh, S. A., Walker, M., & Thako, H. (2019). Karen education and boundary-making at the Thai Burmese borderland. *Journal of Borderlands Studies*, 1–16. DOI: 10.1080/08865655.2019.1685401

Rieckmann, M. (2018). Learning to transform the world: Key competencies in education for sustainable development. In A. Leicht, J. Heiss and W. J. Byun (Eds.), *Issues and Trends in Education for Sustainable Development* (pp. 39–59). Paris, France: UNESCO. Retrieved from: https://unesdoc.unesco.org/ark:/48223/pf0000261802

Sadovnik, A. R., & Coughlan, R. (2016). *Sociology of education: A critical reader*. Third edition. New York, NY: Routledge.

Salem-Gervais, N., & Raynaud, M. (2020). *Teaching ethnic minority languages in government schools and developing local curriculum: Elements of decentralisation in language-in-education policy*. Konrad Adenauer Siftung. Retrieved from: https://www.themimu.info/sites/themimu.info/files/documents/Report_Teaching_Ethnic_Minority_Languages_In_Government_Schools1.pdf

Sammut, K. (2014). Transformative learning theory and coaching: Application in practice. *International Journal of Evidence Based Coaching and Mentoring, 8*, 39–53. Retrieved from: https://pdfs.semanticscholar.org/518e/3e5ed6a5e7ba39d9c6ddf3d625cc64c5362d.pdf

Schulz, W., Ainley, J., Fraillon, J., Losito, B., & Agrusti, G. (2016). *IEA international civic and citizenship education study 2016: Assessment framework*. International Association for the Evaluation of Educational Achievement (IEA). Retrieved from: https://www.iea.nl/publications/assessment-framework/iea-international-civic-and-citizenship-education-study-2016

South, A. (2010). Conflict and survival: Self-protection in South-east Burma. *Chatham House Asia Programme Paper*: ASP PP 2010/04. Retrieved from: https://www.ashleysouth.co.uk/files/17342_0910pp_burma.pdf

South, A., & Lall, M. (2016). *Schooling and conflict: Ethnic education and mother tongue-based teaching in Myanmar*. The Asia Foundation. Retrieved from: https://asiafoundation.org/resources/pdfs/SchoolingConflictENG.pdf

Taormina, R., & Gao, J. (2013). Maslow and the motivation hierarchy: Measuring satisfaction of the needs. *The American Journal of Psychology, 126*, 155–77. Retrieved from: https://www.researchgate.net/publication/249964580_Maslow_and_the_Motivation_Hierarchy_Measuring_Satisfaction_of_the_Needs/citation/download

Thuzar, K., & Matthews, Z. (2020. May 7). *Microcosms of civic education in Myanmar*. Tea Circle. Retrieved from: https://teacircleoxford.com/2020/05/07/microcosms-of-civic-education-in-myanmar/

UNESCO. (2020, May 7). *Working with Myanmar Ministry of Education to improve quality of pre-service teacher education*. Retrieved from: https://bangkok.unesco.org/content/working-myanmar-ministry-education-improve-quality-pre-service-teacher-education

UNESCO-IICBA. (2017). Transformative pedagogy for peacebuilding: A guide for teachers. Retrieved from: https://unesdoc.unesco.org/ark:/48223/pf0000261349

United Nations. (2015). *Transforming our world: The 2030 Agenda for Sustainable Development*. Retrieved from: https://sustainabledevelopment.un.org/post2015/transformingourworld

Vinterek, M. (2010). How to live democracy in the classroom. *Education Inquiry, 1*(4), 367–80. Retrieved from: https://www.tandfonline.com/doi/pdf/10.3402/edui.v1i4.21951

Wegerif, R. (2006). Dialogic education: What is it and why do we need it?. *Education Review*, 19, 58–67. Retrieved from: https://www.researchgate.net/publication/236950610_Dialogic_Education_What_is_it_and_why_do_we_need_it

Chapter 2

LESSONS LEARNED FACILITATING DIALOGUE TO BRIDGE DIVIDES WITHIN AND BETWEEN DIVERSE COMMUNITIES IN MYANMAR

Kaung Zan and Joanne Lauterjung

Introduction

This chapter presents the perspective of two practitioners from very different cultures and backgrounds who have found themselves allied and aligned in philosophy and approach in promoting education for peace in Myanmar. In this chapter, we look at the current conditions that foster and/or challenge meaningful dialogue in Myanmar and share culturally specific observations and recommendations of our work. Since dialogue is crucial for agency, the chapter fits well within this section, whose focus is agency. Together we represent two sides of a coin: an insider and an outsider who seek to build bridges and find ways to communicate different perspectives and ideas. We believe that understanding and appreciating cultural norms and practices is key in creating an environment where connection and understanding can happen. Facilitating experiences that fosters openness for something new and an expanded peripheral vision is at the heart of our work. We share our observations and lessons learned working with NGOs, government, civil society organizations, and religious leaders. Collectively we have worked in nearly all of the states and regions of Myanmar, and with a wide variety of learners from all sectors. We enjoy unpacking language and culture, meanings and metaphors, and finding ways to open channels of communication to foster understanding and empathy. We offer an overview of dialogue in Myanmar today, lessons learned from our individual and collective experiences as educators, and some thoughts on ways we can improve our peacebuilding skills within the Myanmar context.

Dialogue in Myanmar

An online search for "dialogue in Myanmar" results in millions of hits including initiatives encouraging, teaching, and convening dialogue, such as political, interfaith, and community dialogue among others. We know of six different dialogue manuals for the Myanmar context, each written to accompany a specific

NGO-funded project, and only one or two of them used beyond the life of the project or shared to an audience beyond the original participants. When we ask local people in trainings how they understand dialogue, there is often an assumption that dialogue means Track 1 (national level) or Track 2 dialogue (sub-national levels) between the government and armed ethnic groups engaged in ceasefire negotiations as part of the formal peace process. While there are historical traditions within different cultures of dialogue as a means to come to greater understanding, there is little awareness of dialogue as a learning tool. There is a perception that dialogue should be used to make decisions and resolve conflict at an elite level, among leaders and decision-makers.

Communication in Myanmar is a complex web of relationships, languages, and power dynamics. In the Burmese language, when speaking with someone older, you address them differently than those who are the same age or younger. Informally, people call each other "brother" or "sister" using different words depending on whether they are older or younger than the speaker. Christians from different ethnic minority groups may address their leaders as *Sayadaw* (great teacher, your venerable, or your highness). When speaking to a Buddhist monk, the same can be used as well as specific words in Burmese that are used only with monks. Burmese language itself has these structures built into it, which acts as a constant reminder of your relationship to that person, and the speakers' standing in the social order in relationship to each other. For some minority group languages, this formality is not as prevalent, although when speaking with someone older, you address them differently than those who are the same age or younger. While these structures can provide clarity and understanding in knowing your place in society, they can also limit people's understanding of others—particularly those in a higher status who are tasked with representing a particular constituency. As a result, decisions are made that may or may not address what is actually going on.

A pedagogical paradigm shift has started to emerge in education in Myanmar from rote memorization to engaged learning, and this impacts how dialogue is viewed and used and, to some extent, supports peacebuilding efforts. Before the 2021 coup, Myanmar's educational system was undergoing sweeping reforms, moving from a system of rote memorization and teacher-cantered learning to experiential and student-centered learning. It will take time for all the pieces to fall into place—teacher training, parent support and buy-in, smaller class sizes, and development of robust resources. An Education for Peace Working Group (EPWG) was established in 2017 to promote communication and collaboration among those working on peace education. The National Education Strategic Plan (NESP) contains several references to "twenty-first-century skills" and "innovation," thematic areas that offer opportunities to mainstream peacebuilding principles and practices into both formal and informal education sectors. The EPWG defines "education for peace" as "a multi-disciplinary and transformative process that develops competencies to realise human dignity; social equity; harmony; respect for diversity and non-violent conflict-handling capacity" (EPWG, 2017, p. 1). We will use this definition as we present the context within which our creative dialogue structures are designed and facilitated.

When I (Joanne) began working for US-based Karuna Center for Peacebuilding (KCP) in 2017, I had already been working on interfaith dialogue in Myanmar for a few years. KCP was funded by the US Department of Human Rights and Labour (DRL), and the project was to run for two years and focus on interfaith dialogue. Working with three local partner organizations, the project was slow to get off the ground due to long discussions about the safety and effectiveness of focusing on religion as a topic of dialogue. The KCP team made site visits to all six target areas—Mandalay, Sagaing, Lashio, Bago, Mawlamyine, and Yangon. Sittwe, in Northern Rakhine State, was later quietly added but never discussed publicly. The Arakan Rohingya Salvation Army (ARSA) had attacked police posts in 2016, beginning a clash with the Myanmar military, the Tatmadaw, that continues to this day. Anti-International Non-Governmental Organization (INGO) sentiment in Northern Rakhine required a quiet approach in support of local efforts. After interviewing community leaders and stakeholders, it was decided the project would focus on adaptive leadership as an "umbrella" topic with which to talk about peace concepts, and we would begin with intra-faith dialogue within faith groups—Buddhists, Muslims, Hindus, and Christians.

Beginning in 2014, Myanmar experienced a so-called gold rush of peace projects. Most organizations started to promote peace, either implicitly or explicitly. In 2017 I (Kaung Zan) worked for a local organization oriented toward peace and cohesion. I focused on diverse communities in Rakhine seeking to build bridges between divided communities by training them in community development, leadership skills, and project management skills. The program included discussions of the underlying values of human rights and democracy. We trained community members separately at first, then would bring them together in the next training to try to build trust and relationships through shared field assignments. I went to Buthidaung Township (in Northern Rakhine) to facilitate the training in civic education and project management skills for the more marginalized target groups in villages where movement outside of it was limited.

The training was stopped midway through because it was the one-year commemoration week of attacks by the ARSA. The Myanmar military shut down the whole township and imposed a curfew. That training, and a few other similar projects, tends to draw people together too quickly, putting youth on the spot by asking them to achieve social cohesion despite unresolved and deep-rooted trauma. Whether it was a civic education training, where the word "tolerance" might be mentioned, or dialogue sessions, where divided communities sit face-to-face, what we would hear in side conversations during tea breaks was, "*Well, they want us in the same room for three days, so we will endure that before we go back to our own realities.*" Half-closed minds, though not at all their fault, are not prepared to absorb new ideas or learning, and sometimes they even shut us out. The dialogue culture or the practice of tolerance and other democratic ideals has to start from within, and that tends to be more realistic in less heterogeneous groups.

In peacebuilding we talk about fractals—patterns where subsets of a system reflect the same patterns as the larger parts of the system. In terms of dialogue, we can see the dynamics at the community level play out at the state, regional, and national levels as well. There is tension between cultural norms to preserve hierarchy, and lack of communication skills to speak across status and power differences. The peace process is an unmediated one, relying on formal structures that reinforce power imbalances and do not support meaningful dialogue, preventing awareness of the shared needs across all groups in order to foster win-win solutions when negotiating. A scarcity mindset feeds competition, and many of the most powerful leaders do not recognize the benefits in peaceful alternatives in meeting the needs of all.

Challenges in Education for Peace in Myanmar

For many years the thinking among most peace workers was that bringing diverse groups of people together for workshops would lead to greater understanding resulting from increased contact, and therefore a higher likelihood of some kind of relational transformation. However, there is rarely adequate time in a typical five-day training to build the necessary trust that would allow for deeper sharing, and therefore deeper learning. And while relationships are the main currency in Myanmar society (not much happens without first establishing a relationship) trust is in very short supply. This is to be expected after decades of military rule, weak rule of law, and strong hierarchies of entrenched power and privilege. However, this reality is often underestimated by foreign donors who may be unaware of just how deep the mistrust runs and the extent of the challenges inherent in projects with only two- or three-year time frames.

In addition to inadequate time frames, the lack of understanding of and appreciation for how people in Myanmar view diversity is also a challenge. For the sake of NGO projects, diversity is often seen as ethnic and religious diversity. Funded projects and workshops also often require an attempt at gender parity. However, there are many other groups that are marginalized. Disabled people are rarely visible in society, LGBTQ issues are still taboo, and cultural communication norms related to age and status limit meaningful dialogue between the generations. A challenge in promoting dialogue in Myanmar is finding ways to honor these cultural norms, while offering an opportunity for people to learn about each other. Most groups in Myanmar have a tradition of dialogue. The Burmese phrase *laphat yae wine* ("tea circle") is commonly understood, regardless of religion or ethnicity, to refer to tea shops as places to gather and discuss the issues of the day (Min Lu, 2000). In the 1990s, following the 1988 student uprising and subsequent military crackdown, government informants were known to spend time in tea shops to eavesdrop and report back to the military, quieting normal conversation to a near-silent hush. Mistrust flourished. This began to slowly shift following the 2010 elections, and picked up more speed after the 2015 elections, when tea shops were once again bustling hubs of lively conversation. With international tea and coffee chains opening in Yangon and Mandalay, traditional tea shops are maintaining the tea-circle culture by adapting to compete for business by offering expanded food menus and nicer looking store fronts.

While workshops attempt to create "safe" gathering spaces for dialogue and learning, the global pandemic of 2020 created challenges to bring people together for in-person trainings. Many schools and educational programs explored online delivery for the first time. Not only did this require trainers and teachers to learn new teaching skills for an online environment, it also presented accessibility issues for those living in rural areas or poorer communities where not everyone has a mobile phone and access to the internet. Up until 2013 in Myanmar, SIM cards for mobile phones and access to the internet were a luxury for the elite. When the monopoly of cell phones was lifted that year, millions of people suddenly could purchase smart phones and have access to the internet, as the price for a SIM card went from $2,000 on the black market to less than $2 at the local market (Heijmans, 2017). Applications like Facebook come pre-loaded on mobile phones, and for many, many users, Facebook was their only experience of the internet. There is very little awareness of search engines, and while there are several organizations promoting digital literacy, it will take time to catch up with what most of the rest of the world has learned in the past two decades. The digital divide also exists in Myanmar, as access to mobile phones varies greatly between different communities. One CSO in Rakhine State estimates that while 70–80 percent of Rakhine Buddhists have mobile phones, coverage in Muslim communities is only 30 percent, with very few women having their own mobile phone. This disparity illustrates the likelihood that bridging the gap between these different communities will increase rather than lesson with the advent of online learning.

Project Design and Time Constraints

Education for peace requires a long-term commitment over time so that concepts are deeply understood and result in behavior that will create an enabling environment for a nonviolent society. The NGO model of project-based funding is problematic in that we are working within donor-prescribed constraints of time, budget, and country strategies, some of which are developed half-way around the world without deep, on-the-ground knowledge and wisdom (see Waters' chapter in this volume for more on these issues).

Many peace education projects are within programs that are funded in one-, two-, and three-year increments. A typical NGO-style training runs anywhere from three days to five, and up to ten days for Trainings of Trainers. Workshops typically have thirty participants, and often challenging topics are covered in two or three days. These workshops are often held in hotels ballrooms, normally associated with formal, ceremonial events, and not always conducive to reflective learning. In terms of participants, there is an odd mixture of those who are "over-workshopped," representing a somewhat elite, smaller circle, and the vast majority of those who have never been exposed to this kind of creative learning experience.

When it comes to monitoring and evaluation, there tends to be a bias, or perhaps habit, of giving preference to focusing on quantitative data. These projects tend to have a technical approach that measures success in terms of quantitative data: how many workshops were conducted, how many participants attended, perhaps some pre- and post-workshop surveys on levels of comprehension, and sometimes the number of community projects implemented after the trainings are documented. Without rigorous qualitative indicators, the small glimmers of behavior change are difficult to see within these short time frames. What we often find missing are the psycho-social metrics that would allow for meaningful qualitative measurements—confidence, motivation, agency. It is ironic that arts-based activities are sometimes seen as less rigorous, when in fact, if done correctly using evidence-based practices, these activities often provide rich qualitative data because at their core, it involves personal expression.

Target Areas and Participant Selection

Workshops are most often held in cities such as Yangon or Mandalay; however, an increasing number of organizations are looking to more rural areas to bring venue costs down and allow participants an experience away from their day-to-day lives and jobs. The number of participants varies greatly, although an average size is between fifteen and twenty-five attendees. There has been increased funding in recent years for youth trainings, which is defined in Myanmar as ages eighteen to thirty-five. Trainings for older participants are often shorter, with a more focused theme such as leadership, interfaith dialogue, mediation, or governance.

Myanmar has a wide gap between rural and urban areas, and trainings are often held in hotels in big cities. Rural participants are sometimes at a disadvantage because they are uncomfortable in such a formal and foreign setting, which is not always conducive to reflective learning. Also, as NGOs select target areas based on existing relationships, this often results in multiple organizations holding competing workshops in the same locations, and courting the same active youth to participate. In some locations permission is required to host a workshop, and during Covid-19 this is often based on the number of participants so as to stay in compliance with the government's changing policies as the pandemic waxes and wanes. And while it is common for the government Special Branch to occasionally drop in on workshops, it rarely presented a problem if the organization had a good relationship with local authorities. Having a good relationship usually means that the authorities don't believe the workshop will present any threat to keeping "calm and order," which sometimes means that the organization putting on the training has "appeased" the authorities either by giving small gifts, or other gestures that may be considered bribery. This is a cultural norm, and understandably stringent donor requirements sometimes mean a limited ability to engage directly with local authorities due to the prevalence of corruption.

There are times when nepotism and corruption enter the picture. For example, field staff working for an INGO may feel pressure to get enough participants to hit the desired attendance numbers promised to the donor. They may have a relationship with a local authority, who then asks their niece, nephew, or cousin to help by attending the workshop. The NGO thinks it is training civil society leaders, only to have some participants drop out of the project half-way through because they weren't prepared to commit to the work necessary to carry out the project, let alone reflect on issues such as bias and discrimination. As for corruption, we have learned there are two sides to every story. Gift giving is a very common practice throughout Myanmar, where establishing a relationship must precede any other interaction. This can cause great stress for donor countries that have anti-corruption clauses that do not allow for gift-giving or require a signed contract before any formal discussions can begin. Such cultural differences sometimes hamper projects from the outset, where the tension between relationship building, transparency, and accountability creates confusion and a lack of goodwill that is hard to recover once activities are underway.

Learning Styles and Cultural Issues

There were significant changes happening in Myanmar's formal education systems with top-down reforms and goals and recommendations from the NESP. The new direction for education focused on experiential learning and moving away from rote memorization. However, teacher training to lead these kinds of learning experiences remains inconsistent and under-funded. We can see generational differences, between older adults who were never taught how to learn, and often come to trainings expecting the instructor to simply "pour" knowledge into their heads, what Freire calls the "banking model" of education. Younger adults who have been online and allowed to develop their curiosity are quicker to understand the benefits of being responsible for their own learning.

There are cultural norms of modesty and selflessness that also limit participant willingness to "take up space" or be in the spotlight. This shows up in workshops as participants happily discussing the communities they work in, but less confident to engage in self-reflection. This greatly limits the ability for participants to connect with each other, in seeing their common strengths and challenges. There is also the issue of language. It is more common in the West to use "I" statements, whereas in Myanmar it is considered impolite to do so. Speaking as "we" reflects people's preference to not put themselves front-and-center, but also encourages expressions of representation that may or may not be accurate. As well, reticence to speak up can also result from power dynamics in the training room, where the presence of a "higher up" (an older male Bamar community leader, or monk, for example) can prevent meaningful sharing or willingness to take a creative risk. Most trainings seek to reduce this power differential, as evidenced by the amount and kinds of funding for youth work versus working with older adults such as government workers.

Another interesting dynamic is a cultural preference for harmony over disagreement. Often trainers push for participants to come to agreement, to come to agreement under the guise of, "We are more alike than we are different." I (Kaung Zan) had a teacher in my Masters of Interfaith Dialogue program, a Hindu religious leader, who lectured on how similar Hinduism and Buddhism are, despite these two religions being very different. We, the students, were fine with those differences, but this instructor wanted to emphasize the commonalties between the faiths. If we rush to only look at similarities, not only do we develop a limited view of each faith's richness and diversity, we also miss out on the message that it is acceptable to be different and that we can manage these differences.

Confluences: Opportunities for Change and Innovation

We believe that the link between dialogue and learning can support overcoming these challenges by finding structured and creative ways to give voice to the voiceless. We discuss recommendations in the final section of this chapter, and will discuss here the opportunities that are presenting themselves to shift entrenched mindsets in support of adaptation and resilience to move Myanmar further along its path of transition.

Covid-19 is likely to ebb and flow over the coming year or two. It has led to more people receiving training online. Already we can see people are more comfortable with technology. There is greater awareness that the internet is much more than Facebook, and that a video chat in place of an in-person meeting can save people the five-hour drive to the capital of Napyidaw to meet with Union Ministers. While there are definitely downsides to this extreme reliance on technology, not the least of which is that people in poor, rural areas who lack internet or mobile phones now have no access to education. However, in the long run, NGOs and CSOs will have new tools to add to their toolkit in how they engage with communities, how they network and share information.

State Counsellor Aung San Suu Kyi's support of the NESP with its emphasis on skills for the future presented some opportunities for meaningful reform. Before the coup, parents were slowly adapting to the new textbooks and interactive approaches, and teachers were supported by the Ministry of Education in partnership with UNESCO to learn the skills they needed to update their teaching methodologies. Support from such high places goes a long way in shifting attitudes toward education reform. One important, prominent proponent of education is Ashin Nyanissara, known as Sitagu Sayardaw, a meditation teacher who established the Sitagu Buddhist Academies which support education reform in Myanmar. He is a very powerful, influential, and well-connected figure in both education and politics.

Other changes that were taking place in workplaces in the cities before the 2021 coup, where organizational systems and structures that allowed for more democratic forms of communication and feedback. The private sector, with its emphasis on efficiency, was leading this change, followed by INGOs with Western ideals of fairness and opportunity. What these workplaces share are essential structures for dialogue that can sometimes tip traditional power imbalances toward more equal opportunities for participation. Teambuilding is a commonly used phrase, and these kinds of activities provide opportunities for people from diverse backgrounds to learn more about each other, and hopefully come to appreciate those differences.

National forums are another area for increased activity and opportunities for intra-group dialogue. Women's forums, youth forums, and CSO forums were becoming more common. When I (Joanne) worked on an interfaith project in 2018, we held both intra-faith and interfaith national forums, and many of the participants were seasoned NGO trainees—some had been to as many as fifty workshops over the past few years. But for many of those participants, this was the first time they had attended an event that allowed for meaningful dialogue with others from their own faith group from diverse locations throughout the country. After they had worked on building understanding with others from their own faith group, this helped them learn how to interact with others from diverse religious backgrounds. This had a profound impact on some of the participants, and even a few years after the project, many of these participants continue to stay in touch.

Retreat-style workshops, pre-Covid-19, were becoming very popular. These provide an opportunity for people to get away from their day-to-day lives, engage in more reflective activities, and have the time to build connections with other participants. These are often focused on youth, who don't have as many work and family obligations and are able to go away for a week. Many of these retreats include trust-building activities such as theater games, sports, or arts activities—all of which help people relax and get to know each other before introducing activities that require a higher perceived risk, such as dialogue.

Lessons Learned and Recommendations

Using the arts as a springboard for dialogue is not new; however, it is fairly new in Myanmar and we have learned many lessons along the way. Arts-based methodologies are strongly linked to culture and identity and must be approached with care and consideration to create the necessary trust and sense of inclusion. This is extremely important for trainers who may be unaware of cultural norms, or metaphorical meanings inherent in a given art form, story, theme, or gesture. Working with local trainers is key to adapt exercises to be culturally appropriate, and this is especially true for remote regions in Myanmar. What works in Rakhine State may not work in Kachin or Kayin States. What works in Yangon or Mandalay may not work in a small village.

One of the biggest benefits of these approaches is that the instructor does not need to be an artist, musician, or poet to use them. A trained facilitator can easily learn to lead a collaborative poetry writing exercise, or to have participants analyze song lyrics on a given topic. Theater games require a basic understanding of positivity and appreciative inquiry, but no formal acting training is needed.

I (Joanne) learned an important, and difficult, lesson about the importance of matching participant needs with the right creative tools. A colleague of mine, another international consultant, brought together a diverse group for dialogue at a retreat setting in Shan State—Generation 88, NLD members, Saffron Revolution monks, and ethnic political leaders. Those who understand the context know that this grouping presents many challenges because of the tension between politics and religion that exists in Myanmar—despite the involvement of religion in national politics. My colleague pushed for a particular activity in the spirit of trying something new with such a challenging group. The activity required that participants work in their own affiliation groups, and discuss moments of chosen glory and chosen trauma from their collective past, write those down, and then place them along a timeline on the floor. Knowing what I know now, I shudder to think about this very activity with monks, who dedicate their lives to the concept of non-attachment—to thoughts, feelings, and the past. The resistance to the exercise was clear from the beginning and, in the end, there were very few pieces of paper along the timeline.

For the political leaders, not enough trust had been built, and the trauma was evident in their behavior, which was highly competitive and sprinkled with inappropriate humor. The lesson learned is that people must self-select to participate in anything creative or new. They came anticipating dialogue the way they had always experienced it, and then were asked to do something they were not expecting nor prepared for. This situation had the potential to re-traumatize many of the people there, which did not happen thanks to the relationship the convener had with these participants. He was able to move on and steer the group back into more neutral territory, and go back to a style of discussion they were more familiar with.

For groups that are ready for something new, sometimes these more creative forms of expression result in a deeper, more emotional conversations. This was true for the Kachin case study, where participants spanned a broad range of both age and status. Baptist ministers shared stories of hardship and difficulties, and young participants shared stories of abuse. Tears were shed most days of that workshop, and it was extremely important to end each day with some kind of ritual closing, some mindfulness activities to come back to the present moment so that participants could leave feeling grounded and centered, and able to cope with their lives beyond the workshop.

Another key learning is that it is extremely helpful when the skill set of the instructor includes the ability to help participants manage and regulate their own emotions, without resorting to a Western therapeutic paradigm. Myanmar is still emerging from six decades of military rule, with many people over the age of forty having lived most of their lives with high levels of fear and suspicion. It is highly likely they have suffered some form of trauma, and any experience that opens the door for them to express themselves, their hopes and fears, must be carefully designed and set clear boundaries. It can be a fine line to walk—asking participants to express themselves, while not laying bare all the trauma in the room. In light of the violent and tragic events following the February 2021 military coup, being aware of the trauma that training activities might stir up in participants needs to be considered for all age groups.

On the other hand, there is also the potential for incredible joy and delight in discovering one's creativity. Theater games are deceptively simple, but convey meaningful lessons of acceptance and trust. Most shy participants who hold back on the first day are happily participating by day two, surprising themselves and encouraged by a kind of positivity from other participants that many have never experienced before. It is as if when we expand our range of emotions, it expands in both directions—by experiencing a greater depth of sorrow, we experience greater joy. There is no "cookie cutter" approach when it comes to creative dialogue structures, and some trial and error is to be expected. We hope the following recommendations guide you in using these approaches and adapting them to your specific context.

Process Design

One of the advantages of using these creative approaches is that they work for a wide variety of themes. Topics for instruction and discussion can be drawn from many different sectors—hygiene, social cohesion, maternal health, interfaith dialogue, gender-based violence, etc. The Five Steps to Change (described in Chapter 3), for example, can be modified to any situation where change is desired, and where participants will be required to think through the smaller steps to make a bigger change.

We find that the Kolb (1984) model of experiential learning works well. Put simply, the Kolb model includes four stages of learning: (1) a concrete experience; (2) reflection and observation (reviewing the experience); (3) abstract conceptualization (concluding, learning from the experience); and (4) active experimentation (planning out, trying out what was learned) (Kolb, 1984, p. 42). In terms of process design, decide what the actual arts-based experience will be, and then allow time for participants to unpack what they have just experienced, reflect on what it means to them, and discuss how they can apply this in their lives beyond the workshop. Let go of hard-and-fast outcomes, and allow space for creativity to guide participants where they want to take the conversation. We typically design two topics per day—one in the morning covered by two activities, and one in the afternoon. Asking participants who have only experienced rote learning to think creativity and think critically is a tall order. Allow time and go slowly to give people time to process and digest what they're learning.

In our experience, fifteen or more participants are needed to create "safety in numbers" when trying new and creative things. A group of twenty to thirty is better, and up to fifty can work if the instructor knows how to manage that big of a group. These activities work for a wide variety of ages, and whether or not you blend those ages into one workshop depends on how well the group knows each other. This worked in Kachin State, but may not work if you try to mix government workers and youth community mobilizers. For younger participants, they will be more willing to try new things than older participants. With older people it helps if the instructor is close to their age—that way the willingness to take a creative risk is modeled by someone they consider a peer.

Whether you design a shorter workshop or longer experience depends greatly on the participants, and the nature of the learning objectives. It also depends on whether you are training other trainers, or offering a capacity-building workshop for a specific project. For a training of trainers, seven to ten days is needed. For capacity building, a minimum of three days is recommended as it often takes participants two days to relax into a more creative style of learning, and five days is a preferred duration. For corporate settings, a one- or two-day workshop can work to infuse a team with a sense of creativity and collaboration.

In terms of location, if the subjects could potentially get quite emotional, a retreat-style workshop works well so that people are away from their day-to-day lives, and can get outside in nature to feel grounded and centered after an emotional discussion. This is rarely realistic for older participants, but works well for youth. In general, hotel ballrooms are not ideal—they feel quite formal, and participants associate them with speeches and the use of a sound system. (Which should be avoided, if possible.) A dedicated training space can usually be transformed into a creative space.

Preparation: Setting the Stage

Setting the tone with the right kind of environment is extremely important. Anything you can do to surprise and delight participants will convey that this is not a typical workshop or training—playing music as they arrive, covering surfaces with butcher paper for doodling, providing colored pens and/or other art supplies, and preparing colorful, hand-drawn "Welcome" posters or banners. Decide what tone you want to set, and then factor in the physical environment when selecting a venue and developing the curriculum. Keep the space uncluttered by dedicating a corner of the room for supplies at the end of each activity. Post what participants have created throughout the workshop to remind them of their own creativity.

Dialogue must begin with suspension—of thoughts, impulses, judgments, and involves attention, listening and looking, which is essential to exploration (Bohm et al., 1991). Providing a creative and inviting space helps learners step "out" of their day-to-day life, and "into" what Bhabha (2004) called "third space"—"a 'shared space' where the flow between different realms of meaning and being are interconnected and shared between autonomous yet interdependent subject. This third space introduces an inevitable aspect of ambivalence, openness and fluidity into the act of interpretation, as it is controlled neither by the one nor the other" (Bhabha, 2004, pp. 95–110). Shepard (1995) refers to this as a "developmental container where attitudes are 'caught, not taught,'" which requires a certain amount of ownership on the part of the learner, to "catch" what's being presented.

Facilitation

Engaged, active learning has been a major component in many NGO-style workshops in Myanmar for over a decade now, and still today presents a big departure from traditional teaching styles used at government schools. It takes strong facilitation skills to build the necessary bridges that help learners know how to take advantage of the opportunity to take charge of their own learning. While Myanmar may seem like a collectivist culture to newcomers in the beginning, decades of mistrust have actually created a kind of individualism born of fear and suspicion. So collaborative, collective learning that relies on willing participation requires strong facilitation skills and awareness of these cultural issues. Building trust is key, and we have found that creative structures can do this more quickly than dialogue alone. We believe this presents an opportunity for transformative learning where "meaning is actively co-constructed between people." The role of the facilitator is to "shape emerging patterns of communication so that multiple voices and perspective are honored, and the tensions among them are maintained" (Pearce & Pearce, 2000, pp. 405–23).

One theory of practice we share is the importance of modeling the behavior we want to see, and modeling the values we ask participants to reflect on. We are willing to display the same behaviors we ask of participants—be inclusive, be observant, stay centered, and listen well. We work to keep our own emotions in check, and to be comfortable with lack of resolve or highly diverse opinions among participants. Understanding behavior is important in recognizing when someone is acting out to challenge the instructor, or to assert their own identity, or to express frustration with a difficult task. I (Joanne) once had a trainer who taught me that all behavior is that person's best attempt, given what they know, to get their needs met. And when we understand what that need is, or help them understand their own need, we can help them develop better strategies. Cultural norms play a big part in what behavior we perceive as "acting out." It can be a tricky balance between making space for all voices to be heard and allowing an elder to speak freely, sometimes venturing into making a speech. I have found that not using a microphone helps, which often sends a signal that speeches will be made. I also find that many of these creative structures level the playing field and allow "non-traditional" learners (i.e., visual, aural, kinesthetic, etc.) to shine—sometimes for the first time in their lives.

Using a variety of dialogue structures can be very useful for morning check-ins, or activity debriefs, or even small group work. Timed talking in pairs has worked very well with participants of all ages and backgrounds—each person getting equal time to speak and listen. This requires questions that really engage people, so it is important to ask relevant questions about topics they are eager to speak about. Sharing personal stories of confidence or motivation, or stories about their name, helps build common ground early on in a training. Other structures that work well are circle process, fishbowl dialogue, or "chalk talks"—posting questions on flipchart paper, and participants freely go from question to question and write or draw their response to the questions and/or each other's responses. One tip for getting more honest sharing or feedback is to provide ways for anonymous feedback. These kinds of activities take people out of their assumptions about the formality of dialogue and lower the perceived risk of sharing.

Lastly, it is the instructor's responsibility to create "safe enough" space. Given that 100 percent safe space is never a possibility as participants, and sometimes the context, are often unpredictable, there are things that create safer spaces. I (Joanne) make it a rule that when we do theater games, no one can ask anyone else to do something embarrassing (i.e., go to the toilet) or violent (i.e., shoot someone). It's important to promote positivity and acceptance, reduce cultural norms of competition and comparison, while also honoring and making space for differences of opinion.

Evaluation

Methods of data collection can be built into workshops. For example, the artifacts that get created—posters, poems, songs, etc.—can be sources of analysis to assess comprehension or retention. Artifacts that emerge from creative expression are key in facilitating deeper reflection and enhanced ownership of learnings (Boud et al., 1994) and create an opportunity for one's identity to be reflected back through the eyes of others. Another method that works well for low literacy levels is to ask questions, have participants answer by standing along a spectrum, and then document their responses. This is often much quicker than asking for hand-written questionnaires that take up valuable workshop time.

There are many resources online that provide material for developing indicators for arts-based activities: understanding metaphor, shifts in narrative, inclusion and positivity for theater games. Here are some suggested websites:

- ASC Evaluation in Canada—http://www.ascevaluation.ca
- PYE Global—http://pyeglobal.org
- Culture Hive in the UK—https://www.culturehive.co.uk

Cultural Issues

Probably the most important cultural norm to be aware of in Myanmar is *arr nar deh*—a complex concept that includes face-saving, preventing the discomfort of others, and social obligation based on status and hierarchy. Being a teacher in Myanmar is considered one of the most honorable professions and comes with a position of high status. For those of us trained to try and level the playing field in workshops by playing down our status, we need to remember that this may make participants uncomfortable. Navigating cultural norms takes a long time, so a cultural informant may be needed, someone who can discuss and unpack what it means to empower participants while still respecting the hierarchies they live in. For example, organizations may feel *arr nar deh* toward a donor or INGO, resulting in forced participation. Vulnerable groups may feel *arr nar deh* and therefore obligated, though reluctant, to agree to goals and values presented to them because they think they owe the organization something in return for the support they have received, or will likely receive.

It is important to give adequate time to discuss new words and concepts. Many INGO buzz words have entered the Myanmar lexicon, such as social cohesion, advocacy, transparency, and networking. I (Joanne) once asked a local colleague to explain to me the concept of "forgiveness" in Burmese, and he explained three different meanings, none of which mean what I understand of the term from a Western perspective. I have also had the experience of translations given that reflect assumptions of what I want to hear, and that differ from person to person. So, you can see the challenge of introducing new concepts. And given people's norm of *arr nar deh,* there is often quick nodding of heads saying, "Oh yes, we understand" without true understanding. Some of these concepts actually stay in English and float on the surface without being anchored in the many cultures and languages throughout Myanmar. Allowing time for people to digest, discuss, and then bring concepts into their own language is key. Without that step they are operating with limited understanding of the work they're doing, which presents the risk of doing more harm than good when in communities.

Conclusion

Creative dialogue processes can provide helpful structures that allow participants in peace education to sample new ways of communicating and interacting and to develop agency. However, they must be thoughtfully designed, culturally appropriate, and well facilitated. These methods allow for a "safe entry" into dialogue by lowering perceptions of risk, using humor to lower the emotional temperature, and focusing on elements of shared identity to build the necessary trust to advance to more difficult and contentious topics. The need for a known and trusted convener cannot be overstated, especially for something new and innovative. If you are asking people to take a risk, even a creative risk, the location and choice of participants is crucial.

While the appetite within Myanmar is high for these kinds of engagement, funding models do not always support them. There is a need for more adaptive funding to foster experimentation and innovation, which takes time and therefore money. And while many donors have a stated desire for innovative programming, they also have a low tolerance for the risks necessary to support new and creative methods. There is a truism from the business world that applies to donor-supported community initiatives: cost savings, turnaround time, and quality—pick any two. If you need to save money, you will need to sacrifice quality and/or turnaround time. If you want something fast, you will need to adjust expectations of quality and cost-savings. It is important for local organizations to look for appropriate funding, for donors whose values align with their own and who are willing to support creative risks in support of innovative peacebuilding approaches.

Works Cited

Bhabha, H. K. (1994). *The location of culture.* New York, NY: Routledge. doi: https://doi.org/10.4324/9780203820551

Bohm, D., Factor, D., & Garrett, P. (1991). Dialogue: A proposal. (Retrieved from https://infed.org/mobi/dialogue-a-proposal/)

Boud, D., Keogh, R., & Walker, D. (1994). Introduction: What is reflection in learning? In D. Boud, R. Keogh, & D. Walker (Eds.), *Reflection: Turning Experience into Learning* (pp. 7–17). New York, NY: Routledge.

Education for Peace Working Group. (2017). EPWG Vision, mission, member types and principles (p. 1).

Heijmans, P. (2017). The unprecedented explosion of smartphones in Myanmar (Retrieved from https://www.bloomberg.com/news/features/2017-07-10/the-unprecedented-explosion-of-smartphones-in-myanmar)

Kolb, D. A. (1984). *Experiential learning: Experience as the source of learning and development*. Englewood Cliffs, NJ: Prentice Hall. (Retrieved from https://www.researchgate.net/publication/235701029_Experiential_Learning_Experience_As_The_Source_Of_Learning_And_Development)

Min, Lu. (2000). Let me sit. In Sein Yaung Lwin Magazine. Yangon, Myanmar.

NESP. National Education Strategic Plan (2016–2021) *Summary*. Naypyidaw, Myanmar: The Government of the Republic of the Union of Myanmar, Ministry of Education.

Pearce, W. B., & Pearce, K. A. (2000). Extending the theory of the coordinated management of meaning (CMM) through a community dialogue process. *Communication Theories: Perspectives, Processes and Contexts, 10*(4), 405–23.

Shepard, H. A. (1965). Changing inter personal and intergroup relationships in organizations. In J. G. March, (Ed.), *Handbook of Organizations* (pp. 1115–43). Chicago, IL: Rand McNally & Company.

Chapter 3

CASE STUDIES IN USING CREATIVE DIALOGUE STRUCTURES TO FOSTER REFLECTIVE LEARNING IN MYANMAR

Joanne Lauterjung and Kaung Zan

Introduction

In this chapter, we present two case studies illustrating the opportunities and challenges in using creative dialogue structures to foster greater self-awareness and understanding of responses to conflict. This strategy can increase agency, confidence, and motivation to foster an enabling environment in support of nonviolent responses to conflict. We look at the structures needed to foster creativity and expression in service of building trust to the point where meaningful dialogue on difficult topics is possible. As process designers, we see the importance of setting the stage, or, as Bhabha (1994) puts it, creating "shared space where the flow between different realms of meaning and being are interconnected and shared" (p. 5). Bhabha (1994) continues, "This third space introduces an inevitable aspect of ambivalence, openness and fluidity into the act of interpretation" (p. 53). It is the establishing of this shared and co-created space that then allows for a learning environment that encourages exploration and curiosity and lowers the perception of risk that so often limits stepping out of one's existing knowledge base in order to stretch and grow. Zubizaretta (2013) captures the magic that can happen in these spaces as follows:

> As people give voice to their own divergent thought processes, they become aware of a diversity of valid approaches to arrive at given solution. They also discover their own misunderstandings and self-correct their own thinking as needed, all within a supportive climate of experimentation and respect— thus encouraging the emergence of a deeper understanding of the underlying concepts at work.
>
> (pp. 46–53)

We believe that if we set the stage properly we enable participants to learn from their own experience and each other so that they can begin to feel a sense of ownership of their own lifelong learning. Embedded in this is our commitment to fostering an enabling environment in which social justice and self-determination can grow organically and flourish. Now that we have shared our overall approach to peace education, allow us to contextualize the case studies by providing our stories of how we came to this work.

Separate Paths to the Same Destination

I (Kaung Zan) remember the first few times I told lies as a young boy to my friends, parents, and teachers. I did this because I was afraid to disappoint my parents, or wanted an extra snack, or just to see the look of fascination on my friends' faces as I told tall tales. Sometimes I pretended to understand friends' conversations about popular TV shows to hide the fact that we were too poor to own a TV. My interest in communication and trust started at quite an early age. In my teenage years I stumbled onto the writings of the Venerable U Jotika, a prominent monk and author of books on mindfulness and relationships. These books taught me how to overcome my crippling insecurities of having experienced severe poverty, knowing at a very young age that my school expenses were adding to our debts, and fearing the rejection of my friends if they ever found out I was not in the same league as them. Understanding my own feelings helped me understand that others struggle with similar issues. I believe good communication involves a balance between expressing your genuine self, and empathizing with others— understanding on a deeper level how they feel and how they perceive me. My experiences have taught me that greater understanding can be achieved by being mindful about my own communication with others. I have found great pleasure in applying this kind of empathy while teaching English, training, facilitating, translating, and interpreting. I firmly believe that the relationships and lessons people experience in their daily lives can add up to cumulative societal change toward greater communal trust and understanding. These are where opportunities lie in education for peace.

As the youngest of six siblings, I (Joanne Lauterjung) found creative ways to be heard out of necessity, and this coping mechanism later became my life's vocation. I was a shy child, and happy to stay in the background because being seen or heard seemed dangerous. Expressing myself growing up risked inviting criticism, pushback, or negativity that I would rather avoid. However, this strategy didn't work well once I became an adult—particularly when I wanted to speak out against injustice, or to ask for what I needed in relationships. My first career was as a graphic designer, a somewhat solitary job that suited me, but also opened a doorway into visual communication which became a lifelong interest in the many ways that messages are sent and interpreted. Today, over thirty-five years and a degree in conflict transformation later, I am still as fascinated with communication as I was in the beginning. I moved to Myanmar in 2011, at a time a general feeling of paranoia lingered in the air from the previous six decades. One avoided speaking openly with taxi drivers, and there were rumors in the hotel I was living in was bugged. Some of the first workshops I facilitated were spent struggling to get participants, most of them middle-aged community leaders, to communicate with each other openly and honestly. Trust was extremely low, even within communities where people knew each other, and I learned quickly that creativity was needed to navigate cultural norms of status to get to sharing necessary information to work together and find win-win solutions in communities of conflict.

These seemingly divergent paths led us to the same training room for a DeBoer Fellowship workshop in 2017, where I (Kaung Zan) worked with Joanne, who taught conflict transformation concepts to approximately fifty mid-level career professionals from several different corners of Myanmar, spanning a wide variety of sectors and professional paths. I provided simultaneous interpretation, as well as important feedback, during the training on responses from the participants. During this particular workshop, I observed that participants were being gradually led to becoming more comfortable with uncertainty and being open to challenge their own assumptions. The participants in this theater session were fascinated with the possibility of alternative narratives. Some even wished they guessed wrong as they enjoyed the surprise they would experience as the story unfolded. Participants were openly waiting for alternative stories, and enjoyed it when it was different from what they had anticipated. This demonstrated to me the potential that sessions like this could have in forming a mindset conducive for peacebuilding.

When the workshop ended, Joanne and I debriefed about the experience as we shared a ninety-minute taxi ride and hour-long wait at the airport for our flight back to Yangon. Our journey provided an opportunity for a long conversation on the many ways in which we envision education for peace in similar ways. I shared my perspective as a trainer with Mote Oo Education and provided feedback to Joanne that allowed her to later refine her curriculum. We have since co-trained and worked together a number of times and continue to enjoy unpacking cultural and linguistic issues around peace-related topics. This chapter is based on our shared experiences of dialogue training with diverse participants from many parts of Myanmar and the use of creative structures such as Forum Theater, visual arts, and creative writing. Our experiences represent a perspective from the NGO world—informal community education for youth and adults outside the formal educational system.[1]

Creative Dialogue Case Studies

The case studies presented here reflect our personal experiences working in Myanmar. Every situation is unique and methods used here may not be appropriate for other contexts or with other participants. Please take time to learn about your participants and their context and adapt these activities appropriately. We hope these examples will inspire adaptation and creation of activities enhance peace education in other contexts. Specific instructions for each case study are included at the end of the chapter.

---

1. Chapter 2 in this volume also discusses our work of peace education in Myanmar.

Theater of the Oppressed: DeBoer Fellowship Context and Workshop Goals

The idea for the DeBoer Fellowship began when an American couple, Marilyn and Jack DeBoer, visited Myanmar (then Burma) in 1988. The DeBoers were instrumental in establishing the humanitarian organization, World Vision, in Myanmar, and in 2014 launched the DeBoer Fellowship—a program designed to develop the leadership and management skills of emerging leaders in Myanmar, many of whom missed out on educational and vocational opportunities during previous decades.

The DeBoer Fellowship is designed as a year-long leadership development program for mid-level career professionals working in a variety of sectors. Every year, about forty participants are selected from across Myanmar, with a rigorous selection process that seeks a broad and diverse representation of candidates across various geographic locations, ethnicities, and work sectors. Selected participants must commit to an intensive year-long program that involves three five-day (usually) in-person events in retreat settings. At these events, fellows design service learning projects and receive mentorship by both local and international experts. We spend two days every year with the Fellows presenting a module on conflict transformation, as well as sessions on design and presentation skills. It is a short amount of time to present a complex topic. When the training was moved online due to Covid-19, this allowed us more time. What in the past had been two four-hour in-person training sessions turned into multiple, shorter online events that included two hour-long pre-recorded, interactive lecture videos followed by live Zoom Q&A sessions, and an online questionnaire. What took one day of planning in previous years turned into six days of preparation to redesign this for an online learning experience.

Participants come from a wide variety of contexts—some in areas with active conflicts, some from big cities, and some from rural villages that may not be experiencing armed conflicts. They come from many different sectors and work in a wide variety of capacities: senior management, project managers, medical staff, lawyers, educators, accountants. Participants come with equally diverse goals and expectations: career advancement, improve presentation skills, learn about design thinking methodology, ways to respond to conflict, or the opportunity to travel and engage in a new kind of social experience. For many participants, the Fellowship is their first time interacting with such a diverse group. The DeBoer Fellowship takes care to build trust among participants and engages a team of alumni who serve a variety of roles throughout the year. During in-person trainings, alumni serve as table facilitators, working closely with instructors to make sure participants understand key concepts, and are included socially in activities beyond the training room.

The goals of the session related to peacebuilding are as follows: (1) learn to recognize unaddressed needs as drivers of conflict; (2) expand one's "peripheral vision" and be willing and able to question assumptions in order to get a clearer picture; (3) experience storytelling as a participatory activity in order to explore new ways of viewing events and expressing oneself; and (4) equip participants with methods for constructive expression through appreciative inquiry and creative dialogue structures that can balance power dynamics.

Five Steps to Change: Weaving Together Multiple Concepts through Theater

Managing a room of forty or more participants is made possible by having DeBoer alumni as table facilitators, and these alumni are eager to help presenters facilitate activities. These table captains become facilitators for this activity and are given instructions ahead of time and given time to prepare. This way the activity can be facilitated more quickly, and participants can interact and engage right away. The participants are asked to come up with a conflict, as realistic a scenario as possible, that they would act out. The first time this activity was done, they were given several examples of possible conflicts. Each year the scenarios got better as participants heard about what had been done before and built upon that.

One scenario from a couple of years ago involved a man who drank too much and the conflicts that created within the family. Participants were assigned roles, and the actors began with the conflict as step one, and then after working through several steps, came up with a desired outcome as step five. In between they came up with three realistic steps (two, three, and four) to get from problem to desired outcome, hence, "Five Steps to Change." Each step was represented with participants in their ascribed roles, standing as statues. They could not speak or move; they must freeze in place, creating a "snap shot" of what was happening. The participants played the same role throughout, and in each step had a clearer idea of who they were, what their relationship to everyone else was, and how they felt about the situation. Once the actors came up with their five steps, they were reviewed by the facilitators and adjustments made as needed to convey the story as clearly as possible.

The next day, when the exercise began, participants crowded around the front of the room to get a good look at what was happening. People were sitting on the floor, standing on chairs and tables—creating the effective of a theater with tiers of seating. It felt intimate, with the same anticipation you might feel at a play when the lights go out, and the music begins as the curtain rises. The actors struck their first pose—step one, the conflict. They held that pose long enough to engage fellows in a conversation about what's happening. What did they see? What did they think they saw? How did they know? It became a conversation about how quickly we fill in information that we do not have, and how easy it is to assume a story based on limited information. After some discussion, participants are asked which character they would like to hear from, and then that person is tapped on the shoulder and asked, "Who are you, and what are you feeling?" They were not allowed to say anything more than their identity, and an emotion. This is often quite challenging in Myanmar as it is not a cultural norm to talk about feelings. But by identifying a feeling, we learn so much about that person, such as their unique perspective on what is happening. This is especially valuable for marginalized communities, or types of people we tend to write off. Such as the alcoholic in this scenario.

Back and forth the activity went, perspectives and questions from the fellows, feelings from the actors. Gradually the actors went through the five steps, and more of the story was revealed. The engagement was strong, the energy was high, and fellows were prompted to reflect on times in their own lives when they had made assumptions about a situation, or when someone else had made assumptions about them. The desired outcome (step five) is not as important as the process of engagement and reflection, and the "aha" moments that happen along the way. Even for the actors, being asked to think about how that character would be feeling fosters empathy by having to step into their shoes and really ponder what they might be feeling.

What's Happening? Understanding the Pedagogy

The role of the facilitator in this activity is extremely important in shaping the emerging conversation in a way that allows for multiple voices and perspectives to be heard and acknowledged. This allows for what Pearce and Pearce (2000) refer to as "maintaining tensions" among these different perspectives in a healthy, constructive way. This kind of dialogue must begin with a suspension of thoughts and impulses, to be attentive, listening, looking for clues without arriving too quickly at judgment. An essential element for exploration, according to Bohm et al. (1991), involves attention, listening, and looking. In our hyper-speed world with instant messaging, tweets, and other digital drivers of behavior, slowing down to explore a situation more thoroughly can be lifesaving in certain circumstances.

The facilitator/trainer must create a space that allows for ambiguity and help participants manage their desire to arrive at a "solution" or understanding before having all the necessary information. What helps create this is a playfulness, a creative interaction that "enables transformative interpersonal meaning-making" (Appiah, 2006, p. 151). It is out of the ambiguity that we begin to entertain more options, once we let go of the assumption that we have the answer. This touches on what John Paul Lederach (2005) refers to as "expanding peripheral vision" (p. 120) the ability to keep looking beyond what we think we know, to expand our field of vision so that we are engaged in actively looking for new perspectives, and therefore new solutions and possibilities. It is the ability to tolerate ambiguity and lack of resolve that opens the door for this expanded vision, and in highly traumatized populations this is asking a lot of participants. The playful, creative nature of arts-based activities gives us permission to step outside of a rational, solution-focused mindset to engage with ambiguity.

It can seem a crooked path, an indirect way to get from point A to point B, but activating the imagination and resources that have been untapped becomes the "driving force that enables concrete interconnections with others" (Braidotti, 2008, pp. 1–24). As a generous, positive environment is cultivated through activities such as theater games, a willingness to take creative risks emerges, allowing participants to dive deeper into their own imaginations. Care must be taken, as negative thoughts can lurk in the corners of the mind just as readily as positive thoughts, but by providing an enabling environment that allows for all expression to be accepted and not judged, support among participants grows and increases trust, creating synergy that increases both creativity and trust in a feedback loop of support and willingness.

Lastly, this exercise of participatory theater allows a breaking down of the "fourth wall" that traditionally separates performers and audience. As participants are invited in to engage with the story, a curiosity develops outside of one's preconceived ideas or rush to judgment or solution. The change process is slowed down and dissected, allowing for discussion of the actual, realistic, small, incremental steps that are needed to actually transform a conflict. These smaller steps are where the real world lies, that is, in questioning our own assumptions, in recognizing what we have control over and what we do not, as well as gaining insight into how needs drive behavior.

Collage in Kachin State

Context and Workshop Goals Kachin State lies in the northernmost region of Myanmar, sharing international borders with China to the north and east, and India to the west. This mountainous region is home to eight officially recognized ethnic groups, with an economy that is predominantly agricultural and mineral, including jade and gold. According to Global Witness, the jade trade in Myanmar was worth $31 billion in 2014, nearly half the GDP of the entire country. The lure of these profits pulls laborers from all over the country, sometimes with disastrous outcomes. The Hpakant mine collapse in July 2020 killed at least 174 independent "pickers" who scavenge leftover bits and pieces from large operators (BBC News, 2020). The state capital city, Myitkyina, lies at the confluence of the Maikha and Malikha Streams, considered sacred rivers by the Kachin, that form the Ayeryarwady River, considered the "lifeblood" of Myanmar. This confluence is also the site of the Myitsone Dam, what was to be the first of eleven dams along the Ayeryarwady River and was put on hold in 2011 after massive protests. The trucking of rare earth up to China, however, continued and very few displaced persons have been allowed to return. The Kachin War is one of multiple armed conflicts in Myanmar, and fighting between the Kachin Independence Army (KIA) and the Myanmar Army has been ongoing since 1961, with the exception of a ceasefire lasting seventeen years from 1994 to 2011.

Some Myitkyina-based members of the Kachin Baptist Church set up a foundation to offer support to veterans of the war and wanted to understand how best to support these veterans. A board member working for a Yangon-based INGO received permission to hold the workshop, using the staff and resources of that organization. I (Joanne) worked with the Kachin staff to design a workshop that would offer tools for volunteers with no previous psycho-social training in order to support the veterans, many of whom were highly traumatized. Prior trauma awareness training had been given to the INGO trainers, but yet they did not feel confident to carry on the trainings without the support of international consultants. When asked why, the response was, "We don't know what to do with a room full of crying people." By focusing on the trauma, participants had been re-traumatized, and trainers were not prepared to know how to respond. It was decided that a new workshop should focus on resilience—an appreciative look at what sources of resilience people already had, and could gain confidence to regulate their own emotions and carry on with their lives.

Participants in the workshop initially included board members and volunteers and, as is often the case in Myanmar, later expanded to include community members and youth not connected to the foundation who were available to commit to five days of training. This meant that the age range spanned from eighteen years old to over fifty. Of the twenty participants, there was a good balance of men and women, although having senior pastors presented a challenge in terms of honoring cultural social hierarchies, while also creating a conducive environment to invite all voices to be heard. Religious leaders of all faiths throughout Myanmar hold special status in communities, and many interfaith dialogue efforts are often ceremonial events with speeches rather than true dialogue.

The workshop was designed in collaboration with the local Kachin team, and the decision was made to use arts-based tools in an effort to "level the playing field" and provide an experience outside the norm that might allow participants to listen and learn across the generations. The space was set up with art supplies, tables were covered with butcher paper to encourage doodling, and music played as people entered. The arc of the learning curve was to begin with trust building, introduce dialogue skills such as deep listening and nonviolent communication, and then introduce resilience and self-care once people trusted each other and could self-regulate their own emotions.

Workshop goals related to peacebuilding were to (1) develop the ability to listen empathetically; (2) expand "peripheral vision"—willing and able to question assumptions in order to get a clearer picture; (3) introduce the concept of adaptive leadership for the older participants; (4) equip participants with methods for constructive expression through appreciative inquiry and creative dialogue structures that can balance power dynamics; and (5) develop emotional regulation skills and manage emotions while working with traumatized population.

River of Life: Visual Art as a Tool for Processing and Synthesizing

In the beginning, as participants introduced themselves in a very formal manner, crossing their arms and standing to speak, the facilitation team set the norm of more informal communication, to speak while seated, without using a microphone sound system. Group agreements were done collaboratively, and consequences discussed when one was broken. One participant, an older man, was consistently 20 minutes late every morning, creating anxiety when the trainers wanted to begin on time but other participants felt obliged to not start without him. We learned the man had to come one hour by motorbike every day from his village, but after asking the group if this agreement was important enough to keep, the man decided the workshop was valuable enough to him to make the effort, and was on time every day after that. This small example illustrates the importance of creating a strong and consistent "container" in which participants know where the boundaries are, especially when being asked to take creative risks.

One of the exercises that week was The River of Life—a common workshop activity in which participants draw and map out key events and changes in their lives. In this particular workshop, collage was added so that participants could quickly embellish their rivers with symbols and metaphors cut out of magazines and newspapers. I (Joanne) developed this activity when looking for something that would allow people who don't see themselves as creative to quickly create something that is meaningful, satisfying, and visually interesting. Each participant was given a sheet of large flipchart paper and told to divide into thirds: the left third of the flipchart paper represented their past, the middle third their current situation, and the right third their hopes for the future. Time was set aside every day for three days for each of those sections, and the room would fill with music and voices would fall quiet as people thumbed through photos and illustrations. This helped participants shift into their right brain and provided a break from an otherwise highly verbal life. One pastor surprised everyone with his ability to draw cartoons, and two other older men laughed and said they felt like kids again. Some younger participants shed tears and filled their posters with violent images of the war-torn areas they had grown up in.

When it came time for sharing, the posters were taped up on a long wall to create a gallery. One by one they presented their posters—laughing, crying, sharing, and supporting each other. Everyone was surprised with how beautiful they were, and at how starting with ready-made images out of magazines could result in something to be proud of even with no previous art experience. Even though the theme was resilience, trauma was apparent and came bubbling out with several of the presentations. We ended with a guided visualization to help people calm their emotions and come back to the present moment, asking participants to visualize putting their hurts and wounds into a beautiful box as a way of honoring their experiences, giving them a beautiful place to live, and knowing they can control when to bring the box out and when to put it away.

What's Happening? Understanding the Pedagogy

Most trainers in Myanmar who have learned about pedagogy are familiar with Bloom's Taxonomy, climbing the pyramid from retention and comprehension, through application, analysis, evaluation, to applying new knowledge in the creation of some kind of concrete action (Bloom et al. 1956). A variation on Bloom's Taxonomy is Kolb's (1984) experiential learning cycle, which puts discovery and reflection at the center of learning. The trainer is seen as a facilitator, designing processes of discovery, and then guiding learners through different levels of reflection and application. Kolb (1984) posits learning to be knowledge creation through the transformation of experience. Learning is a dialectic and cyclical process consisting of five other processes: concrete experience, reflective observation, abstract conceptualization, theorizing, and experimentation. Experience is the basis of learning, but learning cannot take place without reflection (Cochran-Smith, 1999). The highest scores in the block on self-regulation of learning refer to reflective learning methodology as a facilitator for the in-depth analysis of emotions in everyday and professional situations (Loughran, 2002). An important rationale for reflective practices is the idea that just having an experience does not equal learning. Deliberate reflection is needed to synthesize new concepts and experiences, to become relevant in one's life, which can then increase confidence and motivation to apply new concepts learned.

At the core of this workshop was the belief that creative expression presents opportunities for reflection outside cultural norms that can limit communication between people where a power differential exists. For example, a young female volunteer sharing her life story in a meaningful way to a middle-aged male pastor. The choice of visual art was deliberate. It was a visual form of communication that allows both personal expressions and processing emotions through the use of metaphor and symbols. Life as a "river," with all its twists and turns, sometimes flowing slowly, sometimes rushing over rocks and cliffs. A collage offers an opportunity to explore metaphors and symbolism through intuitive imagery selection, and a deeper understanding of our lives when juxtaposing different time frames (past, present, and future) side-by-side. According to Lakoff and Johnson (1980), "There is directionality in metaphor, that is, we understand one concept only in terms of another" (p. 112). It is in these comparisons, within our own life stories and also in sharing and seeing them in relationship to others' stories, when our own experiences venture out into the world to then be reflected back to us in new ways. And in seeing our stories reflected back to us in these ways, we can then expand our "peripheral" vision of our own lives, and our place in the world in relationship to others. It is in this expanding of peripheral vision where creative solutions can begin to percolate, where new possibilities become visible (Lederach, 2005).

An activity like this enables and promotes a "narrative identity" (Feldhendler, 2007), whereby the storyteller's own narrative is reflected back through the act of sharing. This opens the door to discovering one's story anew, to be seen and heard in a new way. Its value in terms of dialogue is that it brings the past, present, and future into the here and now, allowing us to examine the stories we tell about ourselves, come to new insights, and perhaps expand our own understanding of given and chosen identities. It also allows us to see more clearly the agency we have in choosing our own identity and how we shape and retell our stories. And in a workshop like this the sharing of individual identities, and the bond that resulted, strengthened their sense of collective identity (Feldhendler, 2007). The sharing of stories using arts-based methodologies also allows a "shortcut," an alternative way of communicating outside cultural norms of hierarchy. Illman (2011) shows that creative forms of communication place a fundamental value of creativity in building the necessary conditions for effective dialogue, including the recognition of a common humanity. She emphasizes the attitudes and values that are key to effective dialogue: respect, curiosity, humor, responsibility, and active solidarity.

Lastly, this case study illustrates how arts-based activities can result in a more emotional conversation. Sights and sounds are more likely to trigger memories, and because of this it's very important to model and build capacity for emotional regulation without venturing into actual therapy. Two things helped participants in this particular workshop to process these strong emotions and then carry on. First, the theme of resilience meant we were focusing all week on what keeps us going during hard times, giving participants an opportunity to apply that understanding to get through such an emotional patch. Second, we included a lot of movement and theater games throughout each day to help move emotions through the body. Every group is different, and it is important for the facilitator to be flexible, prepared, and observant enough to know when to shift the groups energy toward or away from strong emotions. We all need to work within our comfort zone and skill level.

Activity Instructions

The value of these activities is in the combination of a participatory, creative, reflective experience, followed by a rigorous debrief to support comprehension and application in participants daily lives.

Five Steps to Change

Note: This exercise is drawn from the work of Brazilian theater practitioner, drama theories and political activist, Augusto Boal. For more information, see his book, *Theatre of the Oppressed* (Boal, 1985). This activity should be done with participants after time has been spent to build trust and support among them.

Five Steps to Change

Preparation

Time: Depends on the number of participants, approx. 45 minutes
Creative risk level: High—must be comfortable performing
Literacy needed: None
Materials needed: Dry erase board or butcher paper, marker

Facilitation Notes

1. Before doing this activity, it is recommended that you do about 30–40 minutes of warm-up theater improvisation exercises. There are many resources online for theater improvisation, and a good place to start is the Improv Encyclopedia (http://improvencyclopedia.org).
2. One of the key elements of this exercise is to challenge participants to think about how quickly we tend to interpret what we see without knowing the full story.
3. Depending on the conflicts chosen, this has the potential to become an emotional exercise. Therefore, it is important to have a certain level

of comfort and confidence in working with emotional issues to lead this. If people need to process what they are feeling, allow extra time. Be sure participants feel a sense of closure from the activity before sending them off.

Instructions

1. Warm-up with improv exercises. Include some that demonstrate the concept of "statues," that is, a group of people standing still in a pose, without words or movement, to convey a concept or idea.
2. Divide participants into groups of 5–7. Wait until they are in their groups before giving further instructions.
3. On the board or paper, draw a horizontal line and write "conflict" at one end and "solution" at the other. Then draw three tick-marks between the two ends and label those "step 1," "step 2," and "step 3." Explain that this exercise is called "Five Steps to Change" and that they'll be looking at what intermediary steps are necessary to resolve or transform conflict.
4. Groups are to talk about problems or conflict they are experiencing in their lives. This can be at any level: personal, family, community, or national. They must then agree to work on one as a group.
5. Once they have chosen a conflict to work on, they must then agree on a realistic, nonviolent, ultimate outcome that repairs any damage done to relationships.
6. After agreeing on their ideal outcome, they then decide on three steps between the conflict and the final step. These should be realistic steps that would lead to their ideal outcome. For example: Situation: Moh Zin and Kyaw Myo sometimes fight at the office in front of others; STEP 1 Coworkers tell their manager that the fights are affecting their ability to work and destroying a sense of team spirit. STEP 2 The manager speaks to Moh Zin and Kya Myo and listens to try and understand why they are fighting. STEP 3 The manager lets them both know they are valued employees, but that the fighting is not acceptable. STEP 4 In talking with the manager, Moh Zin and Kya Myo better understand each other's issues, and feel greater empathy for each other. They have their differences, but agree to disagree and focus on their work. STEP 5 The office is a happier and quieter place, and people are able to work more productively. Everyone enjoys their job more, and no one leaves.
7. Once their steps are agreed upon, groups then come up with "sculptures" (groups of statues) to convey each of the steps.
8. Groups come back and present their five steps to change with facilitated pacing and conversation as demonstrated in the workshop. The group should freeze in each posture and hold that while the

facilitator asks questions, and only move on to the next pose when the facilitator claps or lets them know to move on. Be sure to ask those watching first for their interpretations of what they see, before you tap someone in the sculpture to reveal who they are and what they feel.

9. Discuss debrief questions: Was that easy or hard? If so, why? Talk about the gap between perception and reality. Do we always know what is really going on as witnesses or outside observers? What are some ideas for using this exercise as a submission? Can you think of steps to change that could be acted out like this?

Collage Instructions

Collage is a technique of art creation, primarily used in the visual arts by which art results from an assemblage of different forms, thus creating a new whole. Using ready-made images allows people to use metaphor and symbolism in conveying personal narratives, sometimes surprising themselves at the synchronicity of finding just the right image to convey what they may have difficulty saying verbally.

Making a Collage

Preparation

Visual art: Collage
Time: 60 minutes
Creative risk level: Low
Literacy needed: None

Materials needed:

1. 1 piece of white construction paper for each group or participant (size is variable—the larger the size, the more time you'll need to allow)
2. Magazines
3. Glue sticks
4. Scissors
5. Optional: colored markers, pens, pencils, paint, and brushes

Facilitation Notes

1. Collage gives participants, especially those that do not think of themselves as creative, a sense of accomplishment because collages usually end up looking good.

2. You may need to remind participants to just dive in and start, and not to worry about selecting the "perfect" image or words. Remind participants that there is no right or wrong way to do this.
3. Collage can be adapted in a number of ways. It can be done individually or as a group, and it can be used for either specific or general topics or issues.
4. If you use this exercise following one of the above activities, you can either brainstorm new issues, or revisit ones that came up earlier.

Instructions

1. Working in groups of four, agree on one issue to focus on.
2. Instruct participants to go through the magazines and select images and words that relate to their issue. Encourage people to trust their first reaction. If an image jumps out at them, tear it out and try to work with it. They can cut out words, phrases, or headlines and add them to the collage. It is recommended that people have a pile of magazine clippings before they start to lay out the collage.
3. Once participants have their pile of clippings, they can then start to tear or cut the images and play around with placing them on the construction paper. They can create background textures, turn images.
4. At the end, post the collages around the room and have a gallery walk where everyone can walk around and see and comment on them.
5. Discuss the following debrief questions: What did you learn about the issue you explored through this process? How can images and metaphor be used as a basis for dialogue in discussing social justice and peacebuilding? How might a visual element compliment traditional approaches to dialogue? What cultural issues might come up, or be addressed through pictures and symbols?

Conclusion

Both of these case studies illustrate the potential for using creative, arts-based processes with people who may not see themselves as creative, or capable of creating art—both instructors and participants. A little knowledge goes a long way, as does a little imagination, in creating a learning environment that invites spontaneous discoveries and a willingness to take risks. And in taking those risks, it can transform our relationship with making mistakes—to see trial and error as a necessary path toward more creative problem-solving, and expanding peripheral vision of what's possible. This is how resilience is built, one risk at a time, and in overcoming that risk every time. We learn to trust our creativity, develop agency, and expand our perceptions of what is possible.

There is a growing weariness with "workshops as usual," and in applying a cookie cutter approach to capacity building. Both trainers and students are hungry for a more engaging experience that directly relates to their lives outside the training room—especially during Covid-19 and the demands of being online and the isolation many people feel. Investment in new skills and new approaches is needed, as is a willingness and tolerance for creative risk. When this is the case, we believe that locally generated solutions and innovative methods of addressing conflict can be generated, sustained, and adapted for a long time to come.

Works Cited

Appiah, K. A. (2006). *Cosmopolitanism: Ethics in a world of strangers.* New York, NY: W. W. Norton & Company.

BBC (2020, July). Myanmar jade mine landslide kills 160. *BBC News.* Author unknown.

Bhabha, H. K. (1994). *The location of culture.* New York, NY: Routledge. doi: https://doi.org/10.4324/9780203820551

Bloom, B. S., Engelhart, M. D., Furst, E. J., Hill, W. H., & Krathwohl, D. R. (1956). *Taxonomy of educational objectives: The classification of educational goals.* Vol. Handbook I: Cognitive domain. New York: David McKay Company.

Boal, A. (1985). *Theater of the oppressed.* New York, NY: Theater Communications Group.

Bohm, D., Factor, D., & Garrett, P. (1991). Dialogue: A proposal (Retrieved from https://infed.org/mobi/dialogue-a-proposal/)

Braidotti, R (2008). In spite of the times: The post-secular turn in feminism. *Theory, Culture, Society,* 25(6), 1–24.

Cochran-Smith, M., & Lytle, S. L. (1999). Relationships of knowledge and practice: Teacher learning in communities. *Review of Research in Education,* 24(1), 249–305.

Feldhendler, D. (2007). Playback theatre: A method for intercultural dialogue. *Journal for Performative Teaching, Learning, Research: Scenario,* 2(2).

Illman, R. (2011). Artists in dialogue: Creative approaches to interreligious encounters. *Approaching Religion,* 1(1), 59–71.

Kolb, D. A. (1984). *Experiential learning: Experience as the source of learning and development.* Englewood Cliffs, NJ: Prentice Hall. (Retrieved from https://www.researchgate.net/publication/235701029_Experiential_Learning_Experience_As_The_Source_Of_Learning_And_Development)

Lakoff, G., & Johnson, M. (1980). *Metaphors we live by.* Chicago, IL: University of Chicago Press.

Lederach, J. P. (2005). *The moral imagination.* New York, NY: Oxford University Press.

Loughran, J. J. (2002). Effective reflective practice: In search of meaning in learning about teaching. *Journal of Teacher Education,* 53(1), 33–43

Pearce, W. B., & Pearce, K. A. (2000). Extending the theory of the coordinated management of meaning (CMM) through a community dialogue process. *Communication Theory,* 10(4), 405–23.

Zubizaretta, R. (2013). Co-creative dialogue for meeting practical challenges: New approaches. *OD Practitioner,* 45(1), 47–53.

Part II

IDENTITY

Chapter 4

CHANGING NARRATIVES AND TRANSFORMING CONFLICT THROUGH NONFORMAL EDUCATION FOR YOUTH IN RAKHINE STATE

Melanie Walker, Soe Khine, and Ko Thant

Introduction

Rakhine State and Its Legacy of Migrations

The great coastline of Rakhine State, Myanmar's westernmost frontier, with its many clusters of islands, is lapped by the steamy tides of the Bay of Bengal and is abutted to the north, over the River Naf, by Bangladesh. Isolated from the main political and economic centers of greater Myanmar to the east by the almost impenetrable Arakan Yoma (Arakan mountain range), in 2017, the state's poverty rate was 78 percent, almost double the national average (Advisory Commission on Rakhine State 2017). I (Melanie) have worked in education and youth empowerment in Myanmar and around its borders for almost two decades, and my first real knowledge of Rakhine State came from Rohingya refugees I met in Bangladesh in 2008. They had fled Myanmar in 1992, some of them fleeing multiple times after their initial expulsion in 1978. Standing on the shores of the Naf, I looked over the great river to the mountains of the Arakan Yoma and I wondered what had and was still taking place over there to ensure that the Rohingya refugees had remained in Bangladesh for so long.

Prior to the formation of the current Myanmar state in 1948 at independence from the British (the people with whom I, Melanie, share ancestry), Rakhine State (or just Rakhine, as it is now often called) was known as Arakan. Located on historical migratory paths from Central and Eastern Asia, and more recent maritime and land trade routes, the development of Arakan proceeded with dynasties and kingdoms culminating in the kingdom of Mrauk U, active between the fifteenth to eighteenth centuries. Professor Michael Charney (2005), Asian military historian in the School of Oriental and Asian Studies in the University of London, explains that

The names Soe Khine and Ko Thant are pseudonyms of two male Rakhine teachers and have been changed to protect their identities.

Arakan history has long been overlooked by scholars of Southeast Asian history at the regional and national levels, even though it "possesses a long and rich history, a unique culture, and many epigraphical and archaeological remains which would seem to make it especially appealing to Southeast Asian historians" (pp. 977–8). Charney (2005) mentions the pivotal roles played by Arakan in Burmese and Thai history, additional to the history of Southeast Asian trade. It was unique in representing all of the major elements of the religions of Southeast Asia: Buddhism (including Mahayana, Theravada, and Tantric sects), Hinduism, animism, and Islam. Many of the primary sources for Arakanese history are unavailable or difficult to obtain, which presents a difficulty to historians wishing to learn more (Amrith, 2013; Charney, 2005; Ghosh, 2016; Thant Myint-U, 2007).

Under the king of Arakan, Min Yazagyi, the ethnic diversity in Arakan was expanded through taxation and the enslavement of peoples from areas as far north as Murshidabad, north of present-day Kolkata in Western Bengal (Charney, 2005; Thant Myint-U, 2020; Yegar, 1972). However, the kingdom's sovereignty was terminated through its conquest and colonization first by the Burmese, and then the British. The Burmese took the Maha Myat Muni statue, Arakan's famed four-meter high bronze Buddha statue, one of the oldest Buddha images in the world, to where it still sits today in Mandalay (Seekins, 2002).

Sittwe city, founded as Akyab by the British who encouraged the influx across the Rakhine border of more migrant labor from India, is now the state's coastal fishing capital. Until 2012, when it suffered what many believe was state-orchestrated communal violence (Wade, 2017) and subsequently segregated along racial lines, the city had become "a thriving, multicultural town where Buddhist, Hindu and Muslim religions, and Rakhine, Rohingya, Kaman and Maramagyi ethnic communities coexisted in relative harmony" (Green et al., 2015, p. 32). Children from different ethnic backgrounds interacted in schools, and communities engaged in shared business as well as social events of festivals, weddings, and other cultural traditions (Peace and Development Initiative-Kintha, 2019). My (Melanie) own memories of my first visit to Sittwe in 2010 are of the town's central market, which backs onto the jetties bringing in the sea's daily catch, being populated by market traders and purchasers who seemed to reflect the town's diversity. Today, the Myanmar state legally enforces ethnic and religious categories through their inclusion on national identification cards, accepting only religious categories of Buddhism (of which 89.8 percent of the country's residents profess; Ministry of Labor, Immigration and Population, 2016), Hinduism, Islam, and Christianity, but not other designations including animism and atheism (Balcaite, 2020). It also sets the number of ethnic groups at 135, eliding the ethnicity of many people whose ancestors have been in Myanmar for centuries (Cheesman, 2017).

While holding teacher training workshops in Sittwe in 2010, I (Melanie) encountered obvious tensions between teachers who identified as Rakhine and Rohingya. Then in 2013, I became involved with a civil society organization (CSO) established by a young former political prisoner, to respond to the violence that had taken place the year before, to normalize collaboration between the communities in conflict and educate a generation of youth peacebuilders.

Myanmar's Statecraft and Politicization of Identity through the National Curriculum

Myanmar's history has been riven by identity politics, spurred on since colonial independence by nation-state building programs. Colonial practices have been continued by presenting ethnic and religious identities as fixed (Cho, 2018), where people are categorized by ethnic and religious identities which are then institutionalized within national identification programs (Carstens, 2018; Cheesman, 2017; Generation Wave, 2020; International Commission of Jurists, 2019) and school curricula (Treadwell, 2013). Oh, Walker, and Hayso Thako (2019), discussing Cheesman (2003), note that "since independence in 1948, government schools in Burma have been used as agents of the state to promote dominant ideologies about nationhood and ethnicity" (p. 2).

Civic values in Burma were taught in primary school textbooks, developed in the 1960s, through the moral framework of Buddhism, as described in Brooke Treadwell's 2013 Indiana University doctoral thesis on the Myanmar state's program of the development of citizenship values in primary school children. Treadwell (2013) demonstrates how the Myanmar state's essentialization of race is conveyed through a Myanmar reader textbook lesson for first grade pupils, entitled "Our Country's Family" (p. 147). The lesson shows a printed color illustration of eight male–female couples wearing the traditional dress of what the state classifies as the eight main ethnic groups of Myanmar, of which Rakhine is one. The couples are smiling and standing around a map of the country, in relation to the areas where they supposedly originate from. Treadwell (2013) shows how obedience and conformity to social hierarchy is taught through three prominent themes to respect elders, fulfil duties, and live and act in unity, and where respect for parents and teachers is elevated to that of the Buddha, his teachings and the monastic order. Treadwell (2013) says

> the repeated emphasis the textbooks place on Buddhism implies that it is the one and only "true" religion of Burma and suggests that if a person is not Buddhist, they are not a truly integral part of Burma in all aspects of their lives. The absence of Christian, Muslim and other non-Buddhist practices and beliefs from the textbooks suggests that students from these religious backgrounds are outsiders, in a sense, who are learning about the "real" Burmese religion from the Myanmar readers.
>
> (p. 163)

In a tandem poetry performance at Myanmar's first slam poetry event that I (Melanie) attended in August 2016, two school friends from Yangon, one professing Buddhism and the other Islam, derided the racism they suffered within the Myanmar education system, in textbooks and through teachers' behavior, which they said leads to racial and religious discrimination and fear and violence within Myanmar society (Aung Kaung Myat, & Than Toe Aung, 2016; Coconuts Yangon, 2016). Than Toe Aung (2019), one of the poets, speaks about his identity crisis suffered as a Burmese Muslim, due to the extreme discrimination he received as the only Muslim child in his class at school and his desire now, as an adult, to contribute toward the creation of an inclusive national identity in Myanmar.

In 2019, Su Myat Mon discussed in Frontier Myanmar how "civic education in primary schools is a lesson in discrimination" (Su Myat Mon, 2019) and centered on an example of a poem in a Grade 3 textbook that vilified people of "mixed blood" (para. 2). In a project funded by the Japan International Cooperation Agency, anthropologist of education Rosalie Metro (co-author of Chapter 8 of this volume) worked on updating Myanmar's basic education curriculum to meet goals outlined in the National Education Strategic Plan (Metro, 2019). The poem in the Grade 3 textbook was removed, but Metro deemed the project only partially successful and says that "more work is needed to promote social inclusion and contribute to lasting peace" (2019). She provided a list of ten recommendations for further improvement. The list covered themes including increasing representation of Myanmar's diversity so that more children can see themselves represented, representing women more broadly to reduce gender stereotyping, and expanding historical and contemporary ethnic and religious references beyond those just of the Bamar ethnic group and the Buddhist religion to allow "more children [to] feel part of the Union [of Myanmar]" (2019).

The national education system has been devastated over the decades since independence by the replacement of critical thinking with rote learning, or memorization (Center for Economic and Social Development and The Global Development Network, 2020). However, critical thinking is a key requisite for the development of civic agency (Treadwell, 2013) and my (Melanie) experience of conducting training workshops with Rakhine youth in 2018 revealed that a lack of civic agency creates significant barriers for the youth to generate the confidence and motivation needed to see through the narratives of hatred espoused within their communities and to begin to rebuild peace.

Subsequently, the belief in a primordial nature of identity held by the architects of the Myanmar state ensures its salience in the minds of its people. This leads youth in Rakhine State, as elsewhere in Myanmar, to align with (and differentiate themselves from) a range of ethnic and religious identities. In Rakhine, the ethnic cultures and identities constructed over the millennia of human migration and settlement refer to themselves as Rakhine, Mro, Kaman, Thet, Khami, Daignet, Maramagyi, Khumi Chin, and Rohingya, although currently, the state contests and does not recognize "Rohingya" (Nyi Nyi Kyaw, 2019; Paddock, 2016). As already stated, state residents also align with, at least nominally, as it is a legal requirement, the religious identity categories of Buddhism, Hinduism, Islam, and Christianity (Balcaite, 2020).

Myanmar's immense diversity could have led to strong ethnic and religious plurality (Walton & Hayward, 2014); however, the state enforcement of these categorizations has instead led to the dominance of people from majority ethnic groups (officially categorized as "main ethnic groups"), over those from minority groups (categorized as "sub-groups"), and from majority religions over those from minority religions. As people identifying as Rakhine are already a minority in the country as a whole, people within this group who further identify with different ethnic and/or religious beliefs are described as "double minority" by Htoo Htet Naing and Kyaw Zin Lin (n.d.) in their student research paper on identity in Rakhine State for Thabyay Education Foundation's Peace Leadership and Research Institute, using the concept developed by Das (2009) and Beeri and Saad (2014) (cited in Htoo Htet Naing and Zaw Lin, n.d.). Peace and Development Initiative-Kintha (2019) report people from these groups to have been further victimized during the communal conflict, by feeling persecuted by Rakhine people who perceive their ethnicities as "inferior" and who mock their use of alternate mother tongues.

This is particularly reported by people who speak languages which are similar to the Rohingya language, such as people identifying with Maramagyi and Daignet ethnicities (Peace and Development Initiative-Kintha, 2019), and people identifying as Hindu (Translators Without Borders, 2019). Perhaps unsurprisingly, debates over "indigeneity" therefore persist throughout Myanmar, which results in people with ancestry in more recent migrations from elsewhere in Asia being derided as "guests" and foreigners and treated differently under the law to those with older ancestral migrations, who are considered by the state to be of "national races" (Arraiza and Vonk, 2017; Cheesman, 2017). This segregation, which is claimed by the state to be racially based, is in fact historically based around the time period of migration and has led many people who identify as Hindu or Muslim, including the Rohingya, being marginalized and at the mercy of individuals and institutions operating from nationalist platforms (International Crisis Group, 2017). Some people in Rakhine with more recent migratory history from South Asia have even conceptualized their more globally acknowledged religious identity of "Hindu" as an ethno-religious identity. This may consciously be a way to elide their ethnic identity which may have become more contentious as hatred of the Rohingya by many in Myanmar has increased since the violence of 2012.

In response to this rising hatred, the government prohibited the nationwide referencing of Rohingya by the ethnic name that they identify themselves with (Nyi Nyi Kyaw, 2019; Paddock, 2016). In addition, the government declared that the term "Bengali," which implies that they are interlopers from Bangladesh, should be avoided and that instead the group be referred to by their religious identifier of "Muslim." This further confounds differentiation of ethnic and religious identities and creates the erroneous impression among Myanmar people that the adjective "Muslim" is an ethnic identity that all Rohingya are Muslims, and all Muslims are Rohingya. Additionally, this elides the ethnic identity of people who identify as Kaman, as they also identify religiously as Muslim. Further demonstrating the irregularity of the nation's list of 135 ethnic groups, the Kaman are officially designated as a Rakhine sub-group, even though they trace their recent history to Persia. Rather than quelling the flames of conflict as intended, this situation has led nationalists to claim that Muslims should not exist in a "Buddhist nation." This action has politicized "Rohingya-ness" so much that it has led Rakhine youth to be confused by Rohingya identity at a time when the civic space to safely unpack the concept of ethnicity and the Rohingya's belonging in Myanmar is being reduced.

Across the country, many people categorized as being from a "sub-group" have expressed that this segregation feels derogatory, is marginalizing, and can lead to communal conflict. This is particularly so when they live among a "main group" such as the Rakhine who also identify with the religion practiced by the majority in the country, this being Buddhism. Furthermore, students of double-minority ethnic and religious identities attend schools in Rakhine State where they have reported they suffer discrimination from teachers who call on them by these identifiers and single them out for different treatment. This includes being forced to sit at the back of the class, being ignored by not being called upon to speak, and being excluded from class events. This extreme racial and religious prejudice results in diversity being downplayed rather than celebrated. Subsequently, the elusiveness of social justice and security in the region contributes toward individual and family migration to more diverse central areas of Myanmar, such as Yangon, where inclusivity in schools is perceived to be greater (Nyein Chan Aung, 2018; Peace and Development Initiative-Kintha, 2019). Migrant youth also report under-representation in government positions in Rakhine State, which leads to discrimination within services and further social injustice (Nyein Chan Aung, 2018).

The Silencing of Rakhine State's Youth

In 2018, interviews with diverse young people in Rakhine State revealed a craving for inter-communal peace (Davies & Saw Lin, 2018). However, the youths' lack of critical thinking skills and civic agency leaves them without capacities to analyze, understand, and address their society's vast sociopolitical problems and achieve the peace they so desperately desire. Consequently, youth growing up in environments of vicious personal criticism were in fear of verbal and physical attack simply for voicing alternate opinions. Furthermore, the obedience and conformity to social hierarchy described previously by Treadwell (2013) means that space to explore alternate views is often nonexistent within students' families, their communities, and their formal education system. These issues contribute to the lack of ability and confidence in youth to form opinions, let alone claim space to voice them. Furthermore, travel outside of the very isolated north and center of Rakhine State, through which the youth could gain exposure to different experiences and perspectives, is difficult at the best of times, and almost impossible during armed conflicts and the coronavirus pandemic. In 2018, inter-generational divisions within their own communities were documented as a barrier for Rakhines wishing to engage with Rohingya communities (Davies & Saw Lin, 2018). In the lead-up to Myanmar's November 2020 election, an empirical analysis on narratives of hate and ultranationalism confirmed that the state's construction and control of narratives toward the Rohingya and their supporters was still strong (Progressive Voice, 2020a).

Detailing the harsh measures that are used to define and regulate the behavior of Rakhine people toward the Rohingya is the 2017 photograph of a woman who was ethnically identified as Rakhine being publicly humiliated in a market in Myebon Township, Rakhine State, after supposedly selling goods to hungry people ethnically identified as Rohingya. The woman was publicly beaten, her hair was forcibly cut off, and she was paraded through the market with a sign around her neck written with the words "I am a national traitor" (Wunna Kwanyo, 2017). Progressive Voice (2020a) warned of recriminations such as this, stating, "Activists attempting to combat hate and discrimination must do so in the face of increased risk of arrests, prosecutions, and attacks on their personal security" (p. 69). Interviewees of Progressive Voice (2020a) stated the following:

> [F]ear, be it of "the others", or loss of one's ethnic identity and religion, is used to justify violence, attributing it as a necessity in defense of one's race and religion. [...] [I]t is the interplay between the physical violence and the psychological effects of hate speech on both the perpetrators and the affected communities that make it so powerful and dangerous.
>
> (pp. 69–70)

Progressive Voice (2020a) has identified key constructed narratives which support this. One narrative is that Myanmar, as a Buddhist-Burman nation, is under threat particularly from Islam. Another narrative is that human rights defenders and journalists should be denigrated as traitors. Systemic discrimination in the education system is identified as one of the key drivers of the narratives, and consequences of the narratives include distrust and violence within affected communities, and increasing difficulties in combatting hate speech, which leads to the closing of civil society space. This closing of civil society space was described as taking place through the targeting of civil society and freedom of expression, which discourages activists who would otherwise seek to build tolerance and inclusion, and also encourages self-censorship.

Progressive Voice (2020a) provides a list of examples of consequences to individuals or groups, spanning 2017 to 2020, who have challenged the authorities or ultranationalists, or spoken out on behalf of ethnic and religious minorities. It was explained that as a result some human rights activists focus their work on only with people whom they identify similarly with and refuse to include others who identify differently. When faced with violence, some activists retreat into their own communities, which create further divides in activist networks. It was found that the fear of physical attack was felt, but the fear of being ostracized from their communities was even greater. This disincentivizes people to engage with activism, and many people reported suffering psychological effects and damaged relationships with friends and family as a result of their engagement. The report was written with the assistance of the International Human Rights Clinic at Harvard Law School and is co-authored by nineteen organizations (Progressive Voice, 2020a.)

Systemic and structural violence is also found in the educational system that normalizes and promotes systemic discrimination, which has been identified as one of the key drivers of the narratives (Progressive Voice, 2020a). Progressive Voice has shown the school curriculum includes derogatory excerpts about ethnic and religious minorities, while glorifying Buddhist Bamar heroes and including only their histories. Moreover, school children have to repeat nationalist slogans which serve to perpetuate the idea that Myanmar is a country for Buddhist-Burmans alone. The voices, histories, and contributions of other ethnic and religious groups are part of null curriculum, that which is not taught. The promotion of Buddhism through school practices and activities at the expense of other religions serves to undermine peacebuilding and social cohesion of Myanmar.

Education Efforts to Support Peace in Rakhine State

In 2017, to address some of the harm done in Rakhine State by Myanmar's state-building programs and policies, a peacebuilding CSO established a college-level one-year liberal arts program in Sittwe city, with residential placements for twenty-four to thirty young people from Rakhine State and the neighboring Chin State township of Paletwa, from where residents can access greater Myanmar only through Rakhine. Approximately 83 percent of the gender-balanced student body identify ethnically as Rakhine, and others identify as Thet, Daignet, Mro, and Khumi Chin. Religiously they identify with Buddhism (80 percent) and Christianity (20 percent). The national policy of apartheid-like racial/religious physical segregation of the Rohingya into different areas of Sittwe township that has remained imposed since the 2012 violence prohibits students identifying ethnically as Rohingya and Kaman, and religiously as Muslim, from accessing the program. However, the CSO strives to provide alternate educational services for these students through facilitating both inclusive environments for Rakhine and Rohingya students to study together and through promoting student interaction with graduates who go on to become teachers in the program.

The program's objective is to develop a generation of grassroots peacebuilders and change-makers. This takes place through the students' engagement in civic and peace-oriented pedagogy and curricula which are developed by individuals with wide experience educating Myanmar's marginalized youth. This curriculum is underpinned by the transformative learning theory of Paulo Freire (1970), as described by Kyawt Thu Zar and Zoe Matthews (2020) (authors of Chapter 1, this volume) in their assessment of this education as leading to conflict transformation taking place in these classrooms around Myanmar and its borders. The authors of this chapter believe that Freire's theory has since expanded further into the realms of global education, decolonial education, engaged Buddhism and borderlands education, lenses through which we will analyze the school's education as experienced by students and teachers.

Global education develops students' competencies to understand and empathize with a diversity of perspectives, to recognize local and global dynamics and the need to take action based on this knowledge as global citizens (Hicks, 2007). In our program, teachers in their early twenties utilize their emerging agency as peacebuilders to foster and teach the attitudes, knowledge, and skills needed for peacebuilding through this curriculum of civic education, human rights, global issues, and conflict and peace studies. The curricula's local-to-global methodology assists students to perceive the broader dynamics behind the conflicts in their region and increases their awareness of processes of "Othering" and ways to address it.

It was in this political tinderbox of Sittwe where I (Melanie) took on a temporary management role in the peacebuilding CSO at the end of August 2017, just after the first cohort of students had arrived to begin their year-long residential on the social sciences program. A week earlier, the Myanmar security forces had been subjected to an unprecedented attack by a recently established Rohingya insurgent group. The Myanmar security forces responded by starting what they described as military "clearance operations" in the area between Sittwe Township and the Bangladesh border. This is where the majority of Rohingya still lived, in villages and towns where they were denied their right to freedom of movement as a result of the 1982 citizenship law which led to the revocation of their citizenship.

Students had been recruited for the program from Sittwe city and other towns and villages in Rakhine and Paletwa Township of Chin State. Some students from rural areas, particularly female students, reported the extreme challenges they faced to convince their parents to allow them to move away from home to attend the program, which like many other non-state-supported programs were not accredited (Loong & Rinehart, 2019). Many of the students had visited Sittwe before but hardly any had traveled outside of the state. As the students and the military settled in, journalists were barred from the area and little information was seeping out about the conflict. We now know that over 700,000 people were expelled into Bangladesh and many died (Wa Lone et al., 2018). In this context of confusion, terrified parents were contacting their children fearful that the violence was going to encroach on the city as it did just seven years earlier, urging them to return home. Consequently, we had a group of twenty-four extremely scared students who were hostile to anyone not Rakhine who we had to build trust with and keep safe while they used Facebook and other social media to post hate speech against the Rohingya. (See Stecklow, 2015, for a description of how Facebook became used as a tool for conflict.) The teachers, all in their twenties and who identified ethnically as Rakhine, Kayin, and Kachin, and religiously as Buddhist, Christian, and atheist, said that although they felt they were being targeted with this hostility, they were committed to seeing the program through. We discussed reducing our expectations from achieving students' full attitude transformation over the year, to just keeping them safe to allow them to complete the program. The syllabus includes a component on media literacy to be delivered in the third term. We discussed bringing it forward into the first weeks of the program but felt that the students' hostility was too high and that without first undergoing the learning in the earlier syllabus, this could lead to the students' views hardening even further and potentially even quitting the program.

It was in this context where I (Melanie) met with the co-authors of this chapter, Soe Khine and Ko Thant, two young male students in the program. They progressed through their studies to become teachers on the same program a year later. I became interested in their personal transformations, their conviction in the sustainability of the program's education to transform the conflict in Rakhine

State, and their bravery in attempting to change the narratives of hate while also facing many of the same challenges discussed by Progressive Voice (2020a). (See Jonathan Head, 2018, BBC's Southeast Asia correspondent, on the narratives of hatred and despair abounding in Rakhine State at the time of the beginning of the program.)

This research has taken place through in-person discussions at first, and then, due to coronavirus-related movement restrictions, through virtual discussions, online chats, and the sharing and commenting on drafts across time zones. This online collaboration was challenged by state-imposed internet shutdown in Rakhine State, medical quarantining and the ongoing armed conflict in the area, and fears for families' well-being and safety. See Enlightened Myanmar Research Foundation (2020) for research on the impact of coronavirus to this population who are also dealing with armed conflict. It is to the stories of the co-authors we now turn.

Personal Transformations and Motivations for Teaching

Ko Thant I (Ko Thant) am Rakhine, from a village in Minbya Township where my family has an agricultural business, growing and selling betel nut. Religion is the most important aspect of many people's lives in Rakhine State, and the majority of residents are Buddhist. One group of Muslim people call themselves Rohingya. Many of their human rights are being denied through the weaknesses of the government and the actions of the military. There is much discrimination here in Rakhine State between people from different religious and ethnic groups, as well as state-led human rights violations. Consequently, most of us living here are quite familiar with inter-communal conflict and civil war.

To be closer to Sittwe to attend a part-time distance bachelor's degree at Sittwe University, my family was able to support me by moving from our village to Mrauk U, an option that is not available to many students. I had wanted to study law and international relations at university, but I could not get the score I needed in my high school exams as students have to memorize everything. This teaching style does not teach us to think critically, and I wanted to learn how to do this. In 2016, I became a member of a youth network in Mrauk-U. Then in 2017, I was lucky to get an international scholarship to study political engagement and organizational development at an international education institute in Yangon. The majority of students outside of Yangon cannot afford this, so international scholarships are crucial to improve our education. After I returned home, I became involved in initiating Rakhine's first state-wide youth conference, held in Taunggup. However, I was still undecided about my future and educational goals. Even though I had studied politics and peace and conflict studies a little, I wanted more knowledge about peace, so I joined the social sciences program in Sittwe in 2017 with Soe Khine. I recall that I was not interested in exploring religious and ethnic diversity too much, but this changed after I joined the program and was made aware of its importance to peacebuilding.

The teachers in the program were skilled in supporting students in being open to new ideas. We debated with our Kachin teacher about religions and ethnicity. In Myanmar schools, we are not allowed to question our teachers, but our Kachin teacher encouraged us to explore our opinions with him through debate. He was open-minded but early in the program, the students were not, and we disagreed with him a lot. But in the second term, I understood his points more.

In the program I acquired the knowledge, values, and valuable teaching techniques that I now use to teach my own students. I changed views on many things. Now I am a peace activist and I am working for a peaceful, developed, and democratic society in Myanmar. Since finishing our program, I have volunteered with a recently established state youth affairs committee as a technical advisor on youth policy and as the international communications officer, which involved active collaboration with government departments, NGOs, social workers, and youth groups. I have also become a freelance trainer on peace and conflict, and local organizations invite me to facilitate trainings. In 2020, I won the first prize in a nationwide essay-writing competition for my contribution entitled "Star," about the diversity and the dignity of all people in Rakhine State. My thesis was that we need to solve our problems with transparency and forgiveness and help each other to shine like stars.

During my studies, I recognized how important the program's subjects are for our society and I now try to understand the feelings and perspectives of others more, to respect diversity, and to help young people. I became deeply interested to promote human rights and peace between young people from different ethnic and religious backgrounds, and to develop a more equal society. The program effectively empowered me to work as a leader in my community as I developed valuable resources in the classroom which I can apply to real life. So, since I graduated, I have also been teaching the subjects of global issues and peace and conflict studies in the program. However, I face many challenges in my teaching, such as some students are older than me and come from different backgrounds, and have different skills and life experiences. When I was eighteen, I occasionally taught as a substitute teacher at a government primary school in Minbya, but teaching in this school is very different. Teachers' roles and students' levels are very different and require more student-centered teaching methods. However, I tried my best and after my first year of teaching, I was promoted to the role of education officer. I like teaching, but we do not fully understand our subjects because we ourselves could only study for one year. We still need more education, too.

Education is powerful. My reason for teaching is to develop and support youth to gain opportunities for quality education, which is difficult to obtain in Rakhine State and Myanmar generally. I want to empower students to build better and more peaceful communities in areas affected by inter-communal conflict and civil war. I want to facilitate learning for youth particularly from different ethnic and religious groups by sharing experiences and knowledge on becoming leaders and peacemakers. I want to help people consider what their values are and to reflect more with a positive mind-set that respects diversity and contests their views of "the Other." If we want a peaceful and developed society, we all have to respect diversity. To achieve this, we must improve our education system to provide critical thinking skills and positive understanding, and I want to contribute toward making this happen.

Soe Khine

I (Soe Khine) am also Rakhine. I was born in Sittwe city, the capital of Rakhine State. I come from a family of civil servants. My mother is a middle school teacher and my father worked for many years in the transportation department. When the communal conflict took place between the Rakhine and Rohingya in Sittwe in 2012, I was just a 13-year-old boy. I used to have negative perceptions of people from different religions and ethnic groups because elders in my community had told us negative stories about historical conflicts between the two communities. I began to generalize about the Rohingya and hate all Muslims and others who did not share my religion of Buddhism. In 2012, I became an actor in the conflict as I started promoting violence in response to the conflicts between our communities (although I didn't become a perpetrator). I began to read about the ancient Arakan kingdoms and their colonization by the Burmese and it made me angry, and I began to think that militarism was the only way to get equal rights and I advocated violence against the Myanmar government to achieve this.

In 2017, I was a first-year full-time bachelor's degree student in Sittwe University. I was also attending a supplementary English class at a local private English-language school. Administrators of the social sciences school came and gave a presentation of their one-year program. Previously, I had never heard about a program with extracurricular clubs like this one, and I was very keen to join. I was not seriously interested in peace studies as I didn't really understand the importance of peace at that time. I was somewhat curious about how they would try to teach me to overcome conflict and achieve peace, but my real motivation was to improve my English-language skills. As I progressed through the program, I was very pleased to find that as well as improving my English, I also gained valuable knowledge from others, developed my skills and attitudes, and was able to extend my network of friends.

I reflected on my opinions while studying in the program, and my perceptions on many social and political issues began to change. In the class on understanding conflict and peace, our teacher was a young Christian from Kachin State. He showed us the common points of every religion and how nonacceptance of others can be a weakness within all religions. In this class I had to research all the religions. I am from a Buddhist community, so I was able to study many documents about Buddhism. I found that the Buddha did not advocate revenge and violence and I came to understand how real Buddhism promotes peace and diversity. Monks and leaders in Rakhine State also teach this, but when I was young, I didn't have a chance to understand it. So in my studies I discovered that the negative things I had started to believe as a result of the conflicts were not according to any of the teachings of any of the religions, and I learned that in every religion we can find peace.

I began to reflect on and understand the value of diversity and social cohesion, and to realize that it is for the common good of society. This brought me to understand the importance of peace and I now accept that every single human being has the same human rights and deserves these rights to be accepted. Finally, I understood the negative impact of violence and I stopped promoting it against the assimilation strategies (what we call "Burmanization") of the Myanmar government, to secure our equal rights. My discovery that there is no hatred in any religion transformed me so much and made me want to teach, to rectify this incorrect message about Buddhism that is being spread through my community. I want to educate youth on the importance of valuing human rights and equality, and the power of dialogue and discussion, in order to bring about change within my community.

During our program, we also learned that we can find diversity not only in race and religion, but also in gender and sexuality. Previously, I didn't understand or respect LGBTQ people. I also promoted patriarchy, but after studying about gender, I understood the negative impact of gender stereotyping on our society and about the rights which are violated due to this. I now accept and respect women and the identity of LGBT people. Overall, I came to understand the importance of peace, social justice, and social cohesion to better our society, as not only communal conflict is taking place here but now there is actual armed conflict too.

As I progressed as a student through the program, I was filled with a desire to share and discuss with young people about the importance of peace, social justice, social cohesion, and gender equality. I felt that becoming a teacher would be the best way for me to fulfill this dream. I was familiar with teaching because my mother and aunt are government high school teachers and I have sometimes tutored their students. So, during community-based service learning in the third term, I chose to teach peace and conflict studies with Ko Thant at a youth center in Ponnagyun town, one hour north of Sittwe. It was my first real classroom teaching experience.

After I graduated from the program, I was asked to teach the next cohort of students. I decided to reduce my university classes to part-time study to enable me to take this great opportunity to follow my dreams and to contribute to my community. This will be more valuable to me than memorization for the university exams. Now Ko Thant and I are teaching our third year. I am teaching civic education, gender, and human rights. Now that I am a teacher, I am discovering that as a student, discussion of peacebuilding is easy, but actually building peace is very hard. When my teaching becomes challenging, I motivate myself by remembering my vision of peace for Rakhine State.

Our Students and Our Peace Education Activities

Soe Khine Most of our students have experienced or been affected by the conflicts between the Rakhine and the Rohingya in some way. When they join the program, many still have memories of difficult experiences and it is hard for them initially to accept and respect diversity. Even though as Rakhine people they have experienced their rights being violated by the state, they are not aware of the violated rights of other ethnic people in Rakhine State and Myanmar. At the start of the program, they easily become emotional when they discuss diversity and they have little knowledge and few skills to identify the root causes of conflict. Moreover, they do not understand the importance of gender equality or the root cause of inequality.

In my subjects, especially through the material on active citizenship from Mote Oo Education, I try to raise students' awareness of their rights, duties, and responsibilities. At first, many students think that because there are many international humanitarian organizations here in Rakhine State working primarily with people who follow the Islamic religion, human rights are just for Muslims and not for people of other religions. So I have to correct them and inform them that all human beings are equal and that we all have the same rights. I also demonstrate that behind our rights, there are also responsibilities and duties. I do this through a number of activities, including using case studies of responsible members of society, by encouraging the students to identify active citizens in their societies and to think about the rights and duties they themselves have.

I also teach about statelessness and how it affects people and their rights. Students begin to understand the lives of the Rohingya and others who are not recognized as citizens, and the importance of citizenship rights. We consider marginalization and social exclusion, so that the students can understand about privilege and the effects of having majority or minority status in society. Rakhines are a minority group in Myanmar compared to those who identify ethnically as Bamar, but even within our group, some people identify with even smaller groups. But many students have never considered marginalization within ourselves before, so in the class I provide space to do this.

Values are harder to teach than knowledge and skills. To explore and strengthen our values, we need to practice them. To do this, I question my students on the kind and quality of discussion they have in class. I explain that sometimes our inner mind can affect us, that even though we discuss in class about nonviolence and peace, sometimes we cannot control our inner mind. When I talk to them about strengthening their values, I warn them that they need to pay close attention every minute to their thoughts and behavior and what values they are supporting.

To facilitate my students' understanding and respect for the value of diversity and social harmony, I searched online for case studies of diverse communities around the world which are living in peace. My search revealed that a lot of communities can do this, so I chose two which I thought my students could relate to. The first was Singapore, where people identifying with many different ethnic backgrounds and religions can live peacefully and the country has become one of the richest and most developed in Asia. The students learn about Singapore through watching a music video of Jay Lim and Lee Wei Song's *Because It's Singapore!* produced for Singapore's National Day in 2017, available on YouTube (Lim & Song, 2017).

I start the lesson that focuses on Singapore with "Good morning students. Today, we are going to learn about the importance and value of living peacefully in diversity. Do you think it is possible?" One student answers, "No. Just look at our country, it is filled with different communal and armed conflicts. I think it will be very hard." I say, "Right, maybe it is not very easy. But let's discuss again after watching this video clip of society in Singapore." After watching the video clip, I ask the students, "What did you see?" One replies, "I saw people of different skin colors and races." Another student says, "Even though they are of different races and religions, they respect and love each other." Another follows with, "They are contributing collectively for their country." I ask them, "What is the most interesting point for you?" One student answers, "The people are living peacefully together, even though they are different religions and races." I state,

Excellent work, everyone. As we saw, the people in Singapore are living peacefully in diversity. Even though they are different in religion and race, they respect each other, and they can work together for the common good. So, there are less conflicts due to religion and race in their country. To ensure this, they focus on developing their country. And right now, Singapore is one of the richest and the most developed countries in Asia. But what about in our country, Myanmar? Is it very hard to live peacefully in diversity here?

A student replies, "I think it's very hard for us. As we know, right now, our country is filling with so many armed conflicts." I state,

Yes, that is also correct. A lot of people say that Myanmar is filled with conflicts and it is hard for us to respect diversity. But this is not the situation everywhere in our country. In some different areas, there are also many people who respect each other and can live peacefully together in diversity. Do you know any of these places? Please have a look at the next video to see one of these places.

The second case study of peaceful coexistence I found was of a group of friends in Taunggyi, the capital of Shan State in the east of Myanmar. They compete in the *Mee-Pone-Pyan* (fire balloon) competition during the festival of *Ta-Saung-Tine*, which takes place annually in October to mark the end of the Buddhist lent period. Even though it is a Buddhist festival, the group of friends from different religions compete together happily. (BBC Media Action, 2019, produced the documentary on Taunggyi's annual fire balloon festival.)

After watching the video about the fire balloon festival, I ask the students about the most interesting points. A student replies, "The balloon festival is a Buddhist festival but a group of friends of mixed religions competed in it." Others reply, "Some are Hindus, some are Muslims and others are Buddhists." I summarize,

Yes, and even though they are diverse, we can see that they can form a team to compete in the festival and they try their best collectively and happily. So, although a lot of people are saying that our country has conflicts and it is very hard for us to respect diversity, actually this is not true everywhere. Some communities can genuinely respect diversity and they can live peacefully together. So even though we are diverse here in Rakhine State, if we respect each other and work for our common good, we will all be successful to live peacefully. If we can do this, the communal and armed conflicts will be reduced, and our community will be a better place for everybody.

Ko Thant

I became interested in the subjects I now teach because we are living in a conflict zone where people need skills to constructively respond to conflict. Most of our students have experienced some kind of violent conflict, so I want them to have the opportunity to develop skills to become peacebuilders. Teaching conflict and peace studies helps students gain a deeper understanding of the reasons that conflicts exist around the world, and the methods for transforming conflicts into sustainable and just peace. Peace education is very relevant for us as it can bring us social justice, social cohesion, nonviolence, tolerance, and empathy. Additionally, it can teach us skills to handle the acceleration of conflict and to promote peace by finding solutions to problems that benefit all parties. I absolutely believe that education can prevent, and also heal, conflict. Studying peace and conflict helps us see that in our location, civilians are suffering from many conflicts and that they should be involved in solving the conflicts and achieving peace. The school's curriculum increases our communities' abilities to participate in doing this.

When I teach about global issues in the first term, we study international conflicts including in Sri Lanka and Rwanda because I want our students to be able to apply understanding of international conflicts to our situation in Rakhine State. For example, when we learn about the Rwandan conflict, most of the students understand that the reasons for the conflict with the Rohingya in Rakhine State are similar with those between the Hutu and Tutsi ethnic groups in Rwanda. I give the example, "We live in Rakhine State and we, the Rohingya and Rakhine people, are the same but we just have different religions and ethnicities." So, when the students study international conflicts, they realize that we can draw comparisons with our own situation and learn different kinds of approaches and responses to conflict.

When I teach about understanding conflict in the second term, most of the students are very interested because our syllabus has many case studies of conflicts in Myanmar as well as international conflicts. However, when I inform them that in the third term that we will learn about understanding peace, most say that they are not interested in this because as conflict is happening in Rakhine State, we do not need to study about peace! When I first heard this, I thought "Oh dear me! In the classroom, when I teach about peace, how can they say this?" So, I can see that when they join our program, some think that studying peace is not relevant to them and their lives. However, I accept this because I know that when I teach about peace, their mindset will change.

There are many interactive classroom activities we can use to teach about conflict. I created an activity that I named "Discussion, Dialogue and Making a Clean Break." In this activity, the students get into groups of eight and they are given role-play characters of different actors in the Rakhine conflict. The first character is Rohingya, the second Rakhine, the third is a Myanmar government official, and so on; other characters are a Myanmar military soldier, a staff member of an international humanitarian organization or United Nations (UN), a member of a CSO, an ethnic army soldier and a religious leader. The first part of the activity is the discussion section and it has three rounds, where in turn each student, in character, speaks their feelings. When one character is talking, others cannot respond or apologize in any way, they must just listen from their hearts to the feelings being expressed. After three rounds, the students make a clean break from their characters and they move into the second section of the activity, the dialogue section. This is where they discuss their characters and their feelings about what they said. The first student reflects on how they feel about their character after they have gone through this process, and how they would like their character's behavior to change. The second discusses which behaviors and actions are beneficial or harmful for their character.

The third discusses what their character dislikes, then the next explains the challenges their character faces, and it continues around the table for three rounds with each student discussing something different about their character. After it is completed, the same groups repeat the first and second sections two more times, but they change characters, so that each student role-plays three characters in total. When they are experiencing their characters' feelings, some talk deplorably, and others speak angrily or in belittling ways. Then the activity finishes and the students express how it was to experience the feelings of their characters. Their feelings range between wonder and being dumbfounded. They say things like "Even in such a short time, my feelings felt real," "I felt anger," "I felt discriminated against," and "I felt like I was second class." One indicated their changing understanding as a result of the activity when they said "Communication is very important to get to know each other and to learn about our different cultures and our religions." They all discuss their feelings as they role-played and how the perceived incompatibility of actors' goals is the basis of all conflict. Finally, they understand all of the feelings, points of view, and challenges of all the conflict actors in Rakhine State. The activity leads them to value diversity so much that there is less tension and misunderstanding between them. They value and do not blame one group and say that we must love each other as we are the same; we are all humans.

Films are another way to explore and learn about peace. I teach using films because this is a very effective method for students to understand problems and to reflect on their values. Reflections on a meaningful film can greatly improve our critical thinking skills and change our views, attitudes, and values. If we watch a movie about gender, peace, and conflict or politics, we get a lot of knowledge through hearing and seeing. Also, students enjoy watching and discussing films. They are interested in learning from educational movies and documentaries that were created with knowledge, facts, and real situations. These kinds of movies can change people's perspectives. Teaching with movies is most effective for learning because students are exposed to and learn from international conflicts, to be able to recognize conflict actors' goals and the underlying reasons for conflict. I want to be able to positively change students' values and to promote reconciliation between diverse groups. I want students to understand the suffering of refugees, to be able to distinguish between constructive and destructive strategies to address conflict, to be able to analyze how conflict escalates through different lenses. Finally, I want students to be able to select appropriate tools for different conflict scenarios.

For example, I use the film, *Hotel Rwanda*. The movie is a fictional re-enactment of a situation that took place during the Rwandan genocide in 1994, between people who were categorized into two ethnic groups by the British colonialists, the Tutsi and the Hutus. After the students finish watching the movie, I organize comprehension and discussion activities using a discussion guide produced by Thabyay Education Foundation and I ask all the students how they feel while watching the movie (Educasia, n.d.). They share their feelings, such as "Why are they killing each other, they are the same?!" They also talk about the role of structural violence in conflict, the drivers of conflict, the presence of win-lose mentality, the suffering of refugees, the importance of third-parties who are outside the conflict and can intervene, and international organizations involved in peacebuilding. When I hear their comments and questions, I answer,

> Yes, you all are right. If we have a win-lose mentality, then we treat people as an obstacle and as an evil enemy, not as a person. If we live together, it is normal that we will have problems and conflict is a normal part of life. We need to use constructive ways to understand each other, and then forgive and forget, and move on. If we use destructive ways to deal with our normal problems, it will lead to violence.

We can talk about peace at different levels such as personal peace, intra- and inter-group, and state peace. At the individual level to be at peace, we need to have positive thinking skills, and to respect diversity and strive for social justice. Social justice is about making sure that all people have equal rights, opportunities, and chances, regardless of their gender, ethnic and religious identities, and social status. Our first goal is to attain peace inside ourselves, otherwise we will be acting in contradictory ways at all levels. The activities described provide much reflection for students and facilitate their understanding of sustainable peace and social justice, and the importance of communication-based peacemaking and negotiation.

Providing peace education for youth is absolutely necessary for peace and social justice to be sustainable in our society because the youth are the leaders not only of the present but also of the future. I strongly believe that youth have the power to build a peaceful society and a good democratic state. I know that we cannot change the attitudes of all youth in Rakhine State, but we can certainly transform the attitudes of our own students so that if they face any problems, they will know how to respond constructively.

Many of our alumni have become committed to working for peace and are involved with the peace process in different ways. Many alumni maintain their membership with the youth network "mother organization" through which they were recruited, and many become peace activists within those networks. Others have jobs in local NGOs and CSOs, and some work with international humanitarian organizations. I have become a member of a global youth movement that promotes hope, peace, nonviolence, and reconciliation. One other alumnus has recently joined a Yangon-based freedom of expression activist organization that supports the Rakhine youth movement against our internet shutdown, which is the longest in the world. See Amnesty International (2020) on the criminalization of human rights defenders and activists in Myanmar that has been continuing during the time of coronavirus. The report includes a case study on the government-imposed internet shutdown to block information flow from the conflict zone in Rakhine State, which ensures that civilians can't keep themselves safe against either encroaching conflict or coronavirus. It also includes other cases referring to Rakhine State (Amnesty International, 2000).

For me, I believe that diversity is more beautiful than a rainbow with many colors. Our future Rakhine State should be formed by many beautiful colors of different religions and ethnic groups without discrimination and hate. Building trust with each other is very important for moving forward. If people trust each other, they are more willing to move forward and not focus on what happened in the past. We have to use constructive strategies to build an inclusive society and involve all, including young people, women, and others who may have been left out. This will help us to attain social justice.

Lenses to Envision a Decolonized, Engaged, and Inclusive Curriculum

We use three theoretical lenses to envision and implement educational experiences that promote peace. These are intellectual decolonization, engaged Buddhism, and borderlands education. The first, Intellectual decolonization, according to Moosavi (2020)

> is said to be necessary to overcome the entrenched exclusion of minority groups and perspectives [...] which does not only harm minorities, but also prevents universities, academics and students from realizing the potential that only the acceptance and inclusion of diversity can facilitate.
>
> (p. 1)

The second, Engaged Buddhism, according to King (2009), is a movement that emerged in the twentieth century as a politically and socially active form of Buddhism. Highlighting the links to Friere's 1970 theories on emancipatory education, King explains that Engaged Buddhism became a large, powerful movement throughout Buddhist Asia capable of giving voice to oppressed people's political aspirations and a path to psychological and practical liberation.

Finally, we view our work through the lens of borderlands education. Su-Ann Oh (2016) describes borders "as marginal spaces at the edge of a nation [which] are in fact sites of social, political and cultural change that impact local and national politics" (p. 1). Scholarly literature on education in borderlands refers to struggles over governance, identity, and nationhood, as described by Oh, Thako, and Walker (2019) in our research on education on Myanmar's eastern borderlands of Karen

State. We conceptualize borderlands education through the analogy of "bridging the Naf," the river which forms Rakhine State's northern border with Bangladesh as referred to at the beginning of this chapter, to ask whether we should be teaching about the divisiveness of the border to the communities straddling the river. The political and social relationships between the communities on either side of the Naf River have further deteriorated over decades as a result of Myanmar's state-building policies, in particular those regarding the Rohingya people. In 2019, this deterioration was recognized by two groups of female photographers in the neighboring urban centers of Yangon, in Myanmar, and Dhaka, in Bangladesh, who decided to engage in cross-border visual conversations on ideas of identity, respect, hope, conflict, and acceptance (Myanmar Deitta, 2019). This collaboration manifested in their photobook named "Bridging the Naf." Of the photographers' creative experience, the portfolio webpage of Myanmar Deitta, the Yangon-based documentary institute that supported the project, explained that "it is only through dialogue and mutual understanding that it is possible to show that the similarities between us as humans far outweigh the differences between us as nation states" (Myanmar Deitta, 2019).

Our program's curriculum has been developed by external curricula developers and the teachers themselves to free students' (and the teachers' own) minds not only of the colonial legacy of my (Melanie) ancestors, the British, who positioned all the country's people as inferior to us (Balcaite, 2020) but also from the more recent colonialism of the Myanmar state which presents the majority Bamar as a superior race. This is being done in a number of ways.

Our testimonies reveal that the fears of the program's first teachers, of potential failure to transform students' attitudes amidst the political unrest in the early months of the program, did not transpire. This was due to the teachers' flexibilities to, as African-American radical transformative educator-scholar Christopher Emdin (2020) describes, reach students "where they really are" (para. 7), this being their psychological state of terror at potentially being subsumed by communal violence. Emdin calls this pedagogy "reality pedagogy" or "pedagogy as protest," as the teachers strived to reflect students' lives and backgrounds in the curriculum and in classroom conversations, and welcomed their engagement in debate. Emdin, seeing his students as co-teachers, says that pedagogy such as this disrupts teaching norms that silence and harm vulnerable students. He explains that when teachers reverse the traditional classroom dynamics, by putting themselves in the position of listener and students in the position of speakers, this engages students more in defining the parameters of their own learning and generates in them a sense of agency that they are typically denied through rote learning. This is the agency that the program's students will need after they finish their studies in order to achieve our goal to transform the conflict in Rakhine State.

Emdin's (2020) "pedagogy as protest" links to theories on decolonizing education, as discussed by another Black educator-scholar bell hooks (1994), who even decolonizes her name by refusing to capitalize it in the Western style, and writes on what she calls "engaged pedagogy." hooks says that "education [is] about the practice of freedom" (p. 4) and links the decolonization of education to

Freire's (1970) work "in its global understanding of liberation struggles" (p. 47). On the oppression of people who identify as African-American in the United States and of particular relevance to the recent Black Lives Matter movement, hooks believes that the important initial stage of personal transformation, particularly the generation of agency, is embodied in "[the] historical moment when one begins to think critically about the self and identity in relation to one's political circumstance" (p. 47). Soe Khine in particular demonstrates that Rakhine perceptions of colonial attitudes and actions that took place in the past and, as many still believe, the current postcolonial period, feature greatly in Rakhine narratives of oppression. This creates a need to doubly decolonize the young minds of this borderland of the deep prejudices that were initiated under the British and which today are still being inculcated through the Myanmar curriculum. See Agence France-Press (2020) and Moe Myint (2019) for how youth in Myanmar embraced the decolonizing Black Lives Matter message to protest against their neo-colonial oppressions with demands of "Don't call me Kalar" and "Rakhine lives matter."

It is these movements, or transgressions against and beyond the traditional boundaries in the classroom, that hooks declares make education the practice of freedom (p. 12). However, she recognizes that when students are encouraged to transgress the passive-learner roles that they are comfortable in and to instead create a more equal relationship with their teachers by engaging in debate, the students would feel fear to do this. In our experiences of being both learners and teachers in the program, we know that as trust between the students and teacher increases, this fear reduces and students begin to learn to expand their communication skills to the parameters of debate. hooks says that in this way, empowerment of teachers can also continue, but not "if we refuse to be vulnerable while encouraging students to take risks" (p. 21).

hooks' (1994) engaged pedagogy, where she describes, "Most professors must practice being vulnerable in the classroom, being wholly present in mind, body, and spirit" (p. 22), clearly resonates greatly with the personal philosophical beliefs and practices that Soe Khine and Ko Thant bring into their classrooms. These practices connect to theories of engaged Buddhism which link Buddhist practice to social action for change and justice. As all the residents of Rakhine State currently continue to suffer not only a civil war but the harsh lockdowns and degradations of the coronavirus that their broken economy and health services are ill-equipped to deal with, the residents' increasing resistance to the oppression of the Myanmar state is revealing the direct links between this oppression and the imposition of nationalist ideologies which stand the Rakhine against the Rohingya and ensure the lack of freedom and social justice for all. It is to raise students' awareness of this externally manipulated positioning and the effect of this upon all residents of the state that the teachers are engaging Buddhist perspectives.

The writing of lay and ordained practitioners of "engaged Buddhism" in Arnold Kotler's 1996 edited volume *Engaged Buddhist Reader* resonates with the situations faced by the program's students and teachers in various ways. Sulak Sivaraksa, leading Thai dissident and founder of International Network of Engaged Buddhism (INEB), recounts a discussion with the world-renowned Vietnamese Buddhist monk Thich Nhat Hanh before the end of the Vietnam War on whether the monk would rather have had peace under the communist regime, which would have brought Buddhism in the country to an end, or the victory of democracy and a Buddhist revival (Sivaraksa, 1996). Thich Nhat Hanh had replied that peace was most important. This speaks of the narratives regarding the Myanmar nation being under threat from Islam (Progressive Voice, 2020a), which the program's teachers are attempting to indirectly counter in their teaching. Thich Nhat Hanh explained how Buddhism cannot "die" and that human lives should not be sacrificed for it "in order to preserve the Buddhist hierarchy, the pagodas, the monasteries, the scriptures, the rituals, and the tradition. When human lives are preserved and when human dignity and freedom are cultivated towards peace and loving kindness, Buddhism can again be reborn in the hearts of men and women" (Sivaraksa, 1996, p. 76). (See International Network of Engaged Buddhists, n.d.)

Thich Nhat Hanh's discussions of the practice of engaged Buddhism to unite the peoples of warring north and south Vietnam in the 1960s and 1970s resonate with the challenges that the teachers face to force themselves to clearly see the dynamics of the conflicts in Rakhine State, to provide a safe space for students to develop critical thinking skills, and to guide them to apply these skills to understand the links between the two conflicts that dominate their young lives (Thich Nhat Hahn, 1996, p. 57). Sivaraksa explains further how religion is related to politics and social justice and that lay Buddhists have a duty to educate even monks who might be isolated from the changing world (1996, p. 74). He writes how in Thailand, many monks couldn't clearly perceive state dynamics of power and violence, "so it is the duty of those of us who have a certain spiritual strength and who can see what is going on to tell them that it is otherwise. This is the duty of any religious person. We have to build up political awareness. Politics must be related to religion" (Sivaraksa, 1996, p. 74). Discussing what he believes is the true spirit of nonviolence, he expands to say that the presence of Buddhism in society must lead to state institutions and politics being "permeated with and administered with humanism, love, tolerance, and enlightenment, characteristics which Buddhism attributes to an opening up, development, and formation of human nature" (Sivaraksa, 1996, p. 76). This is a vision for Rakhine State that both teachers share.

Both of the teachers have been adapting and developing their own curricula. Of this, hooks (1994) says, "Progressive professors working to transform the curriculum so that it does not reflect biases or reinforce systems of domination are most often the individuals willing to take the risks that engaged pedagogy requires and to make their teaching practices a site of resistance" (p. 21). She continues with "professors who embrace the challenge of self-actualization will be better able to create pedagogical practices that engage students, providing them with ways of knowing that enhance their capacity to live fully and deeply" (p. 22). Both teachers provide space for students to reflect not only on their own marginalization but also how they marginalize others, which gives the students a language through which to analyze and articulate their and others' oppression and desires for peace. We believe that this contributes toward decolonizing their curriculum.

Touching upon the teachers' beliefs in the potential of creative sources to teach about peace while living through armed conflict and the related challenges to freedom of expression they face within their communities and at a national level, Thich Nhat Hanh (1996) describes using, in war-time Vietnam, "literature and the arts as 'weapons' to challenge the oppression. Works by anti-war writers, composers, poets, and artists, although illegal, were widely circulated. Anti-war songs were sung in streets and classrooms, and anti-war literature became the largest category of books sold in Vietnam, even infiltrating army units" (pp. 58–9).

The abilities of the teachers to understand the connections between gender, sexuality, and social justice are also significant in conservative, predominantly Buddhist, Rakhine State. Radical Thai Buddhist feminist Ouyporn Khuankaew, former member of the INEB and co-founder of International Women's Partnership for Peace and Justice (IWP) that supports the psychosocial needs of Thai and Myanmar women from northern Thailand, recognizes, as reported through online media, that domestic violence is "a kind of war" and that it is "the worst kind of violence because it can happen every day, at any moment, in your own home" (Buttry, n.d., para. 2). This implies that domestic violence is the greatest and most protracted war many women encounter in their lives. Khuankaew links the oppression of women in Thailand to patriarchy within the Buddhist religion, saying

feminist views and practices are most needed in transforming Thai Buddhism because, as a result of male domination in Thai Theravada Buddhism, the Buddha's teachings have been altered or replaced by the teachings of patriarchy [...] Patriarchal Buddhist institutions and teachings have become one of the main root causes of oppression, particularly against women, transgendered people, the disabled, and other marginalised groups.

(Dwyer, 2019, para. 3)

Khuankaew believes that the improvement of women's situation in Thailand lies in the integration of gender and feminism into high school and university curricula (Dwyer, 2019), a move that we believe could also benefit Myanmar's women and men. She believes that gender oppression is a crucial challenge "because this is the setting in which humans first learn to oppress and to accept [oppression] as a way of life" (Buttry, n.d., para. 5). To de-seat such deeply ingrained principles, Khuankaew offers trainings whereby she supports women leaders in Asia to find male allies, so that the process of challenging gender oppression "becomes more than a 'woman's problem'" and where "men and women begin to work together on solutions" (Buttry, n.d., para. 5). In "intensely Buddhist" Thailand, Khuankaew's training courses "remind both men and women that the Buddha's teachings were not intended to justify patriarchy, violence, and abuse, but rather to serve as a vehicle for liberation—both personal and political" (Duerr, 2013, para. 6).

While the education in this program (and hopefully this chapter) could be described as decolonizing and transformative, we have to ask to what extent? as does Moosavi (2020) in his research on what he calls "the decolonial bandwagon." The fact that the students are border-landers is significant. High levels of ethnic diversity exist in Myanmar's borderlands where many resist what they feel is domestic colonial rule (Sai Latt, 2013) and which, in Rakhine State, is being described by some as military occupation. Comparing my (Melanie) personal experiences of the Myanmar/Karen-Thai and Myanmar/Kachin-China borderlands, I perceive an insularity in this Rakhine borderland, compounded by low awareness of the history of the millennia of migrations throughout the Naf delta. This lack of understanding of Rakhine history is described by Rakhine historian Kyaw Hla Maung in Mrauk U (Hogan, 2018) where Rakhines "were forbidden from speaking their language or studying their history from 1962 under a forced-assimilation policy" (para. 3) but where the identities that were developed throughout these migrations are vast.

The authors of this chapter believe that this calls for the integration into our curriculum of a border studies syllabus which would have a greater focus on rediscovering the numerous histories and how they have affected the construction of identities in the region. This "borderlands syllabus" could utilize a source-based approach to Myanmar's history, developed by Metro and Aung Khine (2013) in their *Histories of Burma* textbook (see Chapter 8 in this volume), to develop students' critical research skills to seek out and assess historical source materials to enable students to develop their own picture of the historical development of the whole area. Particularly this syllabus could assist students on the southern side of the Naf River in Rakhine State to consider their historical links to their cousins on the northern shores in Bangladesh and to ask what they can learn about and understand from each other, their histories and current sociopolitical situations. This would enable greater understanding of the peoples who settled the lands and then found themselves separated at the drawing of the colonial political boundaries, especially the people who straddle the border and identify as the Mro, the Daignet/Thetkama in Rakhine State who identify as Chakma in Bangladesh, and the Rakhine who are sometimes referred to there as "Mogh." Inclusion of comparative studies of peoples straddled across some of Myanmar's other national borders with India, China, Laos, and Thailand, such as the Naga, the Kachin, Akha, Lisu, Hmong, Karen, and Mon, will also aid understanding of how social construction of ethnic and religious identities and belonging is affected by sociopolitical conditions. Would this enable the program to bridge the Naf, and potentially bring peace and social justice to Rakhine State, and maybe even Myanmar as a whole?

Conclusion

This chapter has shown the bravery of Rakhine State's young teachers, both in overcoming the challenges of their own social environments and in their commitment to decolonizing their education to attain peace and social justice in their location. At a time when they are facing head on, not only a pandemic with a barely functioning health system which over decades has left many millions including themselves and their loved ones with underlying health conditions to be exacerbated by coronavirus, but one that is taking place during civil armed conflict. The war in Rakhine State, which is now in its third year, hasn't abated for civilians to protect themselves from the virus. At the same time, many of the teachers' peers and students, if they don't succumb to active combat and its consequences, are being silenced by repressive, junta-era laws which condemn them to disproportionate prison terms for protesting the media blockade of their voices from their war-fields calling for the recognition of their human rights (Khin Hnin Wai, 2020; Progressive Voice, 2020b).

It is therefore perhaps unsurprising that young people in Rakhine State report feeling oppressed from all directions. This is particularly as in October 2020, the national government cited a lack of security (that many have said was exaggerated) to fully or partially cancel voting in November's national election in thirteen townships in Rakhine State which disenfranchised 60 percent of the voters (Arakan State Election Monitoring and Observation Consortium, 2020; International Crisis Group, 2020). In December, civil society groups counted over 200,000 people displaced by the current conflict, just over one third of whom are living in internally displaced people's (IDP) camps and monasteries where delivery of humanitarian aid is greatly restricted by the government (Arakan Humanitarian Coordination Team, 2020). Additional to this number are the 125,000 people who identify as Rohingya and Kaman and have been confined to IDP camps since the violence of 2012 (Office for the Coordination of Humanitarian Affairs, 2020).

The teachers of this nonformal education program in Rakhine State may not have the education and level of content knowledge they desire to teach with, but they themselves are evidence that just one year of the program can transform attitudes enough to enable them to continue to attain teaching goals, which Emdin (2020) admits, took him twenty years to learn to do. This is even though the teachers' starting point is arguably further behind than Emdin's was. Without a doubt, these youth are the future of peace and social justice in Rakhine State, both for people of all ethnic and religious backgrounds who reside there currently and the diaspora who wish to return home in safety and with dignity, including those just across the Naf River, many of whom awaken every day with the Arakan Yoma in their sights and in their hearts.

Works Cited

Advisory Commission on Rakhine State. (2017). *Towards a peaceful, fair and prosperous future for the people of Rakhine: Final report of the Advisory Commission on Rakhine State*. [Research report]. Retrieved from: http://www.rakhinecommission.org/app/uploads/2017/08/FinalReport_Eng.pdf (November 27, 2020)

Agence France-Press. (2020, June.) *"Don't call me Kalar": BML-inspired message reaches Myanmar*. Myanmar Mix. [Online media article]. Retrieved from: https://www.myanmarmix.com/en/articles/dont-call-me-kalar-blm-inspired-message-reaches-myanmar (December 21, 2020)

Amnesty International. (2020). *"I will not surrender" The criminalization of human rights defenders and activists in Myanmar*. London: England. Retrieved from https://www.amnesty.org/en/documents/asa16/2041/2020/en/ (January 18, 2022)

Amrith, S. (2013). *Crossing the bay of Bengal: The furies of nature and the fortunes of migrants*. Cambridge, MA: Harvard University Press.

Arakan Humanitarian Coordination Team. (2020). Presence of violence and resurgence of Covid-19 in Rakhine state after elections. *The Weekly Report*. November 16–20. (Not available online.)

Arakan State Election Monitoring and Observation Consortium. (2020). *Pre-election monitoring study in Rakhine State*. Retrieved from: https://www.kintha-pdi.org/sites/kintha-pdi.org/files/publication-docs/20201103_pre-election-monitoring-study-in-rakhine-state-by_aemoc.pdf (December 27, 2020)

Arraiza, J. M., & Vonk, O. (2017, October). *Report on Citizenship Law: Myanmar*. Country Report 2017/14. Robert Schuman Centre for Advanced Studies, European University Institute. Retrieved from: https://cadmus.eui.eu/bitstream/handle/1814/48284/RSCAS_GLOBALCIT_CR_2017_14.pdf?sequence=1 (December 17, 2020)

Aung Kaung, Myat, & Than Toe, Aung. (2016). *It starts with you*. YouTube. [Online video]. Retrieved from: https://www.youtube.com/watch?v=-xj7lyppN8A (December 23, 2020)

Balcaite, I. (2020, November). Race in Myanmar: Rigid hierarchies, blurred boundaries and the human cost of racism. *Tea Circle*. [Edited academic blog]. Retrieved from: https://teacircleoxford.com/2020/11/12/race-in-myanmar-rigid-hierarchies-blurred-boundaries-and-the-human-cost-of-racism/ (November 14, 2020)

BBC Media Action. (2019). *Taunggyi Tazaungtine balloon festival*. [Documentary video]. Retrieved from: https://www.youtube.com/watch?v=hSqt9to93jw&feature=youtu.be&fbclid=IwAR2hK_ipRBa3KpLJnk69hQwELSUT-rAWitA7NWfYBnTMGdb6E1CEQSgk-eU (December 17, 2020)

Beeri, I., & Saad, M. (2014). Political participation unconditioned by inequality and discrimination: The case of minorities-within-minorities in Israeli-Arab mixed municipalities. *Journal for Ethnic and Migration Studies, 40*, 1526–49.

Buttry, D. (n.d.). Ouyporn Khuankaew (b. 1963): Helping and healing women through feminism and Buddhism. *Interfaith Peacemakers, Read the spirit*. [Online biography]. Retrieved from: https://readthespirit.com/interfaith-peacemakers/ouyporn-khuankaew/ (September 11, 2020)

Carstens, C. (2018). Religion. In A. Simpson, N. Farrelly, & I. Holliday, (Eds.), *Routledge Handbook of Contemporary Myanmar* (pp. 126–7). New York: Routledge.

Center for Economic and Social Development & The Global Development Network. (2020, June). *Country report: Doing research in Myanmar*. Retrieved from: http://www.gdn.int/sites/default/files/u115/Doing%20Research%20Mayanmar%20Country%20Report.pdf (August 7, 2020)

Charney, M. (2005). Arakan, Min Yazagyi, and the Portuguese: The relationship between the growth of Arakanese imperial power and Portuguese mercenaries on the fringe of mainland Southeast Asia 1517–1617 (as submitted in 1993). *SOAS Bulletin of Burma Research*, 3:2, Autumn 2005, ISSN 1479-8484. Retrieved from: https://www.researchgate.net/publication/34088599_Arakan_Min_Yazagyi_and_the_Portuguese_the_relationship_between_the_growth_of_Arakanese_imperial_power_and_Portuguese_mercenaries_on_the_fringe_of_mainland_Southeast_Asia_1517-1617 (August 31, 2020)

Cheesman, N. (2003). School, state and Sangha in Burma. *Comparative Education, 39*(1), 45–63.

Cheesman, N. (2017). How in Myanmar "National Races" came to surpass citizenship and exclude Rohingya. *Journal of Contemporary Asia*, 47(3), 461–83.

Cho, V. (2018). Ethnicity and identity. In A. Simpson, N. Farrelly, & I. Holliday (Eds.), *Routledge Handbook of Contemporary Myanmar* (pp. 43–51). New York: Routledge.

Coconuts Yangon. (2016, August). Please read (and share) this powerful poem against racism in Myanmar. *Coconuts Yangon*. [Online feature article]. Retrieved from: https://coconuts.co/yangon/lifestyle/please-read-and-share-powerful-poem-against-racism-myanmar/ (December 14, 2020)

Das, S. K. (2009). Minorities within minorities: Gender implications for minority policies in India and Bangladesh. *European Yearbook of Minority Issues*, 8, 483–98.

Davies, J., & Saw, L. (2018, November). *Rohingya crisis Myanmar: Strengthening inter-communal cohesion through storytelling, dialogue and community engagement*. Situation analysis. Peace and Development Initiative-Kintha. Retrieved from: https://www.kintha-pdi.org/sites/kintha-pdi.org/files/publication-docs/18-11-19_situation_analysis_storytelling_project_rakhine.pdf (August 31, 2020)

Duerr, M. (2013, October). Can religion be a force for transformation? *Transformation, Open Democracy*. [Online biography]. Retrieved from: https://www.opendemocracy.net/en/transformation/can-religion-be-force-for-transformation/ (September 11, 2020)

Dwyer, C. (2019, December). Toward a Thai feminist movement: Ouyporn Khuankaew. *Buddhistdoor Global*. [Online feature interview.] Retrieved from: https://www.buddhistdoor.net/features/toward-a-thai-feminist-movement-ouyporn-khuankaew (September 11, 2020)

Educasia. (n.d.). *Comprehension and discussion activities for the movie "Hotel Rwanda"*. Thabyay Education Foundation. Retrieved from: www.educasia.org/wp-content/uploads/Educasia%20Myan%20page/Movie%20Modules/Hotel%20Rwanda.pdf (December 18, 2020)

Emdin, C. (2020, July). Teaching isn't about managing behavior: It's about reaching students where they really are. *On Teaching, The Atlantic*. [Online essay.] Retrieved from: https://www.theatlantic.com/education/archive/2020/07/reality-pedagogy-teaching-form-protest/614554/ (September 9, 2020)

Enlightened Myanmar Research Foundation. (2020, September). *Rapid situational analysis of Covid-19 in Rakhine and Chin States*. Retrieved from: https://assets.researchsquare.com/files/rs-18159/v3/11988655-73d1-49da-8879-5ae3dc51062e.pdf (December 6, 2020)

Freire, P. (1970). *Pedagogy of the oppressed*. New York: Seabury Press.

Generation Wave. (2020, March). *The challenges of racial and religious minorities in accessing national registration card and passport*. [Research report]. Retrieved from: https://drive.google.com/file/d/1-9ToPsnAQRilw8VntV9nAYtdh4rj7tZu/view (November 26, 2020)

Ghosh, D. (2016). Burma-Bengal crossings: Intercolonial connections in pre-independence India. *Asian Studies Review*, 40(2), 156–72.

Green, P., Macmanus, T., & De La Cour Venning, A. (2015). *Countdown to annihilation: Genocide in Myanmar*. International State Crime Initiative, Queen Mary University of London. [Research Report]. Retrieved from: http://statecrime.org/data/2015/10/ISCI-Rohingya-Report-PUBLISHED-VERSION.pdf (August 27, 2020)

Head, J. (2018, February). Rakhine state: Hatred and despair in Myanmar's restive region. *BBC News*. [Online media article]. Retrieved from: https://www.bbc.com/news/world-asia-42899242 (December 17, 2020)

Hicks, D. (2007). Responding to the world. In D. Hicks, & C. Holden (Eds.), *Teaching the Global Dimension: Key Principles and Effective Practice* (pp. 3–13). London: Routledge.

Hogan, L. (2018, March). One man's mission to save Rakhine culture and history. *Al Jazeera*. [Online media article]. Retrieved from: https://www.aljazeera.com/features/2018/3/26/one-mans-mission-to-save-rakhine-culture-and-history (August 23, 2020)

hooks, b. (1994). *Teaching to transgress: Education as the practice of freedom*. New York: Routledge.

Htoo Htet Naing, & Kyaw Zin, L. (n.d.). *Hidden truths of the invisible: The experiences of double minorities in northern Rakhine State during violent conflict*. Peace Leadership and Research Institute, Thabyay Education Foundation. [Research Report].

International Commission of Jurists. (2019, June). *Citizenship and human rights in Myanmar: Why law reform is urgent and possible*. A legal briefing. Retrieved from: https://www.icj.org/wp-content/uploads/2019/06/Myanmar-Citizenship-law-reform-Advocacy-Analysis-Brief-2019-ENG.pdf (August 27, 2020)

International Crisis Group. (2017, September). *Buddhism and state power in Myanmar*. Asia Report No. 290. Retrieved from: https://d2071andvip0wj.cloudfront.net/290-buddhism-and-state-power-in-myanmar.pdf (December 17, 2020)

International Crisis Group. (2020, October). *Majority rules in Myanmar's second democratic election*. Asia Briefing No. 163. Retrieved from: https://d2071andvip0wj.cloudfront.net/b163-myanmar-majority-rules_0.pdf (December 27, 2020)

International Network of Engaged Buddhists. (n.d.). [website]. Retrieved from: https://inebnetwork.org/ (December 21, 2020)

Khin Hnin Wai. (2020, October). Students vow to continue anti-war protests as court increases activists' sentences to six years. *Myanmar Now*. Retrieved from: https://www.myanmar-now.org/en/news/students-vow-to-continue-anti-war-protests-as-court-increases-activists-sentences-to-six-years (December 27, 2020)

King, S. B. (2009). *Socially engaged Buddhism: Dimensions of Asian spirituality*. Honolulu: University of Hawai'i Press.

Kyawt Thuzar, Matthews. Z. (2020, May). Microcosms of civic education in Myanmar. *Tea Circle*. University of Toronto. [Edited academic blog]. Retrieved from: https://teacircleoxford.com/2020/05/07/microcosms-of-civic-education-in-myanmar/ (August 26, 2020)

Lim, J., & Song, L. W. (2017). *Because it's Singapore!* NDP 2017 Theme Song. [Music video]. Retrieved from: https://www.youtube.com/watch?v=DI2TeyDJ7Zo&feature=youtu.be&fbclid=IwAR1Otl0ufBGp6za81m3bWsNpoYidiVuA-Ksnq_gqTE5eLjXAPxO_707Lo8g (December 17, 2020)

Loong, S., & Rinehart, G. (2019, February). Post-secondary education in Myanmar: Reform from the ground-up. *Tea Circle*. University of Toronto. [Edited academic blog]. Retrieved from: https://teacircleoxford.com/2019/02/18/post-secondary-education-in-myanmar-reform-from-the-ground-up/ (July 18, 2020)

Metro, R. (2019, November). A missed opportunity for schoolroom reform. *Frontier Myanmar*. [Online feature article]. Retrieved from: https://www.frontiermyanmar.net/en/a-missed-opportunity-for-schoolroom-reform/ (December 23, 2020)

Metro, R., & Aung, Khine. (n.d.). *Histories of Burma*. Mote Oo Education. [Education textbook]. Retrieved from: https://www.moteoo.org/en/social-science (December 23, 2020)

Ministry of Labour, Immigration and Population. (2016, July). *The union report: Religion*. Census Report Volume 2-C. The 2014 Myanmar Population and Housing Census. The Republic of the Union of Myanmar. Retrieved from: https://myanmar.unfpa.org/en/publications/union-report-volume-2c-religion (December 17, 2020)

Moe Myint. (2019, July). "Rakhine life matters" protesters sought by police in Sittwe. *The Irrawaddy*. Retrieved from: https://www.irrawaddy.com/news/burma/rakhine-life-matters-protesters-sought-police-sittwe.html (December 21, 2020)

Moosavi, L. (2020). The decolonial bandwagon and the dangers of intellectual decolonisation. *International Review of Sociology*, *30*(2), 332–54.

Myanmar Deitta. (2019). *Bridging the Naf*. [webpage]. Retrieved from: https://www.deitta.org/portfolio/bridging-the-naf/ (December 21, 2020)

Nyein Chan Aung. (2018). *Minority ethnic migrants and social justice*. MA diss., Myanmar Institute of Theology, Yangon.

Nyi Nyi Kyaw. (2019). Interreligious conflict and the politics of interfaith dialogue in Myanmar. *Trends in Southeast Asia*. 2019 No.10. ISEAS – Yusof Ishak Institute, Singapore.

Office for the Coordination of Humanitarian Affairs. (2020, December). *Myanmar: Humanitarian update no. 2*. Retrieved from: https://reliefweb.int/sites/reliefweb.int/files/resources/OCHA%20Myanmar%20-%20%20Myanmar%20Humanitarian%20Update%20No%202.pdf (December 24, 2020)

Oh, S-A. (2016). Introduction. In S-A. Oh (Ed.), *Myanmar's mountain and maritime borderscapes: Local practices, boundary-making and figured worlds* (pp. 1–36). Singapore: ISEAS – Yusof Ishak Institute.

Oh, S-A., Walker, M., & Hayso, Thako. (2021). Karen education and boundary-making at the Thai-Burmese borderland. *Journal of Borderlands Studies*, *36*(4), 637–52. DOI: 10.1080/08865655.2019.1685401

Paddock, R. C. (2016, May). *Aung San Suu Kyi asks U.S. not to refer to "Rohingya"*. *The New York Times*. [Online media article.] Retrieved from https://www.nytimes.com/2016/05/07/world/asia/myanmar-rohingya-aung-san-suu-kyi.html (December 17, 2020)

Peace and Development Initiative-Kintha. (2019). *The impacts of language barriers on inter-communal relationships: Among Rohingya, Kaman, Rakhine, Daignet, and Maramagyi in Sittwe, Thandwe and Buthidaung*. [Research Report]. (Not available online).

Progressive Voice. (2020a, October). *Hate speech ignited: Understanding hate speech in Myanmar*. [Research Report]. Retrieved from: https://progressivevoicemyanmar.org/wp-content/uploads/2020/10/20201007-PV-Hate-Speech-Book-V-1.4-Web-ready.pdf (November 26, 2020)

Progressive Voice. (2020b, October). *Defiant in the face of oppression*. [Online weekly update]. Retrieved from: https://progressivevoicemyanmar.org/2020/10/31/defiant-in-the-face-of-oppression/ (December 27, 2020)

Sai Latt. (2013, June). Alienation and ethnocide in Burma. *Asia Sentinel*. Retrieved from: https://www.asiasentinel.com/p/alienation-and-ethnocide-in-burma (December 27, 2020)

Seekins, D. (2002). *The disorder in order: The army-state in Burma since 1962*. Bangkok: White Lotus Press.

Sivaraksa, S. (1996). Buddhism in a World of Change. In A. Kotler (Ed.), *Engaged Buddhist Reader* (pp. 70–8). California: Parallax Press.

Stecklow, S. (2015, August). Hatebook: Inside Facebook's Myanmar operation. *Myanmar Burning, Reuters Special Report*. [Online feature report.] Retrieved from: https://www.reuters.com/investigates/special-report/myanmar-facebook-hate/ (December 14, 2020)

Su Myat Mon. (2019, February). Civics education in primary schools is a lesson in discrimination. *Frontier Myanmar*. [Online feature article]. Retrieved from: https://

www.frontiermyanmar.net/en/civics-education-in-primary-schools-is-a-lesson-in-discrimination/ (December 23, 2020)

Than Toe Aung. (2019). Identity crisis. *Frontier Myanmar*. [Online feature article]. Retrieved from: https://www.frontiermyanmar.net/en/identity-crisis/ (December 17, 2020)

Thant Myint-U. (2007). *The river of lost footsteps: A personal history of Burma*. London: Faber and Faber.

Thant Myint-U. (2020). *The hidden history of Burma: A crisis of race and capitalism*. London: Atlantic Books.

Thich Nhat Hahn. (1996). Love in Action. In A. Kotler (Ed.), *Engaged Buddhist Reader* (pp. 57–63). California: Parallax Press.

Translators Without Borders. (2019, September). *Misunderstanding + misinformation = mistrust: How language barriers reduce access to humanitarian services, reduce the quality of those services and aggravate social exclusion for Rohingya communities. Part III: Sittwe, Myanmar*. [Research report]. Retrieved from: https://translatorswithoutborders.org/wp-content/uploads/2019/09/ENG-Myanmar-Report_online_FINAL.pdf (December 27, 2020)

Treadwell, B. (2013). *Teaching citizenship under an authoritarian regime: A case study of Burma/Myanmar*. Indiana: Indiana University.

Wade, F. (2017). *Myanmar's enemy within: Buddhist violence and the making of the Muslim "other"*. London: Zed Books.

Wa, Lone, Kyaw Soe, Oo, Lewis, S., & Slodkowski, A. (2018, February). Massacre in Myanmar. *Reuters*. [Online media article]. Retrieved from: https://www.reuters.com/investigates/special-report/myanmar-rakhine-events/ (December 17, 2020)

Walton, M., & Hayward, S. (2014). *Contesting Buddhist narratives: Democratization, nationalism, and communal violence in Myanmar*. Policy Studies 71, East-West Center. Retrieved from: https://www.eastwestcenter.org/system/tdf/private/ps071.pdf?file=1&type=node&id=34800 (September 2, 2020)

Wunna Kwanyo. (2017, September). *Arakanese woman publicly humiliated for being a "traitor"*. Democratic Voice of Burma. [Online media article]. Retrieved from: http://english.dvb.no/news/arakanese-woman-publicly-humiliated-traitor/77435 (7 December 2020)

Yegar, M. (1972). *The Muslims of Burma: A study of a minority group*. Wiesbaden: Otto Harrassowitz.

Chapter 5

REFRAMING POLICY AND PRACTICE: LANGUAGES IN EDUCATION AS RESOURCES FOR PEACE IN MYANMAR

Jasmine Tintut Williams and Erina Iwasaki

Introduction

It was spring 2017, and we both had the day off from school: I (Jasmine) was an assistant teacher in the banlieue just outside of Paris, and Erina was finishing her first year as a doctoral student at Teachers College (TC), Columbia University. Two strangers separated by the Atlantic, by luck, connected through Dr. Carol Benson. We had scheduled thirty minutes out of our day to talk about Erina's experiences at TC, what it was like to study the intersection of human rights and languages in education. Two and a half hours, and we were still on the same Skype call—passionately talking about our personal relationships with languages, belonging, the role of education in shaping our identity, and most of all, our entangled relationship with the place we both considered our second home: Myanmar.

Three years later, we found ourselves sitting with our new colleagues around desks that had been pushed together to form a makeshift conference table for our workshop. It was our first day with our new team in Myitkyina, and we were about to embark on a six-month-long endeavor to document mother tongue-based multilingual education practices in Kachin and Northern Shan States. Some of us had experience working in the development field, most of us had been teachers, but all of us were multilingual. Jinghpaw, Burmese, Lachid, Zaiwa, English, French, Japanese—we jumped in and out of our multiple language pools, connecting linguistic riverways and laughing together as we learned new words and got to know each other.

In the summer of 2019, we began working on two multilingual education projects in Myanmar: a revision of a multilingual literature curriculum for a private school in Yangon and technical support for a multilingual education project for an ethnolinguistic group in Kachin and Northern Shan States. While these two contexts differ in the ethnolinguistic and socioeconomic backgrounds of the students, languages, and communities they serve, both had addressed Myanmar's proclaimed democratization, its commitment to educational equity, and its transition to a market-based economy.

In a country of 120 languages (Eberhard, Simons, & Fennig, 2020), Myanmar is linguistically and culturally diverse. However, the Burmese language (also called Myanmar) is Myanmar's only statutory national language as stated in the 1974 Constitution (Article 198) and reaffirmed in the 2008 Constitution (Article 450), and it is the main language of instruction in public government schools alongside English. In Myanmar, approximately 80 percent of people are Burmese language speakers; 60 percent of them are reported to be first language (L1) users of Burmese with approximately 20 percent second language (L2) users (Eberhard et al., 2020). Researchers have also reported that the number of L1 Burmese users is increasing every year (Bradley, 2007). However, there is a remaining 20 percent of the Myanmar population who are solely speakers of languages other than Burmese. Despite Burmese presenting as a numerical majority's language, this does not mean that all people, including students and teachers in some non-Bamar ethnolinguistic communities, are comfortable or competent in using Burmese.

State-run education programming in Myanmar relies on the presumption that all learners and educators in Myanmar are functional and comfortable in Burmese as a medium of instruction. Since 1966, state-run education has used Burmese as the medium of instruction—for nation-building purposes—with some transitions to English in subjects like physics and math in secondary schools. This language programming relies on the assumption that all learners in Myanmar are extremely comfortable using Burmese. It is only within the past decade or so that national policy makers and educators are acknowledging that they cannot rely on Myanmar's presumed language homogeneity and total convergence to the Burmese language for education planning and teaching. This presumption has left at least 10,452,880 people or more (those who do not speak Burmese as their first language) (Eberhard et al., 2020) without access to resources or education in a language they understand.

In this context, many ethnic basic education providers (EBEPs) have taken it upon themselves to provide what the state would not: access to quality education for their children in a language they understand. The rise of non-state education actors is deeply intertwined with conflict and Bamar-centric narratives that marginalize ethnic histories and identities in Myanmar (Salem-Gervais & Metro, 2012). In the national peace process, the government had engaged in conversations for official ethnic representation and usage of nondominant languages within education.

Contemporary education laws such as the Basic Education Law (2019) and National Education Law (2014), along with the Local Curriculum Development illustrate that there is some discussion of inclusive, culturally and linguistically relevant education for ethnic groups in Myanmar's state-run education curriculum. As Myanmar's first National Education Strategic Plan (NESP, 2016–21) comes to an end and a new ten-year one was being devised (NESP, 2021–30), we saw this as a "policy window," or an opportunity for Mother tongue-based multilingual education (MTB-MLE) or L1-based MLE programming to ensure that all children in Myanmar are able to learn in a language they understand.[1]

This chapter clarifies what MTB-MLE and first language-based MLE (L1-based MLE) are and shares some stories that reveal how a "multilingual habitus" can be facilitated, embodied, and implemented in practice. We argue that educational programs such as MTB-MLE or L1-based MLE that adopt a "languages-as-resource" orientation (Ruiz, 1984, 2010) are opportunities not only to improve the quality and access to education but also support Myanmar's current peace process and proclaimed democratization process in terms of nurturing positive interpersonal and intercommunal relationships.

While we do not go into detail in this chapter about our own work in MTB-MLE development, we share our own self-reflections on our processes, being both an insider and an outsider at times—both escaping and yet conforming to insider norms, aware and critical of our own privilege and how we may be perceived. We, as a biracial Burmese-American woman who grew up in the United States (Jasmine) and a Japanese woman who was born in Japan yet whose family has lived in Myanmar since 1995 (Erina), review our ethical orientation as researchers who bear witness to the work of our dedicated colleagues and the country's socio-political changes. The chapter problematizes our positionality based on our work experience, and the role of "international" consultants and researchers in the country through a self-reflective process that is part of any bearing witness stance. For us, the self-reflective process has been more accentuated with reflections on our own identities, and our recurring dialogues and debriefs on events, attitudes, behaviors, and interpersonal interactions.

Finally, as Myanmar may reform its national educational system, we argue that adopting a "languages as resources" orientation and framework opens up discussions and spaces for diversity and non-essentializing discourses to flourish, and acknowledges the already existing EBEPs' work.

MTB-MLE and Languages-as-Resources Orientation

The term "mother tongue" is indicative of the language(s) we are most comfortable with or have a strong emotional connection toward. The intersection of identity and language are integral to MTB-MLE practice, especially its practice in the context of Myanmar. MTB-MLE (also first language (L1)-based MLE in some contexts) refers to an umbrella term, often used for a range of programs in Asia Pacific and

---

1. On February 1, 2021, the military "Tatmadaw" seized power in a coup d'état. Their actions have halted many of the ministries in the country, including the Ministry of Education (MoE). Thus, education implementation and development has been stalled, leaving the future of the NESP, 2021–30 and its social cohesion and language-in-education progress uncertain. As it was written before the coup, this article does not have direct analysis on the future of governance in Myanmar, but has some footnotes for clarification.

African regions that build literacy and learning in students' own languages while explicitly teaching additional languages. Citing Kosonen and Benson (2013), Benson (2019) clarifies, "[MTB-MLE] was never meant to represent programs that exclude learners' own languages, nor those that use the L1 only for oral explanations or code-switching" (pp. 30–1).

MTB-MLE is also a term that distinguishes "between programs designed for the elite to learn dominant international languages and programs tailored to give speakers of non-dominant languages access to basic education and explicit teaching of additional (dominant) languages" (Benson, 2019, p. 31). This is an important distinction to make as recently, with the globalization of education and the trend of English as the so-called international language, the term bilingual or multilingual education has been co-opted by elites as a means to acquire another dominant language to build their elite status, disregarding the more nondominant L1s of the students. However, it is worth noting that even in the so-called Global North, in countries such as the United States or Canada, the origins of bi-/multilingual education are rooted in valuing nondominant students' languages and cultures in a predominantly white Anglosaxon culture and language to combat submersive, assimilationist pedagogies, and educational programs (Francis & Reyhner, 2002; History of Bilingual Education, 2006; Nieto, 2011). In this regard, MTB-MLE stays true to bi-/multilingual education's first values of promoting social justice and equity in education.

On the pedagogical side, scholars such as García (2008) and Benson (2019) define MTB-MLE programs as those that systematically and deliberately use learners' languages for literacy and learning, accompanied by the explicit teaching of new languages. By the end of an MTB-MLE program, "learners should be multilingual and multiliterate as well as achieving the other goals of the curriculum" (Benson, 2019). In addition, in MTB-MLE programs, languages are used as the medium of instruction depending on learners' previous knowledge and linguistic proficiency. This means nonlinguistic curricular content (i.e., math, social science, science, etc.) is taught in one or more languages. These programs also explicitly teach new languages based on an additive model of bi-/multilingualism (García, 2008; Ouane & Glanz, 2011) in which the emphasis of language learning is put on developing students' interlinguistic transfer competencies or language scaffolding for systematic connections between languages (Benson, 2020; Bialystok, 2001; Cummins, 2009). In this framework, languages are considered a resource (Ruíz, 1984, 2010) for students' learning and self-esteem (Cummins, 2009). By considering languages as a resource, particularly in a highly multilingual nation-state such as Myanmar, this orientation can redefine the educational environment and schooling in ways that it acknowledges the existence of inherent individual and societal multiliteracies and multilingualism. This ultimately provides students with more access to a variety of choices in their future life paths without having to sacrifice their cultural and linguistic identities.

While MTB-MLE has shown to improve students' learning and self-esteem (Cummins, 2009; Ouane & Glanz, 2011), in our practice, we have seen MTB-MLE to be a vehicle for interpersonal relationship-building and opportunities to learn about and from one another. It is a way toward mutual understanding and acknowledgement, respect for differences, empathy, and non-essentializing discourses to flourish—all important elements for a healthier, peaceful, and all-embracing social cohesion. Aligned with Wong's (2019) literature review and analysis, educational programs such as MTB-MLE or L1-based MLE promote linguistic diversity and thus can further catalyze peacebuilding discussions in Myanmar.

Language-in-Education Policy in Myanmar

In 1966, the first Basic Education Law enacted a centralized system of schools and standardized curriculum, positioning Myanmar as the only language of instruction taught at state schools (Salem-Gervais & Metro, 2012, p. 34). This law has since been rewritten and the 2008 Constitution explicitly mentions that the Union has a duty/role to "promote other nationalities' [or ethnic] languages and culture," though it was not made clear that this is through formal, government-led education. Myanmar's contemporary education laws now include sections dedicated to language inclusion in formal education; such policy documents include the Basic Education Law (2019), National Education Law (2014), and aspects of the NESP, 2016–21.

While teaching other Myanmar nationalities' languages in education is mentioned throughout the NESP, 2016–21, Basic Education Law (2019), and National Education Law (2014), nondominant or ethnic languages are not given the status of a main language of instruction across all curriculum subjects. With the new Local Curriculum in government schools (Salem-Gervais & Raynaud, 2020), the government had created space and a commendable first step forward toward the use of other nationalities' languages as a medium of instruction for a few hours a week with a teaching assistant or language teacher. The Local Curriculum is also supposed to provide space for communities to teach their own cultural histories, literatures, ethnoarts, and handicrafts. However, according to discussions with communities and fellow ethnic education researchers, the actual implementation of the Local Curriculum depends on township and school, with the Local Curriculum being pushed out of the school day to after-school lessons, or ignored completely in some schools. Teacher assistants and language teachers have informally reported they have experienced discrimination by principals and by other government certified teachers. For all of these reasons, the Burmese language continues to dominate government classrooms, with little to no room for other ethnic languages of instruction. Instead, other ethnic languages serve as the medium of translation to explain content for students that are taught exclusively in the dominant language, Burmese, and in higher grades, English.

The absence of mother tongue instruction in government classrooms has not gone unnoticed, with many national and international advocates pushing for educational reform. MTB-MLE had begun to enter the MoE's discussions, particularly in the NESP 2021–30, which would determine education policy for the next generation of Myanmar's learners. The MoE had identified two key transformational shifts related to basic education in the NESP, 2016–21: "all children can access, progress through and successfully complete quality basic education and all school children develop knowledge, skills, attitudes, and competencies relevant to their lives and to the socio-economic needs of 21st century Myanmar" (p. 25). EBEPs and their NGO partners had been in conversation with the government not only for EBEP system recognition, but for the implementation of a national mother tongue-based multilingual curriculum. This dialogue was a step forward for Myanmar as it seemed to be shifting toward more inclusive educational policies.

Languages in Education and the Emergence of EBEPs

Myanmar is the site of the longest running civil war in the world between the Karen and Bamar starting in 1949, with numerous other ethnic groups also fighting for their rights for decades, including various Kachin, Mon, Shan, and Chin groups, amongst many more (South & Lall, 2016a). Due to the conflict and division between government and nongovernmental areas, ethnic organizations and their armed groups have developed their own civil society organizations (CSOs). While there had been positive developments in partnerships between the Myanmar government and Ethnic CSOs, there are still many partnership aspects that need to be discussed and mutually agreed upon.

Throughout Myanmar's history, the central government's position vis-à-vis ethnic groups has fluctuated, particularly in the area of education access and accurate representation. In a textbook analysis study, Salem-Gervais and Metro (2012) identified that textbooks from each era reveal different underlying sociopolitical motivations of the regime in place. One of the most salient themes was the gradual marginalization of ethnic group representation. During General Ne Win's Burmese way of Socialism (1962–81), history was mainly centered on Burmese patriotism and the histories of non-Bamar people in textbooks were greatly reduced. In tandem with these changes, the 1966 Basic Education Law enacted a centralized system of schools and standardized curriculum, making Burmese the only language of instruction taught at state-run schools.

Following General Ne Win's precedent, the SLORC (1988–2011) regime furthered this ideology by providing a new national identity to the country, changing the name "Burma" to "Myanmar" to introduce a unifying construct across ethnic groups. In history textbooks, references to past Great Kings were increased to justify the military regime, as well as the diminishing of the 1948 Panglong Conference and the role of Bogyoke Aung San (Salem-Gervais & Metro, 2012). Ethnic groups were continuously marginalized through a "folklorized" and rather essentialized version of ethnicity to promote the unity of the country (Salem-Gervais & Metro, 2012). Throughout these two historical periods, ethnic groups did not recognize themselves in the national education system and had created as early as in the 1970s, their own education systems, often referred to as parallel education systems (South & Lall, 2016b).

EBEPs were formed to close the gap in educational achievement and access for their children. While many ethnic groups use the mother tongue as a medium of instruction, three pioneering EBEPs that have implemented MTB-MLE and systematic multilingual scaffolding for many years include the Karen Education and Culture Department (KECD), Mon National Education Committee (MNEC), and the Kachin Independence Organization's Education Department (South & Lall, 2016b). Each of these EBEPs implements different language progression plans for their communities, with some service providers teaching the mother tongue as a medium of instruction throughout all years in basic education. However, as seen in their capacity development work in recent years, it is clear that they are all eager to strengthen their MTB-MLE systems and provide quality education to all of their students.

MTB-MLE, ELB-MLE, or L1-based MLE: Terminology in Policy in Myanmar

With so many ethnic communities across Myanmar implementing MTB-MLE curriculum, there have been discussions around the topic on a national level (Lall & South, 2018; Salem-Gervais & Raynaud, 2020; Salem-Gervais, 2018; Shee, 2018; South & Lall, 2016a). While we see the rise of MTB-MLE as a positive point of advocacy in national educational policy development, as MTB-MLE researchers and consultants, we also noticed that the concept and meaning of MTB-MLE are often filled with varying levels of understandings and perspectives. Even amongst the so-called experts or international consultants, the conception and positionality of MTB-MLE depend on which stakeholders (communities, donor organizations, or governments) they are in conversations and represent.

For this reason, three terms were being debated at the national level for policy use: MTB-MLE, L1-based MLE, and ELB-MLE (ethnic-language-based multilingual education). While each of these terms seemingly overlaps, the slight changes in phrasing may have huge implications in practice. In our practice, we have noticed that EBEPs strongly prefer the term MTB-MLE. As they have been working with international experts and have participated in numerous regional conferences in ASEAN nations (most recently, UNESCO's 2019 Inclusion, Mobility and Multilingual Education Conference in Bangkok), they have become accustomed to MTB-MLE terminology and discourse. They argue that there is international precedent for this preferred terminology, as well as it encapsulates the needs of their ethnic contexts.

In contrast, the MoE argues that ELB-MLE is more representative of Myanmar's context, as the term "ethnic languages" are already included within multiple policy documents (Basic Education Law, 2019; Myanmar Constitution, 2008; National Education Law, 2014). Only 135 ethnic groups are officially recognized in Myanmar, which has led to the perpetual marginalization and conflict with certain ethnic groups—most notably, the Rohingya. With the use of the term ELB-MLE, it can be positioned to exclude unrecognized groups who would greatly benefit from mother tongue-based teaching in their communities. Furthermore, ethnic groups are not confined to particular states or regions, so there are many mixed ethnolinguistic communities (such as the Kachin communities in Northern Shan). If ELB-MLE is to be used on a national level, it must be clear that there are no restrictions with regard to ethnic-language choices by the state.

Ethnicity is not particular to nondominant groups only, and dominant groups also have ethnicity. Bamar or Burmese, the dominant ethnolinguistic community in Myanmar, is listed as one of the recognized 135 ethnic groups in Myanmar. ELB-MLE positions Bamar as somehow separate from the other ethnic groups that are recognized alongside it, even though the current MoE curriculum follows an MTB-MLE progression with a late exit from Burmese to English in upper secondary. As MTB-MLE advocates and practitioners, we caution that with this proposed shift toward ELB-MLE, the term "ethnic" must be mindful, especially coming from dominant groups as it risks tokenizing or "folklorizing" nondominant communities as previously noted by Salem-Gervais and Metro (2012). For example, in contexts like Hong Kong, the term "ethnic minority" reinforced tokenization of other ethnic groups into "idealized" communities by the Chinese dominant ethnic group (Fleming, 2019) or in other instances, their cultural differences were so racialized that they felt othered (Gube & Burkholder, 2019).

As discussions continue around terminologies and meanings, we advocate for the use of L1-based MLE or MTB-MLE on a national level for a lack of a better terminology. Although we understand that there is hesitation to use MTB-MLE nationally, we believe that L1-based MLE escapes essentializing and limiting discourses, and presents language as a critical vehicle by which students are able to access their learnings. This terminology specifically redirects our attention to discussions and action toward concrete educational programming conducive to the implementation of nondominant languages as languages of instruction while providing strategies to learn additional languages—be it dominant or nondominant. However, no terminology is perfect and it is ultimately dependent on the community to define it on the ground, as we share in our next section.

Terminology in Practice and Embodying a "Multilingual Habitus" in Myanmar

Since 2019, we have been working on two multilingual education projects in Myanmar: technical support for a multilingual education project in Kachin and Northern Shan States and a revision of a multilingual literature curriculum for a private school in Yangon. While these two contexts differ in the ethnolinguistic and socioeconomic backgrounds of the students, languages, and communities they serve, both have addressed Myanmar's proclaimed democratization, its commitment to educational equity, and its transition to a market-based economy.

January 2020, Kachin State

Our colleague raised his hand—we had arrived at the discussion section of our introduction workshop for MTB-MLE. "But what if it's not the mother tongue," he mused. "What if my daughter speaks her father's tongue? What if?" he posed. It appeared as such a succinct question but overflowed with so much more: Where does language come from? What more does a language carry beyond words? Who passes a language on, and is it innate within us? Does it run through our blood lines as the Myanmar Government's preferred translation implies (taing yin tha ba tha za ga)?

While the terminology "mother tongue" has its flaws, we see these flaws open a space for people to talk about our own language histories, hidden languages, and belonging, precisely because we value multilingualism and all languages regardless of our proficiency levels. We then opened the floor to discuss the use of L1 as another preferred term, when a colleague asked: "What if I learned Myanmar at school but spoke my mother tongue at home? What if I didn't learn how to read or write my mother tongue until adulthood? What do I call my L1?"

This comment raises some interesting issues. Most of us have not had the opportunity to learn all of our languages systematically in a formal school setting. We acquire them from home, church, monastery, out-of-school lessons, and time spent with friends and family members. While we may have learned the same languages, how we use them may differ. A few of the group, us included, had become competent in languages in adulthood through formal language classes. We considered ourselves functional to work in places where these languages were used.

The order in which we learn languages may not be representative of how we perceive our identities. As an activity, we had each member draw a flower to map our language histories (ÉLODiL, 2010). The roots that produce a stem may change into a different language, and the petals bloom with the other languages we know or use. Our L1s as children are not always recognized by education bodies to be used as the language of instruction. Due to various circumstances, not everyone is given the opportunity to learn their mother tongue or heritage languages to a level of comfort until later in life. This is apparent in ethnic communities across Myanmar, and ultimately shifts languages and reorders them depending on the child. Their mother tongue may shift from L1 to L2, or disappear entirely. Some languages wilt, and others have petals that grow large—but for all of us, our multilingualism budded as children. Our parents were multilingual and it felt natural for us to be multilingual, too.

Although I (Jasmine) grew up with my maternal Burmese family, with days spent with my Pwa Pwa and extended family, I was raised to speak one of my father's languages, English, as my L1. It wasn't until my undergraduate years that my tongue began to embrace my mother's language, Burmese. Without access to formal language learning, I learned new words from pongyi chaung (monastery school), work, and friends, and shared them with my family. They were ecstatic, hearing new vocabulary spill out of my mouth, and giggle when it did not come out right. During the Covid-19 pandemic, I have started to learn Italian, my paternal grandmother's language. English, Burmese, Italian, every one of these languages are important to my family and to carving out our belonging. We are a multicultural family, and our heritage languages—mother tongue, father tongue, grandmother tongue—are the orthographical reflection of our bloodlines.

To me (Erina), "mother tongue" resonates in entangled ways. When I think of my mother tongue, Japanese, I think of something that belongs to me but yet is partially missing because I did not learn to be fully proficient in Japanese through formal schooling. Instead, I went to French schools where my L1 became French. A language of proficiency and functionality. However, despite becoming fluent in French like a "native," my mother tongue remains. Like the motherland that I long for, my mother tongue is both distant and yet so close to my heart. Sometimes it is comforting, and other times uncomfortable. It comes with expectations, both self-imposed and societal but it also represents my deep connection to my family. It is also something that I rejected or felt embarrassed of while growing up. Only in my twenties did I garner the courage to learn Japanese on my own using textbooks for L2 learners with some help from my parents.

After a week of workshops, we had contextualized the *what ifs*. While not perfectly defined, the *What ifs* no longer gave us pause. Throughout our discussions on terms, a shared understanding emerged—that "mother-tongue" or "L1" can evoke different stories and emotions, and even uncover hidden language stories that we may not be aware of. In our group, "mother tongue" meant a language we had strong emotional ties to and wanted to protect and transmit to the next generation. It also meant a language we are the most comfortable with or a language spoken at home with family members. In contrast, "L1" evoked more conversations on proficiency, functionality, and how we define a L1 in comparison to the other languages. However, the difference between L1 and mother tongue is entangled deeper than just functionality, proficiency levels, and schooling. Functionality, sure, was important, but what drove us all to learn and be comfortable in our mother tongue alongside multiple languages was our desire to speak, to share our lives and our ideas with others. Our desire to speak our mothers' and fathers' tongues was driven by our love for our families, our communities, and to share that love with others.

The mother tongue is the language of *belonging*. The bond between our languages and identity was inseparable. Our multilingualism and discussion around it has expanded our belonging, developed our characters, and built our friendships across our diverse languages and cultures. Despite the proficiency levels or how we acquired it, our mother tongue is something we want to preserve. We recognized throughout our discussions that people can have multiple mother tongues, especially in Myanmar.

Multilingual education development facilitates an opportunity to discuss language, culture, and diversity. This didactic space is what builds awareness and empathy within communities, particularly because no community is perfectly uniform. By explicitly discussing language diversity, we also created a space to talk about identity, gender, ethnicity, and inclusive practices in general. Through these discussions, we had opportunities to explore and share our intersectional identities and discomforts. Our conversations did not leave us passive in our situation, but rather it inspired us to be more empathetic and develop better solutions and educational tools in our work. We observed that empathy is not only a key pedagogical tool for peace education, but also multilingual education, as it stimulates a connection between people to not only recognize differences but to embrace them. These peace education practices are aspects of social-emotional learning and grievance acknowledgement for community building (Zembylas, 2017), and can be facilitated within multilingual education as well. From our experience, it was clear that language conversations can serve as community-level foundations of reconciliation and peacebuilding as they create a space for a shared lived experience and empathetic interpersonal relationships.

July 2019, Yangon

We conducted a multilingual socio-emotional development workshop for teachers in a multilingual private school in Yangon. This workshop was co-designed with the faculty there as we inquired what kind of workshop they wanted based on what they struggled with. Already a multilingual school, with Myanmar, Japanese, and English being languages of instruction in elementary and middle school, students there are used to navigating a multilingual environment and learning alongside peers with varying language proficiencies in different languages. Students have different linguistic profiles. Myanmar children, children of Myanmar "repats" educated in the language of their host country, Japanese-Myanmar biracial students, Japanese and other country expat students attend this school. To be more effective in their teaching and pedagogy, the teachers asked us for more tips and strategies with interlinguistic transfers within their classroom while recognizing the children's linguistic backgrounds. Since teachers are not all multilingual in these three languages as well, they requested ways to promote interlinguistic transfers that would allow them to communicate better with their students—particularly in the realm of sharing emotions and feelings—who don't necessarily speak the same language as they do or rely on the teacher that speaks that language. Hence, we came up with a multilingual socio-emotional development workshop focusing on how to design classrooms and spaces that would build on children's languages and literacy skills.

In the workshop, we discussed making a language survey at the beginning of the year to learn about the languages (especially the hidden ones) of each child. A simple way to get to know your students and their families and opening up conversations on languages and hidden linguistic identities. Then, we modeled a classroom with the teachers as students and utilizing drawings as a means to engage with emotions. Most of the teachers were from Myanmar, with a few Japanese and Filipino teachers. Alongside Burmese and Japanese, English is used as a language of wider communication at the school, so we conducted the activity in English and French as mediums of instruction. We chose French as it was a lesser known language amongst the teachers so everyone would experience what it felt like to make connections to a language no one understands to level the playing field.

First, we split the teachers into groups of four and we wrote a variety of emotions in French on the board—content(e), triste, fatigué(e), en colère, satisfait(e), et frustré(e). We said the words aloud so that the participants could associate sound with orthography. Each group had a mixture of languages, so no group was linguistically homogeneous. We gave each group a collection of drawings in a random order and asked the teachers to guess which matched the French words.

The teachers took time before matching the pictures, looking for connections across their existing linguistic competencies. By providing space for them to discuss, we could see that the teachers were making their own interlinguistic connections. We could hear as we wandered through the room, "this word looks like … in this language" and "this word sounds like" across Burmese, Japanese, and English. After debating for about five minutes, they placed their best guesses on the board and explained to the other groups the reasons behind their choices.

We allowed for groups to make last minute changes after the presentations before we mimed each emotion for them. Teachers cheered when they had connected the languages correctly, and we could hear the "ohs" of realization when corrected. We then asked them to reflect on their language connecting processes and how they could apply this in their classrooms. Each group discussed for a few minutes, and then shared their ideas. They shared that the charts could be used to help students point to their emotions if they were unable to describe them comfortably to the teacher and their peers. It was also important that they provide space and opportunity for their students to make these language connections themselves in their learnings, but with guiding strategies. These guiding strategies could be multimodal, such as drawings, actions, and multilingual projects.

We gave the teachers the opportunity to use their own languages and create new pictures for these emotion words in Japanese, Burmese, Tagalog, and English. The teachers made multiple and shared them across the language groups. Since the workshop, the teachers have incorporated in their own ways the emotion wall in their classrooms and added the emotions in the languages of their students. Some expanded the multilingual approach to other subjects, creating multilingual vocabulary charts with the lesson's keywords that students can add their languages alongside the other languages of instruction present at school. The workshop has opened up new ways of exploring languages through already existing resources within the classrooms in a seamless fashion.

Teachers have since reported that recognizing languages as resources rather than barriers helped them communicate better with their students and colleagues. As a school community, they are continuing to develop the tools to express their own emotions and feel heard or acknowledged across multiple languages. By approaching languages as resources and using them to make systematic connections across subjects, the multilingual and multimodal pedagogy liberated teachers from a limited way of learning and made them realize that teachers and students can rely on one another. It also allowed them to integrate the students' different linguistic profiles and proficiency levels existing in the classroom.

Both contexts in which we work illustrate that using multiple and relevant languages can provide an innovative, learner-centered pedagogical environment for students to engage in critical thinking and to discuss *essentializing* and *dominant* discourses. We have witnessed how positioning languages as resources has allowed teachers and researchers to build their confidence as practitioners and learners. It also has provided space for personal validation and mutual understanding between ethnolinguistic communities.

Conclusion

With the second democratic election under the NLD completed in November 2020, Myanmar's reform is far from over.[2] Literature in transitology, which "explores the factors that lead to the demise of autocracy, the turbulent pathways of change and the choice for an eventual consolidation of democracy" (Mohamedou & Sisk, 2017. p. 1), suggests that during a transitional period, governments tend to engage in specific social, political, and economic reforms that either distinguish them or continue the works of its predecessors. Examples of recent transitional countries include Egypt, Morocco, Tunisia; and Myanmar was cited alongside these countries given its recent political change (Mohamedou & Sisk, 2017). With the peace process and rise of inclusive education legislation over the past ten years, ethnic groups were not absent from the public light: EBEPs and Language and Culture Committees were in dialogue with the government to develop a more inclusive basic education curriculum.[3] Though the national recognition of diversity as a strength is still ongoing and the Local Curriculum program still has room to grow, it was no small feat that Myanmar's ethnic groups' individual cultures and languages were showcased in legislation and curriculum.

According to transitology scholars, in transitional phases, "education is [often] given a major symbolic and reconstructionist role in [...] social processes of destroying the past and redefining the future" (Cowen, 2000, p. 338), and Myanmar is no exception to this phenomenon. At this critical moment in Myanmar's historical transition,[4] researchers must bear witness alongside diverse communities, recognizing the intersection of different knowledge systems and how this requires navigating concepts of belonging in a society experiencing political and socioeconomic change. In doing so, a new understanding of identities, languages, and cultures can emerge, one that is more multifaceted and embracing of diversity and differences. In Myanmar, a future of sustainable peace relies on recognizing and embracing diversity as a strength. Many EBEP

---

2. With the future of the country's leadership in flux, it is unclear how reform will be shaped over the coming months and years. However with regard to education, the country's history and progress with language rights and MTB-MLE are grounded in the programmes developed by EBEPs. It is clear that their leadership and experience are integral for any national reform to be successful and sustainable.

3. The peace process has become irrelevant as the Tatmadaw has further strained the relationships with the ethnic organizations by breaking ceasefire agreements and attacking villages and schools in ethnic-leadership areas. Moving forward, the future national government will need to mend these broken relationships with ethnic organizations if there will be any possibility for peace or federal coordination in sectors like education or health.

4. While this article was written before the coup d'état, the sentiments and recommendations still apply. Myanmar is experiencing a historical transition, with Myanmar's people as the changemakers and the leaders of reform as made overtly clear throughout the Spring Revolution.

communities have taken the initiative and implemented ethnic languages as main languages of instruction in basic education alongside Burmese. The MoE's Local Curriculum program was also a step in the right direction by including ethnic languages in the national curriculum as a subject, but had room to grow so that it better supported nondominant language speakers in their learning across all core curriculum subjects such as Science, Math, and humanities.

However, it is one thing to recognize multilingualism in the community, but it is another to implement it effectively into education spaces. As implementers, we are often asked the same questions: MTB-MLE/L1-based MLE is nice, but how does one implement the mother tongue in education spaces? What if the teachers don't know all of the languages of the children in their classes? Isn't it just easier and more efficient to use one language of instruction? These questions are valid and often arise because MTB-MLE pedagogy, such as language scaffolding, is not often explained in practical ways. We cannot run away from these questions. Our workshops have taught us that language issues are central to education. Teachers and educational implementers need the space and time to discuss these matters so that they can support all learners from diverse backgrounds. These discussions—along with community engagement and patient curriculum planning that systematically connects languages through language scaffolding—are necessary so that there is sustainable implementation of multilingualism in classrooms. By taking time for advocacy and facilitating workshops that teach MTB-MLE pedagogy, we are able to develop new learning solutions while also supporting the teaching and learning capacity in communities.

Languages serve as a means to share ideas and learn about the world around us. In education, languages serve as a way to access curriculum content and create lasting relationships with peers. We have seen in our work that by creating space for Burmese and ethnic languages (along with other nondominant languages) to be systematically connected and used in education, a natural dialogue and cultural sharing is stimulated. Through multilingual education programming, teachers, students, and community members naturally foster peace education practices, such as empathy building. Community partnerships begin through utilizing languages as resources, catalyzing a shift not only in education, but in the wider communities as well.

In Myanmar, MTB-MLE is *possible* and *desirable*. The reason why MTB-MLE, L1-based MLE, and ELB-MLE are hyphenated suggests that one could remain loyal to their mother tongue yet strengthen their relationship with the larger world through development of other languages. In this sense, multilingual education is a method of building intercommunity understanding and national unity. It is a way to signify multiple facets of learners' identities, finding belonging beyond linguistic boundaries and exploring beyond essentializing discourses. Teaching the mother tongue alongside other languages is about recognizing the fluidity of identities and that all languages are valuable to build a cosmopolitan community. By cosmopolitan, we draw from philosopher of education, David Hansen (2011), who defines educational cosmopolitanism as "the human capacity to be open reflectively to the larger world, while remaining loyal reflectively to local concerns, commitments, and values" (p. xiii).

Languages in education have a direct impact on improving access to and quality of education. Mother tongue or first language access and use is an integral part of community building and maintenance. By embracing nondominant languages as mediums of instruction alongside other languages, children and teachers will be allowed to flourish their entire linguistic repertoire and nurture empathy. We see these discussions around MTB-MLE as an opportunity for Myanmar to further strengthen the education system while also building mutual understanding and trust between all for sustainable peace.

Works Cited

Basic Education Law. (2019). Retrieved from https://pyidaungsu.hluttaw.mm/uploads/pdf/EeN59x_29-11-2019President%20return%20Basic%20Education%20Law.pdf

Benson, C. (2019). L1-based multilingual education in the Asia and Pacific region and beyond: Where are we, and where do we need to go? In A. Kirkpatrick, & T. Liddicoat (Eds.), *The Routledge International Handbook of Language Education Policy in Asia* (pp. 29–41). London: Routledge.

Benson, C. (2020). An innovative "simultaneous" bilingual approach in Senegal: Promoting interlinguistic transfer while contributing to policy change. *International Journal of Bilingual Education and Bilingualism.* DOI: 10.1080/13670050.2020.1765968.

Bialystock, E. (2001). *Bilingualism in development: Language, literacy and cognition.* Cambridge: Cambridge University Press.

Bradley, D. (2007). East and Southeast Asia. In C. Moseley (Ed.), *Encyclopedia of the World's Endangered Languages* (pp. 349–424). London: Routledge.

Constitution of the Union of Burma. (1974). Retrieved from: https://www.burmalibrary.org/docs07/1974Constitution.pdf

Cowen, R. (2000). Comparing futures or comparing pasts? *Comparative Education, 36*(3), 333–42. DOI:10.1080/713656619.

Cummins, J. (2009). Fundamental psycholinguistic and sociological principles underlying educational success for linguistic minority students. In T. Skutnabb-Kangas, R. Phillipson, A. K. Mohanty, & M. Panda (Eds.), *Social Justice through Multilingual Education* (pp. 19–35). Clevedon: Channel View Publications.

Eberhard, David M., Simons, Gary F., & Fennig, Charles D. (Eds.). 2020. *Ethnologue: Languages of the world. Twenty-third edition.* Dallas, TX: SIL International. Online version: http://www.ethnologue.com.

ÉLODiL. (2010). La fleur des langues. Retrieved from: http://elodil1.com/pdf/activites_prescolaire/Les%20fleurs%20des%20langues.pdf

Fleming, K. (2019). Who is "diverse"?: (In)tolerance, education, and race in Hong Kong. In J. Gube & F. Gao (Eds.), *Education, Ethnicity and Equity in the Multilingual Asian Context* (pp. 89–104). Springer: Singapore.

Francis, N., & Reyhner, J. A. (2002). *Language and literacy teaching for Indigenous education: A bilingual approach.* Bristol, UK: Multilingual Matters.

García, O. (2008). *Bilingual education in the 21st century: A global perspective.* Retrieved from https://ebookcentral-proquest-com.tc.idm.oclc.org

Gube, J., & Burkholder, C. (2019). Unresolved tensions in Hong Kong's racialized discourse: Rethinking differences in educating about ethnic minorities. In J. Gube, & F. Gao (Eds.), *Education, Ethnicity and Equity in the Multilingual Asian Context* (pp. 105–21). Springer: Singapore.

Hansen, D. (2011). *The teacher and the world: A study of cosmopolitanism and education (1st ed.).* New York: Routledge.

History of Bilingual Education. (2006). In K. L. Lerner, B. W. Lerner, & A. W. Lerner (Eds.), *Immigration and Multiculturalism: Essential Primary Sources* (pp. 401–3). Detroit, MI: Gale.

Kosonen, K., & Benson, C. (2013). Introduction. Inclusive teaching and learning through the use of non-dominant languages and cultures. In C. Benson & K. Kosonen (Eds.), *Language Issues in Comparative Education: Inclusive Teaching and Learning in Non-dominant Languages and Cultures* (pp. 1–16). Rotterdam: Sense.

Lall, M., & South, A. (2018). Power dynamics of language and education policy in Myanmar's contested transition. *Comparative Education Review, 62*(4), 482–502. https://doi.org/10.1086/699655

Mohamedou, M.-M., & Sisk, T. D. (2017). *Democratisation in the 21st century: Reviving transitology.* New York, NY: Routledge.

Myanmar Constitution of 2008. Retrieved from: https://www.constituteproject.org/constitution/Myanmar_2008.pdf?lang=en

National Education Law. (2014). Retrieved from: http://www.ilo.org/dyn/natlex/natlex4.detail?p_lang=en&p_isn=100493&p_count=3&p_classification=09

National Education Strategic Plan 2016-2021 Summary. Retrieved from: https://www.unicef.org/myanmar/media/1771/file/National%20Education%20Strategic%20Plan%202016%E2%80%932021.pdf

Nieto, S. (2011). Speaking truth to power in educational research. Commissioned essay for the American Educational Research Association Conference, Vancouver, CA. Retrieved January 5, 2012 from http://www.aera.net/

Ouane, A., & Glanz, C. (Eds.). (2011). *Optimising learning, education and publishing in Africa: The language factor. A review and analysis of theory and practice in mother-tongue and bilingual education in sub-Saharan Africa.* Hamburg: UNESCO (UIL)/ADEA. http://unesdoc.unesco.org/images/0021/002126/212602e.pdf

Ruíz, R. (1984). Orientations in language planning, *NABE Journal, 8*(2), 15–34. DOI: 10.1080/08855072.1984.10668464.

Ruíz, R. (2010). Reorienting language-as-resource. In J. E. Petrovic (Ed.), *International Perspectives on Bilingual Education: Policy, Practice, and Controversy.* Charlotte, NC: Information Age Publishing.

Salem-Gervais, N., & Metro, R. (2012). A textbook case of nation-building: The evolution of history curricula in Myanmar. *Journal of Burma Studies, 16*(1), 27–78. DOI:10.1353/jbs.2012.0003.

Salem-Gervais, N. (2018). *Teaching ethnic languages, cultures and histories in government schools today: Great opportunities, giant pitfalls? (Part II).* https://halshs.archives-ouvertes.fr/halshs-02512851

Salem-Gervais, N., & Raynaud, M. (2020). *Teaching ethnic minority languages in government schools and developing the local curriculum. Elements of decentralization in language-in-education-policy.* Konrad-Adenauer Stiftung Ltd., Myanmar Representative Office. https://halshs.archives-ouvertes.fr/halshs-02512416

Shee, N. K. (2018). Karen education department's multilingual education for language maintenance. *Kasetsart Journal of Social Sciences.* https://doi.org/10.1016/j. kjss.2018.07.007

South, A., & Lall, M. (2016a). Language, education and the peace process in Myanmar. *Contemporary Southeast Asia, 38*(1), 128–53.

South A., & Lall, M. (2016b). *Schooling and conflict: Ethnic education and mother tongue-based teaching in Myanmar.* USAID and The Asia Foundation. https://www.themimu. info/sites/themimu.info/files/documents/Report_Ethnic_Education_MTB_teaching_ in_Myanmar_Feb2016_0.pdf

Wong, M. S. (2019). The peace dividend of valuing non-dominant languages in language-in-education policies in Myanmar. *The Forum for International Research in Education,* 5(3), 49–68. https://fire-ojs-ttu.tdl.org/fire/index.php/FIRE/article/view/143/64

Zembylas, M. (2017). Emotions, critical pedagogy, and human rights education. In M. Bajaj (Ed.), *Human Rights Education: Theory, Research, Praxis* (pp. 47–58). Philadelphia: University of Pennsylvania Press.

Chapter 6

DESIGNING PEACE EDUCATION FOR COMMUNITY-BASED ACTION WITHIN MYANMAR: REFLECTIONS OF A COLLABORATIVE APPROACH

Grace Michel, Arkar Phyo Thant, and Katie Zanoni

Introduction

This chapter draws on the collective experience of three practitioners who contributed to the Learn and Share Together (LST) educational initiative, developed and piloted in Karen State,[1] Myanmar (2017–18). The LST program is part of a social cohesion initiative led by a non-governmental organization, People in Need (PIN). Co-authored by a peacebuilding practitioner from Myanmar, a Karen-American peace educator, and a peace educator from the United States, we embody the methodology of reflective practice to consider key questions and strategies employed in the project as we collaborated remotely across different time zones and geographical borders (see, for example, Lederach, Neufeldt, & Culbertson, 2007 on reflective peacebuilding strategies). As part of a larger team we look upon our curriculum development process to ask ourselves key questions such as: How do we teach peace within a context where the concept of peace is so politicized that even the utterance of the words "peace" and "conflict" could elicit a negative reaction from the community of learners? This question captures one of the dilemmas we faced in our effort to practice a conflict-sensitive approach (INEE, 2013) to curriculum development for the LST project. Through the process of collective reflection, we highlight four key principles employed by our international team and share key practices and lessons learned through our process.

---

1. Karen State is also called Kayin State, the name (transliterated to English) that was given by the Myanmar military government in 1989 when the military junta imposed name changes to states and regions (this occurred at the same time they changed the official name of the country from Burma to Myanmar). For the purposes of this project we choose to use the name Karen as it reflects one author's (Grace's) self-identity and the authoring team's preferred nomenclature.

The LST project emerged out of an existing program initiated in 2015 in Mon, Karen, and Rakhine States called the Social Cohesion program. The objective of the Social Cohesion program was to "contribute to the mitigation of the effects of inter-communal/religious violence and promotion of peaceful coexistence through community development and peace education" (PIN, 2017, pp. 1–2). Due to the rising instability within the Rakhine State and forced displacement of the Rohingya people (Alam, 2019), PIN narrowed their geographical focus to implement the next phase of this effort within Karen State. Funded by the US Department of State, Department of Democracy, Human Rights and Labor, a call to hire educational consultants was put out for a project working towards "bridging religious and ethnic divides in Burma through supporting civil society in promoting tolerance, conflict resolution, and peace education" (PIN, 2017, p. 1). It is important to note that PIN welcomed the opportunity to implement the US-funded initiative, but with the integration of conflict-sensitive language. To this end, PIN aligned the project with more neutral terms such as "social cohesion," the concept of "togetherness," and collective community-based learning. Thus, the LST team was created with local Myanmar peacebuilders and international staff members at PIN, alongside two contracted curriculum developers from the United States with expertise in peace education. This US authoring team in turn brought together a curriculum production team including two Myanmar translators, a US American graphic designer who had previously worked in Myanmar, a Myanmar graphic designer, and a US-based artist who had worked with Burmese refugee communities in Thailand and the United States.

The LST curriculum consists of eleven key modules and was implemented at the school and community level. At the school level, teachers working with middle school youth were trained using the train the trainer (TTT) approach and were invited to pilot the content in their respective classrooms. Simultaneously, representatives from local civil society organizations (CSOs) in Karen State were selected as Peacebuilding Champions (PBCs) to participate in the TTT then act as facilitators and agents of change to train learners in the target communities. The culmination of both the school and community-level LST program was for participants to integrate these peacebuilding skills to design and co-create a "Learn and Share Together Project" in their school or local community. Due to space limitations, this chapter focuses primarily on the community-level activities; however, key lessons are drawn from both the school and community implementation approaches. The following section outlines the context within which this project was piloted, Karen State.

Context of the Learn and Share Together Project in Karen State

Karen State in southeastern Myanmar was the implementation area for the LST project. The state is named after the Karen ethnic group and Karen sub-groups which predominate in this region of Myanmar. Karen State is also home to people from other ethnic groups including Pa-o, Mon, and Bamar people. Buddhism is the predominant religious identity in Myanmar. In Karen State 84.5 percent of the population is Buddhist, according to the 2014 Myanmar census (Government of Myanmar, 2015). There are also significant Christian (9.5 percent) and Muslim (4.6 percent) minorities in Karen State, as well as small population segments that practice Hinduism and traditional or animist practices (Myanmar Information Management, 2020).

Karen State is marked by a long and violent history of armed ethnic and religious conflict with complex dynamics whose analysis and explication are beyond the scope of this chapter. The conflict has been marked by lines of division along ethnic lines, as Karen has sought self-determination within the Bamar-majority nation, as well as religious lines, predominantly between Buddhists and Christians. Ethnic and religious conflict narratives can be traced back to divide and conquer policies and ethnic favoritism enacted by the British during colonial rule, as well as the influence of Christian missionaries and the conversion of significant numbers of Karen to Christianity. These influences led to the formation of a Karen nationalist movement with predominantly Karen Christian leadership. This movement formally organized under the umbrella of the Karen National Union (KNU) in 1947, and shortly after Burma's independence from British rule in 1948, violent conflict emerged between the KNU (with its Karen National Liberation Army, or KNLA) and the Burmese military in a struggle for control over the Karen territory (South, 2011). The conflict escalated into what has become known as one of the longest running civil wars in the world, lasting more than sixty-five years and resulting in the forced displacement of millions of Karen people. While the majority of Karen are Buddhist, the leadership of the KNU has historically been predominantly Christian. Dissatisfaction with this imbalanced representation in leadership led to factions within the KNU and the establishment in 1994 of the Democratic Karen Buddhist Army (DKBA) (South, 2011). This faction was then supported by the Myanmar military (Tatmadaw) in fighting against the KNU, leading to the fall of Manerplaw, a tide-turning event that severely weakened the Karen national movement. In 2012 the KNU signed a ceasefire with the Tatmadaw, then in 2015 signed the National Ceasefire Agreement (NCA) (Myanmar peace monitor, 2019) along with many other ethnic armed groups. However, much of the region is still heavily militarized, and skirmishes and military attacks in parts of Karen State have still occurred since the ceasefire has been in place.

In addition to the long-standing Karen/Bamar ethnic tension and Christian/ Buddhist religious divisions, there are other complex conflict dynamics that impact Karen State. Muslims have long been a persecuted religious identity in Myanmar. There is a broad lack of recognition and understanding of the ethnic identities of people groups who also identify as Muslim, but conflict narratives have been created targeting these groups. In particular, the Rohingya, an ethnic minority group who predominantly practice Islam, are excluded from recognition as one of Myanmar's 135 official ethnic groups, and have been the target of ethnic cleansing campaigns by the Tatmadaw. Many anti-Muslim campaigns have been spearheaded by organized Buddhist monks, in particular the 969 movement, which created a narrative that Muslims in Myanmar are attempting to establish supremacy and destroy Buddhism in Myanmar. While an in-depth analysis of the causes of intercommunal conflict concerning Muslim-identifying communities will reveal contests over geographical areas, questions of political management, control and use of natural resources, and access to services, the ideological threat of Islam has become the issue people are mobilized around. The impact of intercommunal violence and Islamophobia at a national level is also felt in Karen State, though Muslims are a small segment of the population there, and there are active 969 movement leaders in Karen State. As a result, the PIN team observed existing tensions and negative views held toward Muslims from both Buddhists and Christians in Karen State.

In addition to and as a result of violent conflict and various structural impediments inhibiting sustainable and inclusive development practices (Karen Human Rights Group, 2018), Karen State, like much of Myanmar, is characterized by high levels of poverty and vulnerability, including poor quality and access to education, and lack of job opportunities. The need to pursue economic opportunity fuels large-scale migration to neighboring Thailand. Though both men and women migrate in large numbers to Thailand for work, the balance of men is higher, leaving many women to tend to families and provide community leadership at the civil society level (Wilkins, 2017).

The educational system across Karen State is fragmented with some parts of the state having schools under the Myanmar government-sponsored Ministry of Education (MoE) and others managed by the KNU's Karen Education Department (Jolliffee & Mears, 2016; Ritesh Shah & Lopez Cardoza, 2018). School facilities are often severely under-resourced, lacking in learning materials, chairs and desks, and sanitation facilities. In the MoE schools, students learn a government-sponsored curriculum using a highly traditional teaching system of rote memorization (Shah & Lopez Cardoza, 2018). In these schools, Burmese is used instead of mother tongue-based language instruction, leading to poorer educational outcomes for Karen and other ethnic minority students who do not speak Burmese before beginning their formal education. Many children drop out before completing secondary school due to a number of factors including being forced to work in order to support their families economically, the distance to travel to reach a school being too far, or not having the support of their families to continue their education (Higgins, et.al., 2015). Many parents consider spending on educational fees to be a waste of money given that youths may complete their formal education without any meaningful prospects for work. Many youths are also exposed to drugs and suffer from drug addiction as early as grades 9–10, leading further to lack of completed education (Simbulan, 2016).

Outside of the school environment, there is a dearth of learning opportunities. International NGOs play an important role in supplementing formal educational opportunities for children as well as non-formal community education for adults, and local CSOs are involved in supporting non-formal education. Many families do not prioritize accessing informal learning opportunities given their need to focus on livelihood-generating activities. For some students, the PIN LST curriculum was the only opportunity to learn subjects beyond the government curriculum offered in school, as travel from a village to a township to study things such as computers, music, English language, or other skills-based programs are out of reach.

It is against this backdrop of conflict and obstacles to development that the LST project emerged as a response to equip local teachers and community leaders with skills to foster social cohesion and community engagement at the school and village levels.

Building Our Team: Drawing Knowledge and Expertise from across the Globe

At the onset of our virtual team meetings, it was evident that our team eased into a set of commonly understood peacebuilding practices as our theoretical framework for project design and implementation. The first centered around the need for the Learn and Share curriculum to be designed with engaged pedagogy as the baseline standard of practice (Freire, 1970; hooks, 2010). All team members acknowledged engaged pedagogy as a critical component of a transformative learning and development process, yet also recognized the challenges this might present due to the traditional rote style of learning often found in formal schooling. The second was the need to remain conflict sensitive in all stages of the project including design, stakeholder input, implementation, and evaluation (INEE, 2013). The third component grounded the work within the communities of Karen to ensure that an inclusive approach was taken to include key leaders in the community such as religious leaders, village leaders, existing peacebuilding organizations, and government representatives in the stakeholder engagement process. As we focused on our collective strategy to center local voices (De Coning, 2018), our team also acknowledged the need to remain gender sensitive (INEE, 2019) as we designed content. PIN formalized this process of reflective peacebuilding through an internal evaluation of the LST project after the team piloted the curriculum in the community.

In the spirit of LST, what follows in the rest of this chapter is a sharing of the lessons learned through three team members' reflections on the aforementioned project design and implementation process. We distill the experience into four guiding principles of peace education practice: (1) conflict sensitivity, to ensure the content designed by our team did not impose unintentional harm within the communities served (Anderson, 1999; INEE, 2013); (2) contextualization of content through a consultative process involving reflective cycles of feedback; (3) ensuring the content was collaboratively designed and co-created (Zembylas & Bekerman, 2013); and (4) centering local wisdom and voices to prioritize local peacebuilding knowledge and practice (Autesserre, 2017). Each of these principles will be discussed in further detail. However, in an effort to exercise the process of reflection we first share our positionality to situate ourselves within this work and invite the reader to consider how our individual knowledge, experience, cultural background, and socially constructed understanding of our worldview may have contributed to this work.

Arkar Phyo Thant

At the time of this project I worked with PIN as Project Manager for the social cohesion program in Mon, Karen, and Rakhine States. I came to the field of peacebuilding via the road of student activism. While studying public health, political science, and philosophy, I became an activist and worked as co-secretary, president, and advisor of the Student Union at my university. I have been involved in supporting the political transition movement of Myanmar. My perspective and lens on peacebuilding is informed by a lifelong commitment and a long-range vision. For me, peacebuilding is not a project; it is a process. Working in the context of a global NGO with a combination of both international and local staff, I have observed how peacebuilding is approached by international actors from the point of view of project implementation.

I contend that peacebuilding is a long process that extends beyond the limitations of project cycles. It is important to approach peacebuilding from a local perspective and reality, which requires immersion in local context and a level of relationship and engagement that goes beyond consultation. A project implementation approach may emphasize the importance of consultative processes, including local stakeholder engagement as a key part of project design and implementation; however, this approach is limited. Through consultative processes, outside actors may gain information about a local situation, but they will not experience the local reality. They may know in their head but not understand with their heart. From my perspective, if you want to know about the Karen people you need to go there, eat with them, sleep with them, then you will know how their energy is working, how and what they believe. I see this gap in international actors' lived experience and heart-level understanding of local contexts as one of the problems in the current approach to peacebuilding in Myanmar.

Grace Michel

One of my earliest family memories was attending a Christmas celebration of the Karen community in Bakersfield, California. This group of several dozen Karen families had relocated as refugees in the early 1990s to escape violent armed conflict in Karen State. Singing Christmas carols in a Baptist church, then sharing a delicious communal meal in our host's living room was my introduction to what it meant to be Karen. My own mother and her family had come to the United States from Burma three decades earlier shortly after the 1962 military coup. I grew up hearing stories about my mother's childhood, playing among the haunted Banyan trees with her siblings and splashing in monsoon rains, as well as the suffering of the Karen and other ethnic peoples who endured violent armed conflict at the hands of an authoritarian military regime. I was raised a world away in a small, mostly homogenous white town in northern California, where as a multiracial child I was constantly faced with the question, "What are you?" I took pride in my Karen heritage, though most people who I tried to explain it to looked at me with a puzzled gaze when I said my mother was from Burma. By the time I was in high school, I was fascinated with other cultures and longed to visit my mother's homeland, though none of my family had ever returned. In college I chose to study International Relations and I devoted much of my research to the political situation in Burma, and made it a goal to one day devote myself to working for peace among Burma's many ethnic and religious identity groups.

After completing an MA in Peace and Justice Studies, I finally made my long-standing dream a reality by moving to Burma in 2016 and became involved in peace education research and curriculum development work. I arrived in Burma (which I eventually reluctantly adapted to calling Myanmar in some contexts)[2] at a time of great energy and hope for prospects of peace during the time of the twenty-first-century Panglong Conference (Beyond Panglong: Myanmar's national peace and reform dilemma, 2017). Over the course of the following year I went through a personal reckoning of my own positionality, role, and identity in Burma. Despite my deep ancestral connections and heartfelt desire to belong and contribute to this place of my heritage, I was an outsider. I didn't speak either Burmese or Karen language. Though I had studied the country for years, I still didn't have a full grasp of the nuanced and delicate political dynamics and sensitivities. And while I witnessed many international workers swirling around me building their careers in the NGO industrial complex, I couldn't quite bring myself to join them. When I was honest with myself I knew that I would need to devote many years of cultural immersion and language learning to begin to meaningfully contribute in a transformative way to Burma's transition. Instead, after one year living in Burma I chose to return to the United States and devote myself to efforts to build peace and understanding across cultural differences in my own home context.

The opportunity to work on the PIN project was presented to me after I was already back in the United States. I hesitated to get involved for the reasons mentioned above. Ultimately though, I recognized that the project was going to happen with me or without me, and that I did have valuable technical skills to offer in the area of peace education curriculum development as well as contextual knowledge and experience. I decided to apply the mindset that "perfect is the enemy of the good"—committing myself to applying the best practices I could to the project despite the less-than-ideal situation of being at a distance.

Katie Zanoni

Unlike my co-authors, Grace and Arkar, my connection to this project does not have a personal story linked directly to Myanmar. Researchers assessing this project would label me appropriately as an "outsider" drawing on my content knowledge of peace and human rights education and practice of peacebuilding to contribute to our collective efforts (Kerstetter, 2012). I was invited to this project through my professional connection to Grace, whom I developed a relationship with through our mutual passion in peace education that was further nourished while

---

2. The name of the country was officially changed from the Union of Burma to the Union of Myanmar in 1989 by the ruling military regime. Many who viewed the regime as illegitimate refused to adopt the name Myanmar as an act of resistance and opposition to the regime. Myanmar has now widely become the accepted name, including by the UN and most countries, but the United States still uses Burma as the official name. I (Grace) personally prefer the name Burma as it is the name passed down by my family.

we both held positions within the Kroc School of Peace Studies at the University of San Diego. My work has woven a path steeped both in my local community to co-design Peace Studies programming at the collegiate level and in contexts outside of my own such as Thailand, Kenya, and resettled refugee communities in the United States within the K-12 educational systems. Deeply committed to supporting communities impacted by forced migration and violent conflict, I have devoted my career to increasing awareness of the impact of war on the individual and societal level through my collegiate teaching and peace education curriculum development. When presented with the opportunity to share my expertise and learn from and with peacebuilding experts in Myanmar working toward the same goals of advancing peace education, I humbly accepted the offer.

With these varied backgrounds and relationships to Myanmar, our US-based authoring team and Myanmar project team came together as a broader global team to undertake the curriculum development and project implementation process. What follows is a sketch of our experience framed through the key principles we applied. We offer insight about what worked as well as the challenges and obstacles we faced in bringing these principles to life. Our hope is that other peace educators, peacebuilding practitioners, and donors who undertake peacebuilding efforts in Myanmar and in other complex conflict contexts can reflect upon what we share.

Our Ever-Evolving Four Principles

Conflict Sensitivity

The practice of conflict sensitivity in process and outcome was essential to the LST project. By the time Grace and Katie, as a US-based authoring team, became involved in the project, our Myanmar-based PIN team had already applied a conflict sensitivity framework to the project design, and it was our role and responsibility as curriculum-designers to apply that framework and integrate lessons learned into the design of specific activities and the production of learning materials.

Our LST team was extremely intentional about the terminology we used both to communicate about the project with local community stakeholders/participants and in the published materials. In approaching communities as project sites, the PIN staff did not say explicitly "we want to implement a peace project" because of the highly politicized connotation of peacebuilding activities. Instead, the title "Learn and Share Together" was chosen as an alternative to the politicized term of peace. In order to avoid using language that could potentially cause harm in the written curriculum, we excluded certain specific words and terms including "peace," "conflict," "freedom of religion." Whilst replacing potentially harmful language with more conflict-sensitive terms is a widely accepted and suggested approach of peacebuilders (Shah, Aung, & Lopes Cardozo, 2018; South & Lall, 2016), our team grappled with the tension of designing learning activities that would fulfill the intent of resolving conflict without explicitly calling attention to the fact that learners were practicing this skill. In order to safely implement the project, permission was required from government authorities and such approval would not be granted if terms like conflict resolution or other sensitive learning objectives were used. In the Karen and broader Myanmar context, depending on how they are understood and interpreted by the receiver, these words can put those who use them at risk of being seen as having a specific political agenda or being on a certain side of conflict. They can also be interpreted as an imposition of foreign ideology. Avoiding these sensitive terms, we utilized language that described concrete strategies, skills, and tools that the curriculum aimed to teach, and framed these under the broad objective of building a healthy community. For example, the curriculum included lessons on cooperation, building awareness and appreciation of diverse identities, finding win-win solutions to problems, and communication skills. Thus, the curriculum did not speak directly about conflict or peace but utilized a theory of change that if there is a foundation of a certain set of skills and practices, then there is a potential for peace.

A conflict-sensitive approach was equally critical in the outreach and training process with local trainers as well as learners in the target communities. The selection process for the TTT program to become PBCs began with outreach to CSOs in the Karen capital of Hpa'an, inviting representatives from the CSOs to submit applications. The PIN team then reviewed the applications and conducted interviews to select the PBCs. The selection process involved intentionally selecting diverse participants from different religious and ethnic backgrounds, including Buddhists, Christians, and Muslims as well as Sgaw and Pwo Karen, and ethnic Bamar, while also ensuring that participants had sufficient knowledge, experience, and sensitivity to relate to local community members in the villages where the project was implemented. A lead facilitator from Nyein (Shalom) Foundation, a leading Myanmar peacebuilding organization, was contracted to design and facilitate the TTT program with a conflict-sensitive lens. The TTT program included two phases, starting with a six-day intensive training focused on facilitation skills and practice with the draft version of the first half of the curriculum, followed by a three-day training six weeks later working with the remaining curriculum. This training approach enabled the PIN team and lead trainer to build relationships with the PBCs and see them in action as facilitators to ensure they were prepared to enter into target communities with sufficient sensitivity and skills to engage with local community members in a way that sought to do no harm.

A conflict-sensitive approach also meant dedicating time and energy to trust-building activities. The project was designed with an understanding of the need for trust between PBCs and participants as an essential ingredient for effective learning. Thus, when the PBCs entered target communities their training approach involved dedicating time at the beginning of the program for relationship-building through facilitated games, activities, and sharing in order to build trust. As a result, after spending a couple of days focused on trust and relationship-building, participants became more comfortable with each other and open to sharing their ideas. It is at that point when PBCs were able to introduce more sensitive topics.

In addition to a focus on trusting relationships among PBCs and community participants, effectively practicing conflict sensitivity required building trusting relationships with broader community leaders and stakeholders in order to integrate their perspectives and gain support for the project. LST did not exist in a vacuum but was built on a strong foundation of relationships with community leaders and organizations that PIN staff had cultivated during previous projects and sustained over time through frequent visits and conversations. This relationship-oriented approach reflected PIN's value for listening to and creating open channels of communication with the local community. The PIN team's experience with communities had taught them that it was necessary to build good relationships in order for community members to believe in PIN's people and their work, and only then would they be willing to share their thoughts and feelings openly. These open channels of communication and feedback loops with community members influenced the design, monitoring, and evaluation of the project. For the authoring team, the local relationships that PIN had established were especially critical for the consultation processes to develop the curriculum materials.

Contextualization

One of the approaches we aimed to prioritize in this project was to contextualize the curriculum to make it relevant and reflective of Myanmar reality and culture. When learners see their context and stories represented in a book, curriculum, or educational material, it not only makes it easier to engage with, retain, and implement the content, but also validates and honors learners' lived experiences and cultural worldview. Effective contextualization requires deep engagement and understanding of the belief systems, narratives, artifacts, and behavioral norms of a given context (Autesserre, 2014). As practitioners we recognized that best practice in developing contextualized curriculum ideally means authoring by local people in the local language, centering local knowledge. However, this project faced many limitations and obstacles to this ideal (which are explored in greater detail in the next section). In particular for the US-based authoring team, we recognized the limitations of being "outsiders" without deep lived experience in the local context of Karen State. Working closely as an international team we collectively acknowledged the challenges to linguistic and cultural contextualization. First, in an attempt to have broad impact, the project was conceived with a national-level scope for the curriculum to have use throughout the country. This was in tension with the desire to be regionally contextualized for Karen State. Second, as a result of this national scope and donor expectations, the project prioritized English and Burmese before other ethnic languages. There is a huge diversity of languages in Myanmar (over 100), and among the Karen there are two major dialects—Sgaw Karen and Pwo Karen. Therefore, there is a challenge as to which languages to prioritize in donor-funded projects. The challenging reality of this project was that the limited budget resulted in not prioritizing translation into Karen and other ethnic languages. Recognizing that our contextualization could only go so far, we sought to mitigate these obstacles through writing the curriculum using a consultative process involving reflective cycles of feedback with members of the

PIN team and their organizational partners. This was not included in the scope of work or timeline of the initial proposed work, but something our team prioritized and integrated into the project flow.

Collaboration and Co-Creation

Feedback to better contextualize the content was one ingredient in the broader effort of our globally dispersed team to collaboratively design and co-create the curriculum. Working to our best ability within the constraints of the international NGO system this project existed in,[3] and facing the obstacles of time zone differences, tight deadlines, and language and cultural communication style differences, our team exerted a high level of coordination and patient communication both among the local stakeholders in Karen State and Yangon and with our dispersed team in the United States to uphold the value of co-creation. We approached the project as both learners and teachers. For the US-based authoring team, this meant constantly seeking to learn from our Myanmar colleagues while simultaneously drawing from our formal educational backgrounds in Peace and Justice Studies and offering our expertise in curriculum development. The Myanmar-based team included nationals based in both Karen State and Yangon, and international team members based in Yangon. For our Myanmar-based team, collaboration and co-creation was a complex process of facilitating activities to build a shared understanding of the project among a web of stakeholders including local target community leaders and participants, project implementation partners, and within the PIN staff team. The PIN team then transferred that knowledge to the US-based authoring team and ensured these findings were integrated into the curriculum.

Our collaborative process involved the PIN team first identifying the lesson topics to be included in the curriculum through a consultative process with target community stakeholders. In order to accomplish this task, the PIN team first conducted an analysis of the project context to ensure inclusion of diverse perspectives in the project development process. The PIN team then analyzed and synthesized findings from the consultations and delivered these to the US-based authoring team to prepare them with accurate information to create the curriculum. The US-based authoring team then developed the draft lessons and shared them with the PIN team to continue the cycle of co-creation. The PIN team gathered perspectives on the draft content from their local staff and additional stakeholders when possible, then thoughtfully synthesized their feedback. The PIN team then came together in virtual meetings with the authoring team as well as the lead trainer contracted from another national Myanmar peacebuilding

---

3. This project faced several constraints common to INGO projects. We were under an extremely tight timeline of a few months from curriculum design to training implementation with limited budget, which included not having sufficient budget to allow for the US-based authoring team to travel to Myanmar to participate in stakeholder engagement processes to gather feedback on the curriculum.

organization (Shalom) to report back recommendations and engage in knowledge exchange and discussion on the curriculum content. These feedback conversations included flagging any potentially sensitive terms or topics, reviewing content to ensure gender sensitivity, suggestions for how to make the content more age and learning-level appropriate, and recommendations for how to better contextualize the content. In addition to these collaborative design conversations with the PIN and Shalom team members, there was also time dedicated in the first TTT to get participant feedback on the first five lessons. Unfortunately, due to the constraints of the project timeline and funding, only the first five lessons could be designed and translated into Burmese before the first TTT, and there was not sufficient time or funding to allow for another feedback session on the remaining lessons after the second TTT.

As a result of these feedback loops from both the project team and the TTT participants, the authoring team adapted language, content, and visual design. Sometimes these contextualization attempts were small adjustments, like using a coconut (local fruit) instead of an orange in one of the stories in the curriculum. Sometimes the adjustments were larger and more complex, like re-evaluating and re-framing the concept of "Wants vs. Needs" when speaking to a Myanmar audience as opposed to a Western audience.

As evidenced by the inability to revise the curriculum after the second TTT, the value for co-creation and ongoing feedback was in tension with the extremely short project timeline and limited budget. The tight timeline is an unfortunate but all-too-common reality of the current international NGO system (Fischer, 2006). In this system, time is money, and the reality of the project was that both the funding and the time were experienced by the project team as scarce resources. Because of this scarcity, there were limitations in the approach taken to collaborative design and the voices included in the process of co-creation. Initially the project was intended to be completed in three months from the beginning of the authoring to the completion of the finalized curriculum materials. Furthermore, funding was not awarded to the proposed budget to allow for the US authors to visit Myanmar to conduct stakeholder meetings and focus groups in person as requested. Although the timeline was extended for a few months, we still had to operate on extremely short turnarounds given the many complex elements of the project that needed to be finalized after the lessons were authored, including final translation, graphic design, and illustration. This timeline meant that PIN was only able to take time for a consultation of the draft lessons with one key stakeholder group on the ground in Karen, who organized the TTT. Had time allowed, the team would have aimed to consult with additional stakeholders including religious leaders, government representatives, CSO leaders, community leaders, and Ethnic Armed Organization (EAO) leaders. More extensive consultation would have allowed for deeper understanding of the different perceptions of the curriculum and more inclusive content development.

It is important to note that peace curricula already existed at the time of this project that had been previously developed in and for the Myanmar context by other organizations. The authoring team reviewed and analyzed existing peace education materials and our aim was to not reinvent the wheel with a new curriculum. However, PIN's approach to this particular peace education initiative required the development of additional learning materials not provided in existing curricula. The project approach included a capstone where training participants received small grants to apply the knowledge gained from the training to design and implement projects based upon their assessment of community needs. Ideally, projects like these can tap into a local network with collective knowledge of peace education initiatives to coordinate, collaborate, and leverage existing efforts and best practices.

Another key challenge in the collaborative and co-creative approach to the project was in language-based communication barriers and translation. The language barrier and communication gaps between national and international project team staff was the very first challenge to collaboration. Sometimes there were misunderstandings between national and international team members. Myanmar nationals noted that while trying to share perspectives with international colleagues within the PIN team, they felt there were gaps in what was understood and incorporated into decisions for the project. As a US-based authoring team we attempted to overcome our communication barriers by practicing deep listening and continuously checking for understanding to mitigate miscommunication. We also tried to create a sense of community among our Myanmar-based and US-based team through simple activities including sharing photos and personal updates from our parts of the world.

The language barriers within our team were reflective of a broader challenge in the project as a whole. The reality of the project was that the curriculum was authored in English, though this was not the language of instruction for the vast majority of the facilitators and learners who would use it. There was a fundamental awareness on our team that authoring a curriculum in English to then be translated into Burmese (and potentially other local languages such as Karen) was problematic and an obstacle to effective contextualization. Many of the core concepts within peace education that we as US-based authors brought to the table did not translate. Concepts like "assertive communication" do not exist in Myanmar language and took several sentences to translate conceptually. Even as the authoring team attempted to mitigate our own biases, we were drawing from Westernized peace education frameworks and curriculum theory. The politics of language were admittedly present, and we risked perpetuating the reinforcement of Western power and dominance through using English language to author the curriculum (Wong, 2019).

As Waters (see Chapter 9 of this volume) points out, peacebuilding projects and many research agendas in Myanmar are dominated by the interests and viewpoints of Western donors and thus prioritize English as the language to operationalize these efforts with the goal to ultimately achieve peace. As aptly pointed out by Waters, "Language choice is an expression of power" (Waters, p. 209, this volume). Thus, the role of English language in this project exemplifies the limitations and contradictions of the international NGO system we operated within. In the case of LST, the international NGO system with its frameworks and funding mechanisms demanded a curriculum that met global standards of learning design and a finished product that could be evaluated in the language of the funder–English, and all of this on an extremely tight time frame with limited funding. At the same time, best practice recognized that the most effective learning is achieved through contextualized content in the mother tongue. These competing priorities created a catch 22. There was a lack of local and national professionals to call upon because of insufficient support in terms of time and funding resources to develop local professionals' capacity as primary authors of global standard curriculum in their mother tongue. As such, international authors were contracted for the work. Thus, the work had to be authored in English, furthering it from the best practice of culturally and linguistically appropriate learning design.

Centering Local Wisdom and Voices

"Mae Par Myar Sa Gar Ya" *"The More You Ask the More You Get"* In the face of this dilemma we as a US-based authoring team sought to bridge the gap between ideal and reality by doing our best to center the voices, insights, and knowledge of our Myanmar team experts, who were simultaneously aiming to center the wisdom of local community stakeholders in Karen. This approach was rooted in the belief that peace is an ongoing and long-term process that must be responsive to a local (contextualized) understanding of peace. Our Myanmar team members articulated a number of key practices for centering local voices. First, identifying all the voices to listen to in the given context. It was the PIN's team practice when working in a local community to first conduct a stakeholder analysis to carefully understand who the different actors are and whose voices needed to be heard. Depending on the focus of the project, this meant prioritizing relevant stakeholder groups—for example, focusing on ethnic and religious leaders when doing identity-based peacebuilding and focusing on EAO leaders when doing civic peacebuilding work.

The next key practice to center local wisdom was building relationships and sustaining them over time through continuous contact. The PIN team met with local stakeholders in Karen before the curriculum was created, worked with them during implementation, consulted with them for the evaluation of the project, and then continued to work with them beyond the life cycle of the curriculum project. As mentioned before, this relationship-oriented approach was the foundation to building trust that enabled open dialogue and a conflict-sensitive approach to project implementation.

In the context of these relationships, the next key practice for centering local wisdom was to engage in consultation through deep listening, with neutrality, to understand local perspectives. This meant having a "beginners mind"—trying to mitigate biases by putting aside one's existing knowledge when meeting with local stakeholders, and asking them about their perspectives with the intention of understanding their interpretations of their situation. Such a practice of deep listening can draw forth local wisdom. For example, learning how a local stakeholder defines peace on their terms. Our Myanmar colleagues pointed out that international definitions and frameworks for peace are not necessarily relatable, relevant, or understood in certain local contexts. While an international definition of peace might emphasize governance and human rights frameworks proposed for peaceful coexistence, for local villagers in Karen peace might mean there is food in the village and there is no fighting happening. Drawing on Johan Galtung's theory of positive and negative peace, our team identified a more holistic approach to peace is desired among communities within Myanmar (Galtung, 1969, 1990). While communities desire to reach the overarching goal of ending violent conflict (negative peace), many are focused on accessing basic necessities such as food and education (positive peace). Given that peace is contextually defined and also interpreted in a variety of ways, it was important to center local voices by first listening to them to understand these different perspectives.

While forgetting one's preconceived notions was critical for centering local wisdom, we also learned this needs to be balanced with a practice of discerning which perspectives and interpretations to include in key decisions about the project approach and activities. It was important to differentiate between listening to and taking action based on local perspectives, depending on the stakeholder's understanding of a given situation. The PIN team listened to very diverse points of view and recognized that some stakeholders did not have a nuanced understanding of complex issues shaping their experience. For example, sometimes religious leaders did not understand the multi-factorial root causes of conflict in their regions. They might view the conflict only through the lens of religion and interpret it as an ideological or identity-based conflict, without recognizing or acknowledging other factors that have fueled conflict including the education system, failed political management, and economic factors. Because of this, it was critical for the PIN team to take in all perspectives without being swayed by certain stakeholders' positions on an issue, while drawing on expert knowledge of the conflict and context. Then determinations could be made about how to interpret and include local voices in the project.

The final practice to support the centering of local voices was to keep listening and learning. After the curriculum was finalized, the PIN team conducted an evaluation. At that time, they met with more stakeholders, including CSOs and religious leaders, to ask for their consultation. Though time constraints had been an obstacle to these consultations earlier in the project cycle, the team did not abandon these stakeholders' insights but rather sought to draw them forth to improve the next version of the curriculum and future projects. This is another way in which the approach broke the boundaries of a project life cycle in favor of an interactive and ongoing learning process.

Several challenges have been highlighted in this chapter. However, we would like to pause on this reflective exercise to note the positive impact of the LST project and segue into the lessons learned and caveats for other contexts. First and foremost, "the LST curriculum was found by all engaged stakeholders to be a needed resource to encourage behavioral change and promote social cohesion" (PIN Evaluation, 2018). The formal project evaluation revealed that participation in the LST training led to immediate shifts in attitudes and behaviors among participants in the training group from different ethnic and religious backgrounds. While it is recognized that lasting behavior change and impact occurs over longer time periods, the initial feedback revealed that the project was a building block toward increased levels of inclusion and cohesion in the target communities. The evaluation revealed that the curriculum itself was "sensitively approached and appropriate to the context" (PIN Evaluation, 2018) and at the same time demanded skilled facilitation to adhere to "do no harm" principles. Finally, the evaluation indicated that the curriculum was a successful example of a learner-centered approach with participatory activities that engaged learners in critical thinking and self-reflection, and that the curriculum could be easily adapted for other contexts and time limitations (PIN Internal Evaluation, 2018). It was recognized that the engaged pedagogical approach would be challenging to implement in some contexts and may encounter resistance due to traditional rote learning approaches.

Translating Lessons into Practice in Diverse Contexts

In this final section, we offer three key insights that surfaced as we, the three authors of this chapter, grappled with various questions throughout our process of reflecting on our own work and receiving the feedback from the informal follow-up and formal evaluation conducted after the curriculum piloting phase. These are briefly addressed through a summary of lessons learned along with recommendations for future practitioners, donors, and international peacebuilding teams comprising "insider"/"outsider" experts.

Centering Local Wisdom and Voices

When we say "center local people more" it doesn't mean that we don't want the involvement of international people. We still need the integration of international norms and values, but the approach should be local.

—Arkar

This quote draws out the tensions felt within local peacebuilders as they are held to international frameworks of peacebuilding while simultaneously attempting to translate this knowledge—and the resources tied to consuming this approach— within the local context. However, what if best practices in the field of peacebuilding were drawn from peace education projects that have been funded, designed, and implemented entirely by a local team in Myanmar? Can we imagine new types of partnerships between international funders and local peacebuilders that draw on localized knowledge to design the Request for Proposals (RFP)? How can international peacebuilding and aid agencies collaborate more effectively to enable programming according to the needs identified by the communities? This question is also tied to the dominance of Western ideals as interpreted through the use of the English language to communicate funding opportunities and final reports to international donors. What steps are required for existing international donors to trust local peacebuilders in Myanmar enough to implement projects entirely in the local language without the need to translate the project outputs into reports written in the English language? While answers to these multifaceted questions are beyond the scope of this chapter, our recommendations to future donors and international NGOs are (1) to reconsider granting guidelines to include local capacity building via training opportunities to ensure "insider" peacebuilders are enhancing their technical skills such as learning design and curriculum development using engaged pedagogy; (2) to identify strategies to implement and evaluate a project without the need to spend additional resources on translation to English, but rather focus funding on translation into diverse local languages to expand the reach of the project within Myanmar (Wong, 2019); and (3) to loosen reporting guidelines from traditional monitoring and evaluation frameworks tied to Western assumptions of peace to reflect a more adaptive approach (Waters, this volume). This recommendation requires Western donors to release their grip on a predetermined vision of peace and invite local peacebuilders and stakeholders to demonstrate success markers advancing notions of peace defined by and for the Myanmar people.

"Peace Is a Process, Not a Project"—Arkar

Most donor recipients understand the need to meet and exceed the funding expectations of the donor agency. Yet, as this chapter explored, expectations of achieving targets framed within the field of peacebuilding are translated in diverse ways depending upon the individual, the context and their socially constructed worldview. Processes to build peace take time and cannot be bound in a finite project cycle. Upon the initial evaluation of the pilot project, it was discovered that more training was required to support the PBCs to understand the scope of the project and gain the skills required to translate the lessons of social cohesion into the community.

Our recommendations to both practitioners accepting funding for new projects and donor agencies alike are to expand the timeline to consider the complexities within a goal of sustained peacebuilding activities. For example, in order to fully exercise the principles presented by our team, the timeline of a peace education project ought to be extended to allow for a more in-depth consultative process to ensure the content is contextualized appropriately and designed with ample experiential learning activities. Early on, our team identified the need to build out more time for deep listening and reflection to ensure feedback was understood across the language and cultural boundaries. Had our timeline been extended, our team could have conducted focus groups with the draft curricula prior to the pilot phase. These focus groups could have included checking for understanding, building shared knowledge of Westernized and Burmese concepts and practices of peacebuilding, and identifying cultural references to include from the local context. Such an approach could be undertaken as a multi-year project, which would require a shift in the timeline enabled by donors.

Situating this recommendation within the broader landscape of aid/donor agencies, we present the following questions for further reflection. How can strategic priorities and planning be reconsidered to allow for longer time horizons that reflect an understanding of the complex and long-term process of peacebuilding? When considering how and when communities become more cohesive and therefore resilient to violence (Carpenter, 2014) how do practitioners (and the donors who fund them) design projects that are responsive to a community's timeline and interpretation of peace, rather than predetermined project cycles? Heeding the advice of peacebuilding team John Paul Lederach and Angela Lederach (2011), we echo the need for all peacebuilding practitioners to identify a new understanding of social healing and imagine beyond the linear metaphor that peace occurs directly after violence. As they state, "We propose that social healing cannot be understood as a phenomenon that emerges exclusively after violence ends, in large part because in so many places it simply does not end, and it finds ever new forms by which to express itself locally" (Lederach & Lederach, 2011, p. 11). In adhering to the idea that peace is a process, we call upon "outsider" practitioners, in particular, to reflect on and suspend their preconceived notions of peace. In turn, this can allow peacebuilders to dedicate intentional time and effort to reimagining notions of "success" alongside the local communities within which the work is undertaken. Furthermore, we recommend that funders support projects designed with these locally and contextually envisioned indicators and timelines.

"Peace through Education Alone Will Not Be Enough"—Arkar

In its fullness, peace is a concept that touches all aspects and levels of organization of human society from the interpersonal to the institutional, from the environment to the economy, from the local to the global. This project was implemented through a specific academic and practitioner lens informed by theoretical frameworks of peacebuilding, but we recognize that peace education interventions must be integrated with a cross-sectoral approach to achieve sustainable peace results, and that the field of peace education has much to offer other sectors. Consider actors who are working in sectors such as natural resource management, politics and rule of law, or economic development. To what extent do these actors have an understanding of or an orientation toward peace, and to what extent are they equipped with strategies and skills to foster collaboration, mutual respect, and win-win solutions among diverse groups? To this end, we encourage peace education practitioners to (1) organize themselves to foster ongoing communication and coordination, for example, through working groups[4] and community mapping

4. One example of this is the Peace Education Working Group that Grace was involved in creating in Myanmar in 2017 to encourage ongoing communication and collaboration among peace education practitioners and organizations.

projects to identify potential partners and avoid duplicating efforts; (2) create actionable recommendations from the peace education sector to other sectors, for example, recommendations to the formal education sector to integrate peacebuilding tools, strategies, and frameworks into government education standards; and (3) move beyond the peace education and peacebuilding silos through initiating connections with leaders in other sectors to build networks for positive peace.

In summary, our key recommendations for donor agencies are (1) provide grant guidelines that encourage the inclusion of local peacebuilders, and that honors the local languages in programming, content design, and evaluation; (2) allow for flexibility in timelines, processes, and outcomes that realistically address the complexities of sustainable peacebuilding, and which may diverge from the dominant approach of INGOs and donor/aid agencies that ask for a deliverable package to fulfill a predetermined vision of success; and (3) require the articulation of the broader connections the education sector can make with other sectors to move efforts of sustained peace into new spaces within the structures and systems of a civil society.

It is our hope that these recommendations, coupled with the reflective practice embodied in the four principles presented to co-design conflict-sensitive curricula that is contextualized, co-created in an authentic manner, and centers local wisdom, will support additional efforts to build sustainable peace through education in Myanmar and beyond.

Works Cited

Alam, J. (2019). The current Rohingya crisis in Myanmar in historical perspective. *Journal of Muslim Minority Affairs, 39*(1), 1–25. https://doi.org/10.1080/13602004.2019.1575560

Anderson, M. B. (1999). *Do no harm: How aid can support peace-or war.* Boulder: Lynne Rienner Publishers.

Autesserre, S. (2014). *Peaceland: Conflict resolution and everyday politics of international intervention.* New York: Cambridge University Press.

Autesserre, S. (2017). International peacebuilding and local success: Assumptions and effectiveness. *International Studies Review, (0)*, 1–19. https://doi.org/10.1093/isr/viw054

Carpenter, A. (2014). *Community resilience to sectarian violence in Baghdad.* New York: Springer-Verlag.

De Coning, C. (2018). Adaptive peacebuilding. *International Affairs, 94*(2), 301–17.

Fischer, M. (2006). Civil Society in conflict transformation: Ambivalence, potentials and challenges. *Berghof Handbook for Conflict Transformation.* Retrieved from www.berghof-handbook.net

Freire, P. (1970). *Pedagogy of the oppressed* (30th ed.). New York: Continuum International Publishing Group.

Galtung, J. (1969). Violence, peace, and peace research. *Journal of Peace Research, 6*(3), 167–91.

Galtung, J. (1990). Cultural violence. *Journal of Peace Research, 27*(3), 291–305.

Government of Myanmar. (2015). The 2014 Myanmar population and housing census: The Union report. The 2014 Myanmar Population and Housing Census: Census Report Volume 3 - B (Vol. 2). Retrieved from https://myanmar.unfpa.org/en/publications/union-report-volume-2-main-census-report

Higgins, S., Maber, E. J. T., Lopes Cardozo, M. T. A., & Shah, R. (2015). *Selections of a research report on education and peacebuilding in Myanmar.*

hooks, Bell. (2010). *Teaching Critical Thinking*: Practical Wisdom. New York: Routledge.

INEE. (2013). *INEE guidance note on conflict sensitive education.* New York: INEE.

INEE. (2019). *Guidance note gender: Gender equality in and through education. Guidance Note.* New York. https://doi.org/10.1596/33585

Jolliffee, K., & Mears, E. S. (2016). *Strength in diversity towards universal education in Myanmar's ethnic areas.* Yangon. Retrieved from https://asiafoundation.org/wp-content/uploads/2016/10/Strength-in-Diversity-Toward-Universal-Education-Myanmar-Ethnic-Area.pdf

Karen Human Rights Group. (2018). *"Development without us": Village agency and land confiscations in southeast Myanmar.* Chiang Mai: KHRG.

Kerstetter, K. (2012). Insider, outsider, or somewhere in between: The impact of researchers' identities on the community-based research process. *Journal of Rural Social Sciences, 27*(2), 99–117. Retrieved from http://ag.auburn.edu/auxiliary/srsa/pages/Articles/JRSS201227299-117.pdf

Lederach, J. P., & Lederach, A. J. (2011). *When Blood and Bones Cry Out: Journeys through the Soundscape of Healing and Reconciliation.* Oxford and New York: Oxford University Press.

Lederach, J. P., Neufeldt, R., & Culbertson, H. (2007). *Reflective peacebuilding toolkit: A planning, monitoring, and learning toolkit.* Mindanao: The Joan B. Kroc Institute for International Peace Studies, University of Notre Dame. Retrieved from https://ndigd.nd.edu/assets/172927/reflective_peacebuilding_a_planning_monitoring_and_learning_toolkit.pdf

Myanmar Information Management. (2020). Union data indicators by year data collection. Retrieved from http://themimu.info/baseline-datasets

Myanmar peace monitor. (2019). Retrieved May 1, 2018, from https://www.mmpeacemonitor.org/

People in Need. (2017). Terms of reference for bridging religious and ethnic divides in Burma through supporting civil society in promoting tolerance, Conflict Resolution and Peace Education.

Shah, R., & Lopez Cardoza, M. T. A. (2018). Myanmar's education system: Historical roots, the current context, and new opportunities. In M. T. A. Lopez Cardoza & E. J. T. Maber (Eds.), *Sustainable Peacebuilding and Social Justice in Times of Transition* (pp. 65–86). Switzerland: Springer International Publishing.

Shah, R., Aung, K. M., & Lopes Cardozo, M. T. A. (2018). Education and policy challenges of a situation in flux. In M. T. A. Lopez Cardoza & E. J. T. Maber (Eds.), *Sustainable Peacebuilding and Social Justice in Times of Transition* (pp. 87–113). Switzerland: Springer International Publishing.

Simbulan, K. (2016). *Peace is living with dignity: Voices of communities from Myanmar's Ceasefire areas in 2016.*

South, A. (2011). *Burma's longest war: Anatomy of the Karen conflict. Transnational Institute.* Transnational Institute and Burma Center Netherlands. Retrieved from https://www.tni.org/my/node/1366

South, A., & Lall, M. (2016). Language, education and the peace process in Myanmar. *Contemporary Southeast Asia, 38*(1), 128–53. https://doi.org/10.1355/cs38-1f

Waters, T. (2022). Researching peacebuilding in Myanmar: Framing research questions with our grandparents' moral imagination. In M. Wong (Ed.), *Teaching Peace and Social Justice in Myanmar: Identity, Agency, & Critical Pedagogy* (pp. 191–216). London: Bloomsbury.

Wilkins, A. (2017). Gender, migration and intimate geopolitics: Shifting senses of home among women on the Myanmar-Thailand border. *Gender, Place & Culture: A Journal of Feminist Geography, 24*(11), 1549–68.

Wong, M. S. (2019). The peace dividend of valuing non-dominant languages in language-in-education policies in Myanmar. *FIRE: Forum for International Research in Education, 5*(3), 49–68.

Zembylas, M., & Bekerman, Z. (2013). Peace education in the present: Dismantling and reconstructing some fundamental theoretical premises. *Journal of Peace Education, 10*(2), 197–214.

Part III

CRITICAL PEDAGOGY

Chapter 7

PEACE EDUCATION IN MYANMAR'S MIDDLE SCHOOL CURRICULUM: A QUALITATIVE STUDY OF EDUCATOR AND EXPERT PERSPECTIVES

Kinsa San Yi, Naw Sah Blute, and Radka Antalíková

Introduction

Having attended state schools in Myanmar, we (San Yi and Sah Blute) felt we never had the chance to ask questions during class. Teaching methods were teacher-centered, and we had to learn everything by heart. One of us (Sah Blute) participated in several competitions, such as essay writing, writing in rhymes, and round-table discussions. However, all materials for these competitions had been written by the teachers at our school in advance and we, the students, simply memorized them in order to compete. All the other schools were doing the same. This "winning strategy" had been normalized in our state school culture and so we also thought it was appropriate. All of us wanted our schools to win and viewed the other schools as our rivals. Therefore, not only did we miss the opportunity to express our own thoughts and creativity in these competitions, but we also missed the chance to value and support students from other schools.

Another interesting experience for us was that we never really worked in groups in school. There were no group activities, such as group discussions, group projects, or group assignments in our classrooms. We worked and learned strictly individually. This tended to create an atmosphere of competition among our peers. Moreover, corporal punishment was acceptable. Both of us either faced or witnessed severe physical punishment by our school teachers, such as a teacher beating students in front of the class or in front of the school's flagpole where the whole school could see. Teachers sometimes used their shoes to hit the students.

Fast forward to 2018, when we joined the *Graduate Research Diploma in Peace Leadership* program offered by the Peace Leadership & Research Institute (PLRI), which is a higher education learning center providing social research and leadership skills in peace to Myanmar youth. It was here we met Radka, who became our research instructor and mentor. Coming to PLRI, we were asked to come up with an issue we wanted to research. Growing up in an educational system that was based on competition and focused on rote memorization, both of us were interested in improving teaching and learning in Myanmar. More specifically, we wanted to explore the middle school curriculum, and how it supported (or undermined) peace. We chose this area of inquiry because we believe that education plays a crucial role in promoting peace and unity. Moreover, as our country has been experiencing several decades' long conflict among different ethnic groups and religions, we thought that education could contribute to social cohesion and the promotion and appreciation of diversity. At the same time, we were aware that there was still very little empirical research on the challenges of Myanmar's education system in promoting peace education (e.g., Michel & Saw Myo Min Thu, 2017).

Thus, we set out to investigate whether there were any learning objectives and activities in the middle school curriculum that addressed peace; that is, promoted peaceful coexistence among and between people; or conversely, undermined it. We also looked at the role of pedagogy in promoting peace in the classroom. For this purpose, we began to formulate our main research question and review the available literature on our research topic. We conducted a literature review of forty-five sources in total, including reports from the Myanmar government as well as nongovernmental organizations, news from national and international media, and both unpublished and published books, chapters, and articles. After that, we selected a theoretical framework for our study and developed a research plan. We decided to use qualitative methodology, as we believed this was the most effective way to answer our research question: In what ways is peace education integrated in the national middle school curriculum? Four sub-questions were:

1. In what ways, if at all, does the curriculum address the human rights of children?
2. In what ways, if at all, does the curriculum reflect diversity, and in what ways, if at all, does the curriculum value diversity?
3. In what ways, if at all, does the curriculum provide knowledge of conflict resolution skills?
4. Finally, how do teachers work with and potentially also work around the curriculum in the classroom?

Keeping these questions in mind, we designed focus group discussion and individual interview guides for our participants. We conducted a small pilot study with one primary school teacher in Myitkyina, Kachin State, and one middle school teacher from Mawlamyinegyun, Ayeyarwady Region, to test the appropriateness and understandability of our questions. The data from these interviews was not included for analysis in the study. We adapted the discussion and interview guides based on feedback from the participants in the pilot study.

To identify potential participants for our study, we contacted friends in different parts of the country who work in the education sector and explained to them the purpose of our research. We asked each of them to choose five middle school teachers representing a diversity of genders, ethnicities, and religions. We then conducted three focus groups with three to five middle school teachers in each group who were from the same region; Kayah State, Bago Region, and Kachin State. The focus groups were conducted in Burmese and took place either at a focal person's home or at a local school. The focus group in Bago Region was facilitated by both Sah Blute and San Yi while the other two were led by San Yi alone.

We also conducted three individual interviews with education experts in Yangon and Kachin State. Two experts in Yangon (one local, one foreigner) were selected because of their knowledge on peace education and their experience in working closely with the Ministry of Education on basic education, teacher education, and curriculum development. An education expert in Kachin State was also interviewed in order to include a minority ethnic perspective on the government curriculum in the study as well. San Yi and Sah Blute carried out the three interviews in Burmese and English.

In the end, the study included sixteen participants in total, four males and twelve females. Most of the participating teachers had at least five years' work experience. They also represented different ethnic groups, such as Kayah, Bamar, Kachin, Karen, and Indian. The education experts worked with the United Nations, governmental or community-based institutions, specifically focusing on increasing the quality of education in Myanmar.

Before we began each interview or focus group, we introduced ourselves and explained the study's background and purpose. Then, we handed over an informed consent form to the participants and gave them time to go through the form carefully and sign it if they agreed with the stated conditions. In the consent form, the participants were informed that their participation in the study was completely voluntary and that they could withdraw at any time without any negative consequences. Moreover, they were also informed that all information obtained in the interviews and focus groups would remain confidential and that their identity would not be revealed without their consent. The participants were also asked if they were comfortable being recorded and they all agreed.

After the data collection, the data was transcribed word for word, generating forty pages of text in total. The focus group discussions were transcribed by the person who organized and was present during the discussions, while the conversations with the experts were transcribed by the researchers themselves. In the next step, all transcripts were reviewed by Sah Blute and San Yi several times. Then, the data was combined into one document and important content was highlighted. Sah Blute and San Yi subsequently coded the data and organized it into categories, using direct participant quotes to present and support their findings. The data was analyzed both inductively and deductively. The two researchers cross-checked each other's data interpretation and submitted it to their research mentor Radka. After receiving her feedback, the researchers re-edited the interpretation again. This procedure was repeated several times throughout the data analysis and interpretation process. In the final step, we prepared recommendations based on our findings.

Study Background

Internal Conflict and Its Impact on Education

Through the 1962 coup, the military became the most powerful group in Myanmar, managing the country's administration of education, economics, and all civil and political rights. Long-term armed conflicts between ethnic armed groups and the military government continued to plague the country. Educational institutions, the national curriculum, and its set of pedagogies were managed through a system of centralized administration and the teaching of ethnic languages was forbidden although it took place in remote regions. Soon after the 1962 coup, the education in the different states of Myanmar came to rely on monastic schools implemented by faith-based networks and non-state schools operated by ethnic armed groups, promoting teaching and learning in ethnic languages (Joliffe & Mears, 2016).

After several decades, education started to rebound, but minority ethnic children were still negatively impacted due to armed conflicts. At this time, Myanmar's political system transformed from a military dictatorship to a quasi-democratic (but still military-backed) government when President U Thein Sein took power in 2011 and started to initiate a ceasefire agreement between the military (the "Tatmadaw") and ethnic armed groups (Buchanan, 2016). However, not all ethnic armed groups signed the agreement and the failed peace negotiations caused heavy air and ground offensives by the Tatmadaw, especially in Kachin and Shan State (Joliffe & Mears, 2016). Minority ethnic children's right to education was compromised again. According to Save the Children (2019), the dropout rate of school children from rural areas (where most armed conflicts in Myanmar occur) in 2006–11 was 13.9 percent as compared to only 1.9 percent in urban areas. More recent reports have shown that over 100,000 civilians have become internally displaced people (IDPs) in Kachin State and Shan State due to the ongoing fighting between the KIA and other non-signatory groups on the one hand and the Myanmar military on the other (Burma News International, 2017; United Nations Office for the Coordination of Humanitarian Affairs, 2016).

Communal conflicts as well as escalating armed conflicts continued breaking out around the country despite the change of the government. The civilian National League for Democracy (NLD) government took office at the end of March 2016 after a landslide 2015 election victory. The people of Myanmar had great hopes for the improvement of the economic situation in the country, education reform, and overall progress toward national peace. However, conflicts were still flaring up in the country, most notably in the northern part of Myanmar's Rakhine State, causing extreme human rights violations and hundreds of thousands of people becoming refugees or IDPs (Hammadi, 2020). REACH (2015), in their Joint Education Sector Needs Assessment, showed that approximately 60,000 children aged 3–7 years residing in IDP camps in Rakhine State were not accessing formal education. A needs assessment report by Save the Children (2013) done before the outbreak of violence advocated for the government to take responsibility for providing formal education that would promote values of peacebuilding and peaceful existence among students from ethnically and religiously diverse communities in Rakhine State.

Despite the country's gradual transition to democracy, signaled by both the 2011 and 2015 governments, Myanmar's students' rights to education continues to be a challenge to this day. This is because internal conflicts, whether for political (e.g., failed negotiations) or religious reasons, keep on flaring up in ethnic areas. Enhancing inclusive education in the country is reported to be a major concern for the government (United Nations Children's Fund Myanmar, n.d.), although many conflict-affected areas have been relying on nongovernmental organizations (NGOs) for assistance in this respect. These organizations have been temporarily supporting education staff to reach students in community-funded schools, IDP areas, and monastic schools with the government curriculum. At the same time, the Myanmar government had begun its journey of national education reform, including curriculum reform, supported by international nongovernmental organizations.

Curriculum Reform in Myanmar's Basic Education

The Ministry of Education is responsible for education in Myanmar, particularly in the areas of basic education, higher education, and teacher education (U Han Tin, 2000). Among these levels, basic education is generally given priority when it comes to education reform (Saw Kapi, 2018). Since 2011, successive governments of Myanmar have implemented both short-term and long-term plans to improve the basic education sector, such as the Special Four-Year Plan for Education and the Thirty-Year Long-Term Basic Education Plan (Min Zaw Soe et al., 2017). Moreover, the National Education Strategic Plan (NESP) 2016–21 has also been implemented, focusing on progressing quality education by upgrading the standards of teaching and learning (Min Zaw Soe et al., 2017).

There are numerous reasons as to why basic education curriculum reform is urgently needed. The curriculum is more than thirty years old, with the last amendment occurring in 1985 before recent reforms began in 2014 (Ei Shwe Phyu, 2017). Many researchers and education experts consider the curriculum out-of-date and Myanmar's education system as left behind when compared internationally. This is because, for decades, Myanmar students have practiced a memorization-based learning system, which gives primacy to particular types of academic knowledge rather than the development of life, vocational, and citizenship skills. Moreover, despite diverse student populations, Buddhist culture courses and religious ceremonies as well as historical focus on Bamar leaders are still predominant in the curriculum, while learning about minority ethnic cultures and beliefs has still not been included (Higgins et al., 2016).

Recent reforms in basic education have fallen short in terms of supporting the values that promote peace (see Metro, 2019, for more detail on the primary school curriculum reform). Current curriculum reform in Myanmar's basic education began in 2014, when the Japan International Cooperation Agency and

United Nations Children's Fund started supporting a major review of the content of subject textbooks as well as the national curriculum framework. Even though some reform of the curriculum has been achieved (Aung Phay Kyi Soe, 2019), fundamental challenges continue to exist; specifically, with regards to development of courses and syllabi relating to conflict transformation and peacebuilding. For instance, it has been stated that "the curriculum reform is in line with international standards but not linked to any conflict resolution strategies" (Phyu Phyu Thin Zaw, 2017). Moreover, as Metro (2019) noted, even though the infamous poem stating "Thway hnaw dar nga doe mone, lu myo anyunt tone," which translates as "We hate mixed blood, it will make our race extinct," had indeed been removed from the Grade 5 ethics textbook, "subtle biases favoring powerful groups still permeate the curriculum" (Metro, 2019).

There is considerable need for continued and extensive evaluation of course content when it comes to the country's basic education. This is important for two reasons. First, Myanmar's internal conflicts are long-lasting and complex, so a specific and context-appropriate curriculum could help students understand the underlying causes of the current conflicts, learn nonviolent ways of responding to conflict, and contribute to social transformation. Second, as Myanmar is a diverse country, the curriculum reform should reflect the local context and promote the values of social cohesion and peaceful coexistence. In other words, the curriculum needs to be adapted not only to reflect Myanmar's ethnic, cultural, and religious diversity, but also to preserve it. One of the ways to achieve this is by integrating peace education into the national curriculum.

Integrating Peace Education into the Curriculum

In order to integrate peace education into the curriculum, an understanding of what it is and includes is important. Danesh (2011) defines the term peace education as "a discipline that focuses on teaching students such concepts as human rights, freedom, democracy, and environmental protection, as well as informing them about the negative consequences of conflict and violence" (p. 11). Within the discipline of peace education, different approaches exist, such as international education, human rights education, development education, environmental education, or conflict resolution education. All these "modern" types of education have emerged in the twenty-first century, though each of them has its own way of marching toward peace (Harris, 2004).

There are several ways of incorporating peace education into a curriculum, which each country should consider, based on its own context and capacity (United Nations Educational, Scientific and Cultural Organization, 2015). Yet, there are still some general characteristics that most peace education curricula have. For instance, while most schools educate students on conflict-related issues, peace education curricula focus on the concept of unity. More specifically, such curricula are designed within the framework of a so-called unity-based worldview. According to Bekerman and McGlynn (2007), a unity-based worldview envisions a society in which there is justice, freedom, gender equality, and where all forms of discrimination and prejudice are unacceptable. Therefore, peace education topics, such as gender equality, gender-based violence, and peace leadership skills, are integrated in such curricula.

In peace education, teachers play an important role in creating a peaceful classroom environment by encouraging group-work activities and downplaying competition, which can lead to aggressive behavior. When working in groups, students can become more connected to each other, and their differences, be they ethnic, gender, ability, and so on, serve to strengthen learning. Students are likely to generate more solutions to a problem with greater diversity and can thus also improve their problem-solving skills (Fountain, 1999). When there is a conflict, teachers encourage students to resolve the issue, guiding students in finding the most suitable solution. By doing this, students can come to know the needs of others and develop their empathy (Carl, 1995). Finally, several studies have suggested that peace education curricula must also include the teaching of peaceful ways of conflict resolution at all levels—individual, societal, and global (Fountain, 1999)—and this way, it can help prevent conflicts in the long term (Smith, 2009).

Study Results

No Integration of the Concept of Human/Child Rights in the Curriculum

This study found that none of the teachers that participated in our focus group discussions clearly understood the meaning of the terms *human rights* and *child rights*. One of the participants said, *"I do not know exactly what 'child rights' mean. I did not learn about it when I was studying at the university."* Moreover, all teachers acknowledged that the concept of child rights is not included in the middle school curriculum, and that they have not seen such references in the teachers' guidebooks either. However, the teachers who also taught at primary level knew a little about child rights, because there, the concept is integrated in the co-curricular material (e.g., Grade 4 Morality and Civics subject textbook includes a chapter titled "Our Rights"). Having ratified the Convention on the Rights of the Child in 1999 and pledged to respect its guiding principles (United Nations Children's Fund, 2019), the Myanmar government needs to fulfill its responsibility in this respect and ensure that children in Myanmar are educated about their rights.

At middle school level, we found that some teachers try to teach about child rights and human rights based on their own knowledge and understanding, mostly gained through articles and social media. Yet, teachers who teach more than two different subjects mentioned that they do not focus on topics that are not included in the curriculum, because they need to spend more time teaching what is in the textbooks. One of the participants stated, "The teaching time is limited and I can get complaints if I do not complete the prescribed lessons […] So I am in a difficult situation, even if I want to do activities related to the knowledge of human rights in the class."

Lack of Promotion of Teamwork in the Classroom

The teachers expressed that there is no learning content or learning objectives promoting social harmony and friendship through teamwork and group activities in the textbooks. However, the teachers use group work for activities such as reading, drawing, cleaning, or gardening, depending on the teachers' designation and knowledge. One of the participants said, "*When I teach history, the students get bored and sleepy at that time, so I do some games with them in groups.*" Another participant stated, "*There is no activity guide related to promoting collaboration among students neither inside nor outside class. If I used [such activities] in my class time of my own accord, I am afraid that I would be seen as doing nonsense lessons and irrelevant activities.*"

At the same time, some teachers expressed that they have seen some good results being achieved through teamwork in class. Regarding this finding, one of the participants said:

> *In my class, some students are arrogant and selfish. One student thinks that she is always correct whenever she speaks in front of the other students. When I was teaching using group activities and teamwork, I noticed that this student became conscious of the fact that she could be wrong through her peers' feedback.*

Throughout the school year, there are different events, such as Martyr's Day, essay competitions, or Sports Day, included in the school's calendar. During these events, students from different regions gather and participate in different activities, such as poem and essay writing competitions as well as various types of sports. However, the teachers said that these activities are not intended to help collaboration or better friendships among the students. Instead, schools are trying to gain a good reputation by winning these competitions. One of the participants, who had a similar experience that we described at the start of this chapter, stated:

> *If there is an essay writing competition between the schools, the teachers have to write the essays for the students who will be the candidates on the competition day. After that, the students try to memorize the teachers' essays by heart. It is like the teachers invisibly compete against each other in their ability of writing essays on different topics; not the students.*

The Influence of Burmanization in Schools

All teachers who participated in this study described that students do not learn about minority ethnic groups' cultures, religions, identities, heroes, or histories as these topics are absent from the middle school curriculum. History, Geography, Social Sciences, and Morality and Civics subjects are all focused on only one ethnic group; the majority Bamar. This finding was supported both by our personal school experience, a quick review of the mentioned textbooks, and by our interviews with the education experts. For instance, one of them confirmed:

I consider there to be Burmanization influencing the education system through the curriculum. I think the reason could be that the curriculum developers do not know the other ethnic groups, or do they not read ethnic literature? Or they just do not want to include learning about Myanmar's minority ethnic groups in the curriculum.

Another education expert also said, "*Burmanized teaching affects students. Only the concepts of the Bamar culture, traditions, and identity are included in the curriculum ... there is very little information about the other ethnic groups. Such teaching outcome cannot build a peaceful society.*"

On the other hand, some teachers said that they share information about ethnic heroes and brief history of ethnic people based on their knowledge, particularly during history classes, if they have time. For example, pointing out that General Aung San was not the only national leader of the independence struggle of Myanmar, but that there were other ethnic leaders who sacrificed themselves to build our nation.

All teachers said that school events and ceremonies are enforcing Bamar culture and traditions among diverse students in their respective schools. For instance, as one of the education experts pointed out, "*All students perform 'leouchi'; [making a gesture of respect by putting the palms together and raising them to the forehead] when the teacher enters the classroom.*"

Discrimination among Students

When it comes to religion specifically, students learn about Buddhism in the History and Geography subjects. Moreover, all students have to participate in Buddhist practices and events at the school, because these are officially included in the school's calendar. In contrast, the teachers stated that celebrating minority religions and cultures and organizing related traditional events is not officially allowed in the same way that Bamar/Buddhist celebrations are. One of the teachers said:

I have never experienced visiting a mosque or places of worship of other religions [...] But I told the students as much as I know that there are other types of religions, such as Christianity, Hinduism, and Islam, in order for them to be tolerant and to recognize other religions, even if these topics are not included in the lesson.

Another teacher also said:

I am a Muslim; the only one in my school. In my classroom, two students are Christian and the rest of the students are Buddhist. There is no Christmas celebration at my school. I used to ask to do it, but the school administrator said that no one would want to manage it.

When we asked whether conflicts were happening in their respective classrooms, most participants reported no physical violent conflicts taking place;

however, there was bullying and verbal abuse. One teacher mentioned that "*there is one Muslim student in the class and the other students are teasing him by saying that 'We will give you pork to eat.'*" Another participant mentioned that "*if a Kachin boy attends our school [in Yangon], his classmates would call him a 'Kachin country boy'. Or if he comes from the dry zone, they would call him 'dry zone country boy.'*"

Teachers mentioned that they try to ensure that students do not discriminate against or mistreat each other in class. Despite that, the teachers have witnessed students' daily use of ridiculing words toward each other and discrimination based on ethnicity, religion, physical appearance, skin color, health issues, or disability. One of the participants stated:

> *In my class, a student who has dark skin and is thin is called "kalar" and the students used to make jokes about him whatever he was doing. At that time, I called the students who said "kalar" to the front of the classroom and asked them if they were called names they did not like.*

"Kalar" is a discriminatory term often used in Myanmar to describe people with darker skin, of Indian and Middle Eastern descent, and Muslims (Min Pyae Sone, 2020).

Another participant knew a student that was bullied due to a health condition and moved schools. She said:

> *I used to have one student who suffered from epilepsy seizures. Most students ridiculed her because she was often having epilepsy attacks at the school. After that, I did not see her anymore in the school. When I saw her on the street, she said that she had moved to another school, because another student who had a health problem like her also attended that school.*

Interestingly, the teachers agreed that parents are one of the factors encouraging discrimination among students. Some parents do not want their children to become friends with students who are poor, unhealthy, not intelligent enough, or disabled.

Finally, it appears that the teachers are not formally equipped with conflict resolution skills, since all of them stated that they have not been provided with any guidelines for conflict resolution in the classroom. One teacher simply mentioned that "*when conflict happens in the classroom, the class teacher is the one who is in charge of solving the problem and making a decision. If the problem is big, the class teacher would go to the headmaster for decision-making.*"

Effects of Armed Conflict

In relation to the previous finding, it was found that discrimination also occurs among conflict-affected Kachin Christian students that feel trauma and grievances toward Bamar Buddhist students due to the fighting between the

Kachin Independence Army and the Myanmar Tatmadaw. One of the participants stated:

> When our school was informed that students would get vaccinations by the township's healthcare group, teachers let students know about it in advance and told them to come to school looking neat and tidy. However, all Kachin students were absent that day. We [the teachers] noticed the students' absence and asked about the reason. We found out that their parents as well as the students assumed that the township healthcare group was like the Tatmadaw and that they were coming to kill the Kachin people through vaccination.

These two groups of students bully each other based on ethnicity and religion. Some Kachin students harbor animosity toward Bamar students and do not want to be friends with them because they regard those who are Bamar as the Tatmadaw. One of the teachers said:

> When I was a teacher in a school where most students were Kachin, the students accused the Bamar students [...] saying that Myen [Bamar] were killers, criminals, and rapists. Even though I often punished students who were accusing each other, it was difficult to teach them about this in the class.

Another teacher also said that "*in my school, sadly, the children play by enacting the fighting between the Kachin Independence Army and the Tatmadaw by using toy guns and weapons in the playground.*" Unfortunately, the teachers have not been given any formal guidelines by the school on what to do in such situations. Some schools have an executive teacher committee that is supposed to solve conflicts; alternatively, the school principal can be asked to step in.

Gender Issues in the Curriculum and in the Classroom

Gender representation in the curriculum is not equal. One education expert mentioned that "*almost every hero taught about in the basic education curriculum is male.*" Our quick review confirmed that Grade 5 to 8 history textbooks do not include any female figures whatsoever, while Myanmar language textbooks in the same grades feature only one female, a famous traditional dancer. When we asked about the ways the teachers could promote female heroes in the curriculum context, the expert answered, "*You can bring a story to the class and adapt your own materials a little bit for teaching a project, or maybe you can apply it as homework through which the learners learn more about a female hero.*"

Gender segregation is still present in the classroom environment. For example, one participant mentioned that "*in group activities, students are asked to discuss and study in groups by separating boys and girls.*" Moreover, one education expert shared his own experience that "*in schools, boys and girls have to sit separately; if they sit together, the teacher punishes them.*" Gender stereotypes are also present in the classroom environment. One participant mentioned that if a student who is a boy acts like a girl, his friends would bully him and call him "*a chaut ma*" (a negative term for gay).

Discussion, Conclusion, and Recommendations

The purpose of this study was to investigate the elements of peace education and pedagogy in the national middle school curriculum. The findings show that the current curriculum and pedagogy do not encourage students to learn about human rights, diversity, collaboration, problem-solving, or social harmony.

Curriculum/Textbooks

The courses and content of the textbooks do not address students' rights, the concept of human rights in general, or the diversity of Myanmar. According to the findings, teachers do not discuss human rights content because it is not included in the curriculum. We contend that human rights education is important for the students to increase their interconnection and awareness of other people's rights by speaking about their individual feelings, perspectives, and by participating in discussions in the class. Textbook topics are influenced by and related to the majority ethnic group; they are concerned with the Bamar ethnic culture, leaders, Buddhist religion, and traditions. At the same time, the findings showed that the education experts believed that schools should not practice the culture of only one ethnic group in such diverse classrooms. They discussed that other minority ethnic students have no opportunity to learn about their own identity, culture, religion, and ethnicity together with their classmates. Efforts to improve Myanmar's education system so far have not included promoting components of inclusion through peace education, and this needs to be addressed. Finally, gender perspectives should also be included in the curriculum. It is obvious that the Myanmar basic education curriculum context is dominated by male heroes, while female heroes are underrepresented. This is a form of gender discrimination, as a woman's role is not considered as important as a man's role.

An encouraging finding was that some teachers are finding ways to address human rights in classes teaching at the margins by researching, reading news, articles, and books and using real-life stories. This could be encouraged by asking teachers to develop and share ways they have found to include more inclusive materials into the content that they teach. It is commendable that the teachers talk about diversity when they teach relevant topics, especially history and geography. However, there are many challenges to this, because such topics are not formally integrated in the curriculum. The teachers do not have guidebooks or references for teaching about minority ethnic cultures, religions, and identity. Some teachers said that they had learned about ethnic history, religion, and literature through Facebook and news. This depends on the teacher's ability to select and share such information with the students, but perhaps parents and community organizations could be sought out to help with this.

Pedagogy

Next, the study found that pedagogy, or teaching practices, did not promote cooperation or respect for differences; instead, the students are expected to compete with each other and with the other schools. The teachers also noted that there is little class time for group work to improve collaboration in the classroom. If the classroom encouraged and monitored group work, students could learn to better connect with each other and to value differences in ethnicity, gender, or other characteristics, which could contribute to creating a peaceful classroom environment. Without promoting teamwork and collaboration among the students, this could only hardly be achieved.

In addition, school events are mostly based on the Bamar culture, traditions, and the Buddhist religion. These events are officially set by rules under the school management and all teachers and students have to manage their individual participation. On the other hand, other ethnic, religious, and culturally important ceremonies are not organized by the head of the school and are not included in the school calendar either. Schools need to raise awareness of the importance of learning about and valuing different cultures, which is needed in order to promote values of cultural and social cohesion.

The results also showed that different types of discrimination, such as based on ethnicity, religion, gender, skin type, disability, and other characteristics, occur among the students in their daily communication both inside and outside class. Bullying goes both ways, with ethnic students who are from areas of armed conflict discriminating against Bamar students, and Bamar students in the class bullying ethnic students by using oppressive words, mistreatment, and intimidation. The participants stated that Kachin and Bamar students brought their feelings of trauma and grievances to the school that they learned in their homes due to the long-term human rights violations caused by armed conflict. Teachers saw this in the students' relationships and in the games they play in the class. This shows how essential it is to integrate the concept of peace education and specifically, the learning of nonviolent ways of responding to conflict. Role-playing in teaching training sessions of constructive ways that teachers can respond to bullying and hate speech would help teachers better respond to these critical incidents.

Moreover, the findings showed that parents also promote discrimination among the students by instructing them not to interact with children who are unintelligent, disabled, and of ill health. The community's and the parents' support are essential for students to have better relationships, so parents need to be educated toward and supported in helping their children recognize the importance of other people's rights in order to encourage harmony.

It is surprising that the episodes regarding offering pork to a Muslim student or calling a student a country boy, which is in fact bullying, was considered simple teasing by the teachers. According to Coulson (2015), teasing does not involve a person's identity or characteristics, such as race, religion, or appearance, while bullying does. Michel and Saw Myo Min Thu (2017) argue that students being bullied because of practicing a different religion is a common issue in the Myanmar classroom and that it also leads to school dropout. Such kind of bullying can lead to the mentality of "Us versus Them" between students. Therefore, it is critical for teachers to acknowledge this and become equipped with conflict resolution skills in order to create a culture of peace in the classroom setting. Moreover, not only teachers but also students should be given a chance to express their opinions in resolving the conflict.

Next, gender segregation and gender stereotypes are still very much present in the Myanmar classroom practices. It is important to consider this issue, because if group work is supposed to encourage students to feel connected to each other, regardless of their differences including their gender, separating genders during group activities can be a barrier to promoting a sustainable peaceful classroom and learning environment. Similarly to the teachers' efforts to make students aware of human rights and diversity despite their absence in the curriculum, the findings showed that teachers sometimes use group activities in order to encourage teamwork and self-reflection in and among students, but also to make their classes more engaging. Moreover, the teachers do their best to handle discrimination and conflicts in the classroom, even though they hardly possess the necessary skills and tools to do so. These ways of "peace-building at the margins" should be recognized and encouraged.

To summarize, four recommendations are given based on our findings that reflect the Four R framework (Higgins et al., 2015) and promote a pedagogy that is more critical:

1. Recognition: Teachers, parents, students, administrators, and communities need to recognize the diversity of Myanmar and advocate for the inclusion of peace education content and pedagogy in middle schools at this critical juncture of the educational curriculum reform.
2. Representation: Inclusion and collaboration of all stakeholders needs to be actively sought out so all voices are heard.
3. Redistribution: The government and the Ministry of Education must support these efforts with the resources needed for an inclusive education for all, which includes increasing the budget for education. Moreover, teachers need to be better supported by identifying their challenges and ample learning materials and teaching aids need to be updated and distributed, so that teachers can meet peace education learning objectives.
4. Reconciliation: Immediate incorporation of a context-sensitive peace curriculum in schools that addresses diversity and conflict resolution needs to take place so education can contribute to national reconciliation and long-lasting peace in the country.

Works Cited

Aung Phay Kyi Soe. (2019, August 6). New Basic School Curriculum 'a hit with students, parents'. *Myanmar Times*. Retrieved from https://www.mmtimes.com/

Bekerman, Z., & McGlynn, C. (Eds.). (2007). *Addressing ethnic conflict through peace education*. New York, NY: Palgrave MacMillan.

Buchanan, J. (2016). *Militias in Myanmar*. Retrieved from https://asiafoundation.org

Burma News International. (2017). *Deciphering Myanmar's peace process: A reference guide 2016*. Chiang Mai, Thailand: Burma News International.

Carl, A. E. (1995). Relevant curriculum development in peace education for a post-apartheid South Africa. *Peace Research, 27*, 79–96.

Coulson, J. (2015). *How to tell the difference between teasing and bullying*. Retrieved from https://www.kidspot.com.au

Danesh, H.B. (Ed.). (2011). *Education for peace reader*. Victoria, Canada: International Education for Peace Institute.

Ei Shwe Phyu. (2017, March 9). Myanmar's basic education curriculum gets a makeover. *Myanmar Times*. Retrieved from https://www.mmtimes.com/

Fountain, S. (1999). *Peace education in UNICEF*. New York, NY: UNICEF.

Hammadi, S. (2020, January 24). *A "lost generation" of Rohingya children will have nowhere to go*. Retrieved from https://www.amnesty.org/en/

Harris, I. M. (2004). Peace education theory. *Journal of Peace Education, 1*, 5–20.

Higgins, S., Maber, E., Cardozo, M. L., & Shah, R. (2016). *The role of education in peacebuilding. Country report: Myanmar*. Amsterdam, Netherlands: University of Amsterdam.

Jolliffe, K., & Mears, E. S. (2016). *Strength in diversity: Towards universal education in Myanmar's ethnic areas*. Retrieved from https://asiafoundation.org

Metro, R. (2019, November 12). A missed opportunity for schoolroom reform. *Frontier Myanmar*. Retrieved from https://www.frontiermyanmar.net/en/

Michel, G., & Saw Myo Min Thu. (2017). *Making education policy a force for peace: White paper*. Retrieved from http://www.thabyay.org

Min Pyae Sone. (2020, April 22). How the word "kalar" is a depressing indictment of Myanmar society. *Myanmar Mix*. Retrieved from https://myanmarmix.com/

Min Zaw Soe, Aye Mya Swe, Nan Khin Moe Aye, & Nan Htet Mon (2017). *Reform of the education system: Case study of Myanmar*. Retrieved from http://afeo.org/wp-content/uploads/2018/09/Reform-of-the-Education-System-in-Myanmar-Case-Study.pdf

Phyu Phyu Thin Zaw. (2017, May 19). Reforming education reform in Myanmar. *Oxford Tea Circle*. Retrieved from https://teacircleoxford.com

REACH. (2015). *Joint education sector needs assessment, North Rakhine State, Myanmar*. Retrieved from http://www.reachresourcecentre.info

Save the Children International. (2013). *Education in Rakhine: Next steps for the sector*. Retrieved from https://reliefweb.int/sites/reliefweb.int/files/resources/Education-in-Rakhine_Next-Steps_AssessmentReport-Nov13.pdf

Save the Children International. (2019). *Myanmar: Education*. Retrieved from https://myanmar.savethechildren.net/what-we-do/education

Saw Kapi. (2018). Envisioning a federal education structure in Myanmar: Roles and responsibilities of federal and state/region government. Unpublished manuscript.

Smith, A. (2009). *Education for all global monitoring report 2011: Education and conflict*. Retrieved from www.ulster.ac.uk

U Han Tin. (2000). Myanmar education: Status, issues and challenges. *Journal of Southeast Asian Education, 1*, 134–62.

United Nations Children's Fund Myanmar. (n.d.) *Education: Ensuring all children attend school and develop to their full potential*. Retrieved from https://www.unicef.org/myanmar

United Nations Children's Fund. (2019, November 20). *Government of Myanmar pledges to uphold children's rights on the 30th anniversary of the CRC*. Retrieved from https://www.unicef.org/myanmar/

United Nations Educational, Scientific and Cultural Organization. (2015). *Education for peace: Planning for curriculum reform*. Retrieved from www.ibe.unesco.org

United Nations Office for the Coordination of Humanitarian Affairs. (2016). *Humanitarian response plan monitoring report January–December* 2016: *Myanmar*. Retrieved from https://slidelegend.com/humanitarian-unhcr-data-portal_59d9332d17 23dd827a0291a5.html

Chapter 8

PUTTING DOWN OUR WEAPONS WHEN WE TALK ABOUT HISTORY: USING PRIMARY SOURCE DOCUMENTS TO TEACH MULTIPLE PERSPECTIVES ON BURMA'S PAST

Rosalie Metro and Aung Khine

Introduction

The Weapons of History

Rose: One of the first proverbs I learned when I became interested in the history of Burma was: "Pick up your weapon when you talk about history" (*Tôk tan bi yazawin go pyaw mè*[1]). I heard it repeated many times in the early 2000s while living on the Thai-Burma border and volunteering as an English teacher, and later as a master's and PhD student investigating methods of teaching Burma's history that could ameliorate ethnic conflict and promote national reconciliation. Whether I was talking to a Burman, Chin, Kachin, Karen, Karenni, Mon, Rakhine, Shan, or someone from another ethnic group, people did seem to enter discussions of history on guard. As I entered the classroom myself as a history teacher back home in the United States, I became familiar with how ethnic and racial tensions among my students affected our discussions of the past.

In the mid-2000s, while working on my master's degree, I met a Shan teacher named Saya[2] Sai Loen Kham, who was working at the Migrant Learning Centre in Chiang Mai. We discussed this proverb, and he shared his idea that people needed to put *down* their weapons when they talked about history. This seemed to be the perfect metaphor for what I hoped to do—enable people to disarm their

---

We would like to thank Vengsang Thong and Felix Hessler for their help with translating the words of Aung Khine

1. We italicize Burmese-language terms and use the conventional system for transcription recommended by John Okell (1971, pp. 66–7).

2. "Saya" means "male teacher" in Burmese and is used as a respectful form of address.

defenses long enough to understand others' perspectives. Saya Sai's insight about how to work for peace inspired me deeply.

I took that inspiration into my discussions with teachers from Burma about how they wanted to change the history curriculum. They saw the SPDC's (State Peace and Development Council's) curriculum as one-sided and Burman-centric, and they wanted to center their own group's histories. However, they had trouble agreeing about what was true or false. For instance, Karen, Mon, Rakhine, Shan, and historians all claimed that their group was the first to arrive in Burma. While they agreed that the Burmans were wrong in claiming to be the first inhabitants of the area, they did not concur about what an alternative history should say.

Nonetheless, I hoped to find ways of teaching history that included more than just the Burman-centric story that was in government textbooks. In 2003, a Thailand-based organization called the Curriculum Project asked me to write a textbook called *History of Burma from a Multi-Ethnic Perspective* for post-10th Standard students in refugee camps and migrant schools. They had invited historians from different ethnic groups to write this textbook, but no one had agreed to do so; those historians worried that people from other ethnic groups would not accept what they had written. I did my best to include all the perspectives I had heard and read about, although my knowledge was limited. People seemed to like my textbook better than some other books they had been using, but it was still a simplistic account of Burma's complex history. In 2009, as part of my PhD research, I was gathering feedback about this textbook for a possible revision when I met Saya Aung Khine in Mae Sot, Thailand. He said the textbook was OK, but that together we could find a better way.

Aung Khine: I am currently a civic education trainer for Mote Oo Education in Yangon. I hold a bachelor's degree in Economics from Yangon Institute of Economics, and I'm certified as a trainer by the Reading and Writing for Critical Thinking International Consortium. I was imprisoned for twelve and half years for involvement in Myanmar's democracy movements, and then experienced nine years in exile. I am a disabled person, and I have fifteen years of experience as a teacher, trainer, curriculum designer, researcher, negotiator, facilitator, translator, fixer, organizer, librarian, and consultant. I have worked in nonformal education and conducted research with people from Myanmar and Thailand.

Since my childhood, I have been quite familiar with historical books. Although I studied different historical events in school, I still held the one-sided perspective of a Burman supremacist. My scores in history class had always been high. Apart from that, outside school, I also searched for historical information. The British, Japanese Fascists, ethnic insurgents, and politicians became my main focus. I became convinced that if we could learn what we want to know and how to make decisions, it would not be difficult to reconcile with each other about controversial historical issues. We could build mutual respect and trust.

"Pick up your weapon when you talk about history." According to this ancient Burmese proverb, when people talk about history and try to resolve conflicts, for instance through peace talks, there can be intense friction. I got frustrated seeing it. People who are involved in peace talks hold onto their previous knowledge, they don't want to compromise, and they assume that only their history is right, while neglecting others' history. Selfishly, they are passing one-sided stories down to the next generation and convincing them to get involved in conflicts. This dynamic perpetuates endless war, harming the future for all.

In 2007, I was teaching social sciences in the Child Development Center (CDC) migrant school in Mae Sot, Thailand. In that school, there were many ethnically diverse students who came from all over Burma with different backgrounds and reasons for fleeing. Most of the teachers and students were ethnic Karen. They had lived in refugee camps, along the Thai-Burma border and in areas affected by civil war; while studying at CDC, most of them lived in dormitories.

In my class, 98 percent of the students were Karen. The first day was a big challenge for me. My steps were hesitant under the gaze of their cold, hard eyes. I was not sure why they felt hatred, anger, and grievances toward me—was it my fault because I am Burman or a disabled person? When I introduced myself to teach the history lesson, they said, "We don't want a Burman teacher. The Burma Independence Army killed our Karen people in Myaung Mya township [in 1942], burned down and destroyed our houses and Karen girls were raped by Burmese soldiers." I realized that my identity made me a historical culprit in their eyes. Even though I did not commit those terrible crimes, I had not educated myself about them. Although I did not support the brutal acts, I was a disgusting criminal in their fragile hearts. It was a mournful moment for me. I sympathized with their pains. I accepted that it was my responsibility to help them realize the terrible experiences from my past as well. Dialogue is the best way to eliminate strong discrimination, oppression, hatred, distrust, and hesitation to recognize each other. In 2009, I met Rosalie Metro. She stated, "We have to put down our weapons when we talk about history." Because of her words I felt enlightened and I had confidence to participate wholeheartedly as a co-facilitator with her in workshops for teachers and eventually in writing *Histories of Burma*.

Workshops and Book Project

Rose: Together, Saya Aung Khine and I facilitated workshops in Mae Sot for multi-ethnic groups of teachers, in which we asked them to write a history that all of them could accept. We asked them to "put down their weapons" in these discussions and focus on common ground. These workshops did not succeed. In fact, our participants could not even agree on a title for such a textbook. Burman teachers insisted that the title must include Burma or Myanmar; teachers from other ethnic groups could not accept this word as representing them. We considered titles such as "History of the Place that Some People Call Burma." Even that was unacceptable to some participants. Not only did people disagree about the title, they also could not agree on basic facts about what had happened in the country. For instance, some Burmans insisted that the Panglong Agreement had included all ethnic groups; Karen participants pointed out (correctly) that Karens had only been observers at the conference and had not signed the agreement.

During these workshops, we realized that we needed a new approach that built a common base of knowledge while illustrating multiple perspectives. No matter how many people contributed to writing it, there couldn't be one history of Burma. Instead, there were many histories. A traditional textbook, in which an objective narrator stated what was true and what was false, would not work for a country like Burma where the past was so contested. Instead of creating a traditional textbook, we decided to gather primary source documents and design activities that would allow students to build the historians' skills needed to interpret them. For instance, if we included the actual text of the Panglong Agreement, teachers and students could see for themselves what it said. They might not interpret it the same way, but at least they would have a document to refer to when forming their own theories.

One difficulty we faced was that documents about Burma's history, especially ones that included perspectives of non-Burman groups, were difficult to find. We consulted with historians from various groups, looked in books, and searched the internet. We finally came up with about one hundred documents, from ancient times to the twenty-first century, that could help tell the stories of people from the region: dynastic chronicles, British colonial documents, speeches by politicians from various ethnic groups, newspaper articles, photos, political cartoons, and constitutions. We organized the documents into ten themes (for instance, Rights and Responsibilities of Governments and Citizens; Burmese Unity and Ethnic Self-Determination; and Burma in the World). We added an introductory unit in which students learned historians' skills: identifying their own and authors' biases; analyzing cause and effect; distinguishing between fact, theory, and belief; assessing continuity and change; and finding evidence to support theories. We created activities that allowed students to use these skills to analyze the documents in the textbook. Instead of telling students what to believe—a practice that stifles critical thinking and entrenches conflict—we tried to help students form their own ideas and to respect the perspectives of others.

In 2013, *Histories of Burma: A Source-Based Approach to Myanmar's History* was published by Mote Oo Education. In 2016, Mote Oo published a Burmese-language version of the text. At that time, Saya Aung Khine finally felt comfortable adding his name as co-author. Later in this chapter, we will share peacebuilding activities we did during workshops with teachers, using some of the documents from *Histories of Burma*, as well as activities that Saya Aung Khine did with postsecondary students. First, we would like to explain our ideas about peace, reconciliation, and empathy, and we would like to situate these activities in traditions of education, theater, and activism.

Histories of Burma in Context: Peace, Reconciliation, and Putting Oneself in Others' Shoes

Rose: Today, *Histories of Burma* is used by about twenty community-based postsecondary schools both inside Myanmar and along its borders. Yet changing people's approach to teaching and learning history is not easy, even when the transition to nominal civilian rule occurred. For decades, students have been forced to memorize one-sided histories that foment hatred, both in government textbooks and in ethno-nationalist curricula (Salem-Gervais & Metro, 2012). Additionally, many topics are still so controversial that it is hard to discuss them openly. When we conducted our workshops for teachers on the Thai-Burma border in 2009–10, it was dangerous to talk about history inside Myanmar. In 2020, it was possible to discuss past conflicts, but new issues had arisen. For instance, many people were fearful of discussing the place of the Rohingya people in Myanmar's history, the current conflict going on in Rakhine State, and the accusation in the International Court of Justice that Myanmar is responsible for genocide. Moreover, many people believed that it is better not to raise difficult topics, but instead simply try to "move on." However, we believe that an honest reckoning with history is necessary in order to build lasting peace. As one Burmese poet explains, if you have a thorn in your hand, it is better to pull it out than let it fester. Putting a band-aid over the wounds of history will not help them heal.

Inner and Outer Peace and the Importance of Empathy

Aung Khine: Myanmar bears the wounds of so many successive problems in its history: feudalism, colonial encroachment, ethnic and religious conflicts, political disagreements, enslavement by colonists, the burning civil war, discontentment of dictatorship, economic problems, the repercussions of educational neglect, and lack of development. We have had to endure all of this, and to move forward, we have to embrace all this historical pain. The above reveals how crucially peace is needed in Burma and how difficult it is to achieve. But no matter how difficult it may be, it is the truth. I am determined to go on with perseverance and to explore the beauty of the future with all my abilities. People have developed various perspectives on the origins of conflict. Despite these conflict resolution theories, conflict is still prevalent in many forms. Why do conflicts exist? My perspective may be uncommon. I strongly believe that conflict originates in our inner mind. Internal conflict is one of the root causes that affects our inner peace, but human beings do not usually notice it.

It is crucial to understand that all of our input comes through the five senses. For instance, when you notice a pungent smell, you may get angry with whoever caused that smell. Can you see and accept that this indignation is dwelling in your mind? It can be very difficult to control your mind not to condemn and exclude people as a result of your anger. I am not saying that the person who caused the bad smell is faultless. But how we react is most important. Although there are many ways to react, most people choose problematic ways that can lead to conflict. It is not always easy to follow our knowledge about what is good and bad and to adjust our behavior accordingly. We have to accept that unskillful reactions are part of human nature.

I believe that people often keep the experience of being a victim alive in their minds. Some people want to take revenge, but label it as fair and assume that their actions are innocent. I believe that this dynamic is an adequate motivation for the search for empathy, or *ko-ko-chin-sar-tayar-sa taya,* the ability to put oneself in another's place. Conflicts are taking place on an intra-personal, inter-personal, or inter-group level, but one thing astonishes me. When a conflict occurs, both sides can project the root cause of the conflict onto the other side, making themselves the innocent victim. Both groups are objects and subjects, victims and perpetrators, depending on the perspective. The whole process becomes cyclical. If we could refrain from getting involved in conflicts as a perpetrator, we would have no victims, and ultimately there would be no conflict.

Therefore, we have to learn lessons from the past and look with eyes of forgiveness. We need to learn to look forward into a future that inspires hope, view people of higher rank with appreciation and people of lower rank with sympathy. At the same time, we shouldn't believe everything we hear or see, but develop critical thinking skills. Schools and classes are good places to implement and apply these life skills.

The Cage of the Past

Aung Khine: When we think deeply, we will notice that we are captured in the cage of our past. I, myself, am struggling to escape from this cage. I was a prisoner of the past; therefore I have to overcome my grudges. The best way to overcome resentment is forgiveness. I don't deny the importance of transitional justice, but I believe that if we cannot escape from the past nightmares, our attempts to transform the present will be in vain. There is a saying, "When I look at the open hand that hit me, I still see the mark of my cheek in it." Reconciliation is difficult when constantly remembering one's pain.

My longing for freedom and social justice and my wish to express my own identity made the military imprison me in a small room surrounded by brick walls. Firstly, I was interrogated by military detectives in the No.7 military detention base. When they took off the thick and smelly black hood they'd put on my head, I realized that they had already collected my personal data and that I had been tailed all along. While I was trying to take a deep breath and yearning for air, I saw a pile of documents through my blurry eyes. I could see how skillful the military detectives were, how loyal to their boss and their brutal work. I was thinking that my colleagues would have more time to escape while they interrogated me. We had vowed not to betray each other. In the twelve-by-twelve-foot interrogation room, under six high-voltage neon bulbs, my body was sweating away drop by drop onto the floor, and I thirstily licked the drops flowing down my face to soothe my extremely dry throat.

On the sixth day, they asked me, "Do you want to drink tea?" Actually, I really wanted to drink tea at that time. "We have ready-made tea mix but we don't have hot water here," said one detective. "I have some," replied one skillful military intelligence officer. He put the tea mix into a cup and unzipped his pants. I stared at the urine dripping into the teacup. "You have three options!" he said. "Will you give us the correct answer, shall we pour this into your mouth, or will you drink it yourself?" I tried not to wipe the teardrops from my face and with my shaking hand I took the cup and drank the tea.

It is not surprising that when I close my eyes, those images appear clearly in my mind whenever I am struggling emotionally in my life. I prayed to God several times to give me strength to flee from this terrible past and to purify my blood of the urine tea. My wishes eventually came true. I don't need to blame or hate anyone. Just as I feel fresh in my life, I want my whole generation to avoid the bad experiences I faced, the people who insulted and caused me pain. I want all of us to live with peaceful minds and hearts and to bring about a society which can truly forgive and be accountable for its mistakes. To heal my past trauma and to appreciate myself, I have been sharing those experiences and feelings in classrooms and trainings, in order to eliminate hatred, vengeance, and learn from the past.

Reconciliation as Coexistence

Rose: Understanding the causes of conflict and methods or forgiveness as Saya Aung Khine has explained them, we can also understand better how to work for reconciliation. Sometimes people believe that reconciliation involves consensus or agreement about the past. However, political scientist Andrew Schaap explains that "a reconciliatory moment is not construed as a final shared understanding or convergence of world views, but as a disclosure of a world in common from diverse and possibly irreconcilable perspectives" (Cole, 2007, p. 5). In other words, putting oneself into another person's place doesn't mean that you then agree with everything they say. It just means you are able to understand and accept their perspective. Likewise, South African Archbishop Desmond Tutu (2004) explained:

> Forgiving and being reconciled to our enemies or our loved ones is not about pretending that things are other than they are. It is not about patting one another on the back and turning a blind eye to the wrong. True reconciliation exposes the awfulness, the abuse, the hurt, the truth. It could even sometimes make things worse. It is a risky undertaking but in the end it is worthwhile, because in the end only an honest confrontation with reality can bring real healing. Superficial reconciliation can bring only superficial healing.
>
> (para 7)

Tutu's words show why an exploration of history is so important to building peace. It is difficult for people to move forward from past traumas if they are not given opportunities to bring their wounds to light and to share their truths. This work of confronting past wrongs requires exactly the kind of inner work that Aung Khine has described: being aware of our body's and mind's reactions to the words we are hearing and the sights we are seeing in the present, and to the sights, sounds, and experiences that haunt us from the past. In fact, these techniques for creating inner peace are what enable people to better navigate the difficult work of stepping into others' shoes and sharing their own perspectives.

Role Plays and Theater of the Oppressed

Rose: I and Aung Khine together, and also Aung Khine on his own, have developed activities that put into practice our views on peace and reconciliation, while allowing people with first hand experience of Burma's conflict to develop empathy for each other. These activities can be broadly situated in the tradition of Applied Theater. Applied Theater can be defined as "the use of drama in participatory ways and often in non-traditional settings to address social issues. It can be described as the use of theater as a *tool* rather than simply as *entertainment*" (Mandala for Change, "Applied Theater"). More specifically, Augusto Boal's (1993) practice of "Theater of the Oppressed" allows communities to use drama as a pathway for education and social change. Boal developed this method while working with peasants and laborers in Latin America in the 1970s. He was inspired by his fellow Brazilian educator Paolo Freire (2000), whose book *Pedagogy of the Oppressed* described ways of cultivating marginalized people's agency to educate themselves. Freire and Boal shared the theory that ordinary people have within them the tools to solve the problems in their lives—they are not empty vessels waiting to be filled with knowledge by teachers, but can be active participants in their own liberation from various kinds of oppression.

One of Boal's techniques was "Forum Theater," "a problem-solving technique in which an unresolved scene of oppression is presented. It is then replayed with the audience invited to stop the action, replace the character they feel is oppressed, struggling, or lacking power, and improvise alternative solutions" (Mandala for Change, "Theater of the Oppressed"). The idea is to create possibilities that were not realized in the past, in order to transform social relations in the future. For this reason, Boal (1993) called his methods as a whole "rehearsal of revolution" (p. 155), or as it is sometimes translated, a "rehearsal for the future."

Readers will see that we did not use Boal's exact methods from Theater of the Oppressed—we did various role-play activities in which participants interacted with each other and used primary source documents to explore perspectives different from their own. However, we share Boal's (1993) assumptions that people can transform their relationships in the present and future through exploration of the past; and that ordinary people are capable of liberating themselves from the hierarchies, biases, and limitations that make up systems of oppression and conflict.

Using Documents to Role-Play Multiple Perspectives and ko-hkyìn-sa

Aung Khine: *Literally Stepping into Others' Shoes*

I carried out this activity at the CDC in 2011 with my 11th grade class in Mae Sot Thailand near the border with Myanmar. I started the class by saying,

> Today we are going to do an interesting activity and I believe that it can show our humanity. First of all, let's swap your slippers or flip-flops with your friends. Please remember who you swapped with and how you felt when you swapped

the shoes with your friends. You all will get five minutes to exchange your shoes. Afterwards you can reflect for two minutes in silence about the experience.

I was really happy and thanked them when I saw them following my instructions. At that time, I was worried because some students' faces expressed feelings I couldn't interpret. After five minutes, I told them to go back to their seats and to think for two minutes. I asked, "Who would like to share your experience first?" A few seconds later, a girl raised her hand, "When I tried on his flip-flops, they were too big for me. They are men's size and the tail parts were ripped and old. I felt sorry because I cannot afford to buy him a new pair of flip-flops." One girl stood up and said, "When I tried on another's slippers, one fit me but one was too small for me although his feet are bigger than mine." Another girl said, "Her shoes look nice. I will ask my Mom to buy me the same shoes." One boy said, "When I tried on his slippers, he told me that my feet are so big and asked me not to put my feet into the slippers forcibly, because his slippers might rip. Therefore, I left his slippers without trying them on."

Rose: What I find so useful about this activity is that it prepares students emotionally for what will come next with analyzing primary source documents. It gives them something physical to remember, and it helps them tune into their inner experiences, which, as Saya Aung Khine has explained, is so important for working through conflicts. As an extension, students could try to walk across the room in each other's shoes. It also would be helpful to bring students' awareness back to this activity after doing the document-based activities we will discuss below; if the students wrote their observations about the shoe activity on posters, they could compare at the end how it felt to inhabit others' perspectives using documents and role plays.

Role Play with Teachers of the 1947 Conference between the British, AFPFL, and KCO

Rose: In January 1947, Britain announced its intention to decolonize Burma within one year. Yet the Anti-Fascist People's Freedom League (AFPFL), a major political party dominated by the Burman majority and led by General Aung San, had not secured the support of ethnic minority organizations. The Karen Central Organization (KCO), for example, headed by leaders including Saw Ba U Gyi, was demanding an independent state. It was unclear whether Burma would gain independence as a unified country, or whether parts of the "Frontier Areas," and other areas that had experienced some kind of autonomy under British rule (notably Karen and Karenni States) would have a different status. In January 1947, the British colonial administration of Burma called a conference where leaders of the AFPFL the KCO explained their positions on Burmese independence. Shortly afterward, the British and the AFPFL signed the Aung San-Attlee Agreement, in which those parties stated that Burma Proper would be united with the Frontier Areas, with the consent of its inhabitants. However, the Panglong Agreement, signed in February by Aung San on behalf of the interim Burmese government, and delegations from Shan, Kachin, and Chin areas, was not signed by the Karen,

Karenni, or any other ethnic group (Metro, 2013a, p. 32). Shortly after independence in 1948, the Karen National Liberation Army began armed resistance against the Burmese army, which it continues until today. Thus some roots of civil war can be traced back to misunderstandings or disagreements that occurred among British, AFPFL, and KCO leaders at the January 1947 conference.

In May of 2010, Saya Aung Khine and I led a workshop in Mae Sot where we led teachers in a role play of the 1947 conference based on primary documents that were eventually included in the *Histories of Burma* textbook. The approximately forty teachers who attended this workshop taught in schools for the children of Burmese migrant workers in the area were about 30 percent Burman and 30 percent Karen, with Karenni, Muslim, Rakhine, Shan, and ethnically mixed people also represented. At this week-long training focused on methods of teaching social studies to promote critical thinking and national reconciliation, we first discussed the purposes of teaching social studies, and then walked teachers through several activities using the *Histories of Burma* documents, including the role play we will describe.

Primary Source Documents on the 1947 Conference

While we could not find records of the exact proceedings at the 1947 conference, we did find three primary source documents that illuminated the perspectives that the British, AFPFL, and KCO delegations brought into that discussion. The first documents were two secret telegrams written by members of the British colonial administration. The first was sent by Governor General Sir Henry Knight to Commissioner Lord Pethick-Lawrence, on August 11, 1946. In it, he explains:

> If we want to get out of our obligations to the Frontier Areas with the least trouble to us, we can [...] allow Burma to incorporate at once the Frontier Areas, and leave Burma to hold any baby of complications which may result from such a hasty union.
>
> (Metro, 2013a, p. 31)

The second telegram was sent by Governor-General Sir Hubert Rance to Commissioner Lord Pethick-Lawrence on January 2, 1947, and it explains the British plan for the Frontier Areas given the AFPFL's plan to get independence for Burma within one year. It reads, in part:

> I believe that we have to make an entirely fresh approach to this problem. We should start with the premise that there is only one Burma and that the part known as Ministerial Burma [Burma Proper] and that known as the Frontier Areas [Excluded/Scheduled Areas] are merely parts of the whole. They have been one in the past and they must remain one in the future so that our ultimate aim is always a united Burma in the shortest possible time.
>
> (Metro, 2013a, p. 32)

These two telegrams could be interpreted as showing that the British were eager to be free of any obligation to Burma in order to attend to their own difficulties in recovering from the Second World War.

Another document, "The Humble Memorial of the Karens of Burma to His Brittanic Majesty's Secretary of State for Burma," illustrates the perspective of the KCO. This document was delivered to the British government in London by KCO leader Dr. San C. Po in 1945. It reads, in part:

> Over a hundred years ago, before the British ever set foot in Burma, the Burmese people and Burmese kings literally made slaves of the Karens, and persecuted them generally [...] Then came the British, not only as a Liberator, but also as a Guardian Angel, maintaining Law and Order, and preserving Peace and giving Protection [...] But in 1942, no sooner was the liberator and guardian Angel taken away, than reoccurred both the mental and physical torture in a manner unequalled in the whole history of Burma ... The Karens, therefore, have come to feel very strongly that they must strike out on a course of their own to preserve their National Ideals.
>
> (Metro, 2013a, p. 29)

This document may create the impression that the Karens were eager to get their own state because they feared Burman aggression once British protection was withdrawn.

Finally, General Aung San's address to the AFPFL Convention in May 1947 illustrates his perspective. He explains how he thinks ethnic minorities can be given equality within the union of Burma:

> A minority is discontented [...] because it does not enjoy liberty of conscience, liberty of movement, etc. Give it these liberties and it will cease to be discontented. Thus national equality in all forms (language, schools, etc.) is an essential element in the solution of the national problem.
>
> (Metro, 2013a, p. 34)

This speech could be interpreted as showing that Aung San was aware of ethnic minority groups' concerns that they would not have equality with Burmans in a union, but that he planned to offer that equality as a way to avoid internal conflicts.

It is important when choosing documents for the role play to be careful that the content will not demean any group, but will leave all groups with dignity. There is a risk in historical role plays of retraumatizing people who have experienced oppression (King, 2016). Teachers and facilitators should understand the context of their participants well enough to know which documents are appropriate to choose—hopefully, ones that show each group in a different light than they are usually portrayed by others, and that show the complexity of the situation. We can also consider whether it is better to do role plays in homogenous or heterogeneous groups, and what trust-building activities would be necessary before beginning this sensitive work.

Role Play

During the workshop, we divided the teachers randomly into three teams: British, AFPFL, and KCO. Thus participants were often not aligned with the perspectives they had grown up learning. Burmans might have to represent the British, whom they had been taught by their history textbooks were enemies whose "divide and rule" policies had led to civil war (Salem-Gervais & Metro, 2012). Karens might have to represent the AFPFL, whom they saw as torturing and oppressing their people. People from other ethnic and religious minority groups (Shan, Karenni, Rakhine, Muslim) might be assigned to represent the viewpoint of the KCO, which had some similarities and some differences from their own experiences. Even teachers who happened to take on their "own" perspective had to see it in a new light while responding to questions from their own or other delegations.

We then asked each team to study the documents aligned with their positions. The teams wrote "opening statements" for the conference to summarize their views. Then, they had the opportunity to ask each other questions and respond spontaneously. The sincerity with which participants took on the roles they had been assigned was quite striking. One Burman teacher who had been assigned to the KCO team explained in her opening statement:

> We Karen people have always been close to the British, and not to the AFPFL, because we have had to endure genocide by Burman people. As a result, we have asked the British to give us our own government. We ask the British now to stop ignoring our request.
>
> (field notes, May 7, 2010)

This quotation shows the potential of a role-play activity to allow participants to step into the shoes of others. If a Karen person had accused this teacher of being complicit in genocide as a Burman, she would likely have become defensive. Yet within the structure of the role play, she could explore opposing perspectives without feeling the need to defend herself. Having stepped into the shoes of a Karen person does not mean that she has lost all pro-Burman biases. But, as I explained elsewhere, "stepping into the shoes of others seemed to make one's own shoes fit differently afterward" (Metro, 2013c, p. 158).

This ability to feel empathy is just one part of a nonlinear, spiraling process of peacebuilding that I described after conducting a series of workshops with Aung Khine. I identified six "stepping stones" to reconciliation: Hearing the Other's History, Accepting the Existence of Multiple Perspectives, Stepping into the Shoes of the Other, Complicating Master Narratives of Identity, Exposing Intraethnic Struggles, and Forming Inter-Ethnic Relationships (Metro, 2013c).

This role-play activity allows participants to move along the first three stepping stones. In order to follow up on this experience, participants would then need to be guided toward the next three steps. There are multiple ways to do this. For instance, participants could be divided into "caucus" groups based on their actual identities after the role play, in which they debriefed with each other on how they experienced the role play. They could then pair up with someone from another caucus group to share their insights. As we were still in the process of developing these methods and theories about reconciliation, we did not conduct these follow-up activities during the training.

Nonetheless, surveys we collected after the workshop support the conclusion that participants were able to experience some of these stepping stones. Almost all (98 percent) of the participants agreed or strongly agreed with the statement, "After this workshop, I think I understand more about the perspectives of people from other ethnic groups." Ninety-seven percent agreed or strongly agreed with the statement, "After this workshop, I believe more strongly that there are many perspectives about history and not only one." Almost all (98 percent) of the participants agreed or strongly agreed with the statement, "After this workshop, I can sympathize more with people from other ethnic groups who have suffered." Finally, 94 percent agreed or strongly agreed with, "After this workshop, I feel I can get along better with people from other ethnic groups even if we don't always agree about history." Freeform comments supported this survey data.

Participants commented in open-ended survey responses and in conversation that the opportunity to discuss history "openly" and "freely," to exchange "inner" feelings with people from other ethnic groups, enabled them to "put themselves in the place of others," and to "come to terms with" them. Some participants noted that this had been their first opportunity to gain insight into other groups' histories. A thirty-year-old Burman woman wrote, "When I was in school, I only knew what was taught. Now, because of attending this workshop, I became more interested and I couldn't help wanting to discuss history more" (Metro, 2013c, p. 154).

While these results are encouraging, the role-play activity was also limited in its ability to promote peace. Participants who were not Burman or Karen were less likely to agree with the positive survey statements showing reconciliatory attitudes, and some commented that the focus on Burman and Karen perspectives left out other ethnicities. We learned that it is important to represent the perspectives of as many participants as possible. Additionally, the dominance of high-status (older, male) teachers and the participation of Rose as a foreigner, with the legacy of colonization that her presence represented, may also have impeded the full potential of the role play to touch all participants (Metro, 2013c, pp. 164 & 176). Finally, translation proved to be an obstacle. The workshop was conducted mostly in Burmese, but Burmese was not a first language or equally understandable for all participants. Some people may have been inhibited from participating fully.

While we gathered the documents we found most important, in fact this method could be adapted to students' unique contexts and to evolving realities by using the documents most relevant to their lives. When students examine documents carefully, simplistic narratives that fuel conflict are disrupted, and the divisions between "us vs. them" start to break down. We are happy to share our techniques for helping students put down their weapons when they talk about history, and in the process, pull out the thorns of conflict instead of passing these wounds to the next generation.

Role Play of the Sixty-first Burmese Revolutionary Day and Fifty-ninth Karen Revolutionary Day

Aung Khine: At the beginning of 2011, I decided to make a comparison between the sixty-first Burmese Revolutionary Day and the fifty-ninth Karen Revolutionary Day in my Grade 11 class—similar to the role play that Sayama[3] Rose and I had done with the teachers about the 1947 Conference. I collected as many resources as possible and I was juggling different teaching methods to find out the best way to approach these historical events. Later on, I realized that both events are based on similar ideologies; in both cases human rights violations, oppression, and inequality were prevalent. It is crucial to excavate what happened in the past and how it happened, in order to put oneself in someone else's shoes and to see how other people feel or see the world. This understanding is crucial to building a better future.

I went to the class earlier than the students and prepared the teaching aids and historical documents, while trying to hide my agitated facial expression. I was nervous and excited to help my students to see the other side's point of view, and I didn't know how my students would respond when they had to act as opposing sides in the role play. It might be the first time for some students to actively put themselves in someone's shoes. It was a big challenge for me too because the results could be unexpected, and worsen the situation instead of promoting reconciliation as I hoped.

After doing the shoe exchange activity I described earlier, I used the jigsaw method to form groups and gave them tasks for the groups and each individual. I shared documents about the Burmans' revolution against Japanese Fascism with two groups and documents about the Karen Revolution with another two groups. I gave them fifteen minutes to discuss the topic within their group. After their group discussion, they presented to classmates who had read different documents about points of view from those documents they considered to be especially strong or weak. It was a delightful moment for me seeing all the students engaged in the activity.

I moved to the next step. I told them, "Ok, now let's practice public speeches." I formed three groups. One group had to represent Burmans, one group had to represent Karens, and another group had to represent Mons, who were the audience and would evaluate the two arguments. I could see on their faces how much they engaged with this activity.

The Karen representatives had to give a speech about the sixty-first Burma Revolutionary Day (called Myanmar Army Day by the Tatmadaw), and the Burman representatives had to give a speech about the fifty-ninth Karen Revolutionary Day, originally delivered by the former KNU Chief Saw Mutu Say Poe. Each group had fifteen minutes for preparation. I gave the Mon group a checklist so they could evaluate the speeches. I flipped a coin to decide who would go first and allowed five minutes for each group's speech. The Karen representatives got highest scores from the Mon delegation.

---

3. "Sayama" means "female teacher" in Burmese and is used as a respectful form of address.

Afterward, I asked all the students how they felt during the speeches. Each group shared their feelings: "I felt stressed when I speak." "I forgot myself; who I am." "They [meaning the members of the opposing group] believe that their views are right." "They don't care how civilians are suffering." "Observing the situation, both sides have weaknesses but mostly the government." "The Karen representatives' speech is more reasonable and it seems the government side is presenting false history." "I have to ask many questions after this activity. Please explain why you ask us to do this activity." The students' sincere hearts are clearly expressed in these statements.

When I heard their comments and questions, I was elated, but tried not to show it. "OK," I said, "Let's go to the last step of our lesson today; let's remove the weak points from both speeches and combine the strong points of both into one speech. You will get fifteen minutes to prepare it." The students all worked together. Although the final speech was not flawless, it contained no hatred and revenge. It led toward reconciliation.

Rose: I love the way Saya Aung Khine extended the ideas in the role play we did with teachers about the 1947 Conference, not only by adding the shoe activity first, but also by encouraging students to write one document together at the end. This collaborative document represents the common ground that is so important for reconciliation; we don't have to agree on everything, but we may be able to agree on something. Finally, Saya Aung Khine was able to address some of the weaknesses of our 2009 role play with teachers, for instance, by adding the Mon perspective. Also, he allowed students the opportunity to process their feelings together, which is important in the final three "stepping stones" to reconciliation.

Rehearsals for the Future

The role-play activities that we have shared offer ways to help people put down their metaphorical weapons and move along the stepping stones toward reconciliation: Hearing the Other's History, Accepting the Existence of Multiple Perspectives, Stepping into the Shoes of the Other, Complicating Master Narratives of Identity, Exposing Intra-Ethnic Struggles, and Forming Inter-Ethnic Relationships (Metro, 2013c). The best practices for how to implement these Applied Theater or Theater for the Oppressed (Boal, 1993) activities will depend on the specific group and situation, but we have shown that these activities can be successful in both ethnically mixed groups of adults, and ethnically homogenous groups of postsecondary students.

If we are skillful, history lessons can be, as Boal (1993) explained, "rehearsals for the future" (p. 155), or preparation for a revolution of feeling that allows people in conflict to move forward, without blocking out past traumas, but while embracing new possibilities and identities. If we metaphorically put down our weapons in history classrooms, we are preparing for a future in which people have fewer reasons to take up weapons in real life. These endeavors are all the more important given the recent military coup. We put our faith in the young generation, who are struggling so bravely for democracy. We hope that these methods, ideas, and activities can inspire them in their work for a more just and peaceful future for all of the people of Burma/Myanmar.

Works Cited

Boal, A. (1993). *Theater of the oppressed.* C. A. & L. L. McBride, Trans. Theater Communications Group.

Cole, Elizabeth A. (2007). Introduction: Reconciliation and history education. In Elizabeth A. Cole (Ed.), *Teaching the violent past: History education and reconciliation*, pp. (1–30). Rowman & Littlefield.

Freire, P. (2000). *Pedagogy of the oppressed.* M. Ramos, Trans. Bloomsbury.

King, L. (2016). Epilogue: Black history is more than skin color. *Social Studies Journal, 36,* 72–9.

Mandala for Change. (n.d.). Applied theater. Retrieved from http://www.mandalaforchange.com/site/applied-theatre/

Mandala for Change. (n.d.). Theater of the oppressed. Retrieved from http://www.mandalaforchange.com/site/applied-theatre/theatre-of-the-oppressed/

Metro, R. (2013a). *Histories of Burma: A source-based approach to Myanmar's history*, Student's Book. Mote Oo. https://www.moteoo.org/en/social-science

Metro, R. (2013b). *Histories of Burma: A source-based approach to Myanmar's history*, Source Book. Mote Oo. https://www.moteoo.org/en/social-science

Metro, R. (2013c). Postconflict history curriculum revision as an "Intergroup Encounter" promoting inter-ethnic reconciliation among Burmese migrants and refugees in Thailand. *Comparative Education Review 57*(1), 145–68.

Okell, J. (1971). *A guide to the romanization of Burmese.* The Royal Asiatic Society of Great Britain and Ireland.

Salem-Gervais, N., & Metro, R. (2012). A textbook case of nation-building: The evolution of history curricula in Myanmar. *Journal of Burma Studies 16*(1), 27–78.

Tutu, D. (2004). Truth and reconciliation. *Greater Good Magazine.* Retrieved from https://greatergood.berkeley.edu/article/item/truth_and_reconciliation

Chapter 9

RESEARCHING PEACEBUILDING IN MYANMAR: FRAMING RESEARCH QUESTIONS WITH OUR GRANDPARENTS' MORAL IMAGINATION

Tony Waters

Introduction

Research on peacebuilding is inherently difficult. In large part this is a result of what social scientists call a framing problem. There are multiple definitions of "peace," and perhaps more importantly an equal number of what are known in development-speak, as "stakeholders." The framing problem that occurs in Myanmar is particularly acute because research is funded almost exclusively by foreign donors. As donors, they frame research questions in the context of their own foreign policy interests regarding pre-existing assumptions about peace, war, good governance, and economics. How donors frame these questions is rigidified by narrowly written Requests for Proposals (RFPs), insistence on prescribed methodology, and a right to edit research findings and conclusions. Funded peace research typically emphasizes the "culture of accountability." Emphasized are technocratic approaches which ask basically: "How much does a measure of peace cost per unit in terms of donor dollars?" Such donor-commissioned research has, according to a recent Center for Economic and Social Development (CESD) report, "disproportionately defined the research system in Myanmar" in the last decade (CESD, 2020, p. 36).

In my view, such donor-centric research results from a basic flaw in how "asking the research question" is done, particularly given the unusual nature of peace research. Peace research inherently requires thinking outside the terms of reference insisted upon by stakeholders, that is, those conditions which caused conflict in the first place. This problem for peace researchers is summed up by John Paul Lederach (2005) who writes of the "moral imagination" needed for any search for peace. A "moral imagination" requires that the researcher be permitted to explore that which is "outside the box," that is, the serendipitous and complex. Such serendipity permits the shifting "storying" and "restorying" crucial to peacebuilding. Lederach sums this up by emphasizing "soul of place" as being at the heart of peacebuilding. This paper is about first how the "framing the problem" excludes concepts such as the "soul of place."

This paper is divided into two main sections. The first is about the donor-centric Myanmar research system that emerged since the country opened up to research beginning about 2012. As the CESD (2020) recently noted, most peace research in Myanmar takes place in the context of research consultancies using norms of evidence-based research and donor accountability. These standards in turn reflect a Western cosmology, rigidified in bureaucratic research formulae framed by technocratic issues identified by donors. This is typically done using underlying social philosophical assumptions emerging from Western utilitarianism, pragmatism, and "contract theory."

The second part of the paper focuses on the nature of peace research itself and the "moral imagination." The moral imagination requires, as Lederach (2005, p. xv) describes, identifying an "essence of peacebuilding" rooted in inchoate qualities like a gift of pessimism, the art of social change, serendipity and accidental sagacity. He writes that in doing this, there needs to be an acknowledgement of the mystery of risk, and a view of time which recognizes that "the past that lies before us" (p. 131). In Myanmar, questions might be: How can you design social research in a world which rapidly moved forward between 2012 and 2021, while necessarily gazing backwards at decades of police brutality, universities closed behind barbed wire, torched villages, midnight police raids, false imprisonments, and disappearances? How can research questions be created which acknowledge the persistent memories of terror? How is this done when writers in a country are so habituated to censorship as up until August 2012 all written matter published in Myanmar had to be submitted to the "Press Scrutiny and Registration Division" (Larkin, 2017, pp. 6–7)?[1]

Framing Research Question on Peacebuilding

Research in Myanmar

This paper started with my experiences establishing a PhD program in Peacebuilding at Payap University in Thailand. The majority of our seventeen students are from Myanmar, and most of the students are interested in Myanmar issues. They bring with them decades of experience living in Burma (as it was called pre-1989), and arrived in Chiang Mai asking questions about what peace there might look like, and more importantly, questions about why peace has not emerged despite decades of trying to find an "answer," therefore creating what Peace Researcher Johan Galtung (1964) calls "positive peace." Positive peace is

---

1. This essay was drafted in summer, 2020, before the coup of February 1, 2021, at a time when there was widespread belief that the democratic Myanmar government would continue to develop, and the economy continue to grow rapidly. Final edits were after the military coup of 2021 when democratic institutions were displaced by the military, and economic growth halted by the Civil Disobedience Movement (CDM), and the reaction of the military.

modern, democratic, inclusive, and respects human rights. Positive peace is in contrast to the "negative peace" my students remember while growing up under a harsh military dictatorship. In this respect they echo the popular rhetoric about peace from donors. Peace is assumed to be a "high modernity," which is Western, educated, industrial, rich, and democratic. It is achievable according to what they learned in Myanmar's NGO community, via technocratic state-building and economic development (see Heinrich et al., 2010; Scott 1999).

However, my students, who have all worked on many donor-funded projects in Myanmar (and the Thai-Burma border), brought up a complaint. The programs they worked for rarely, if ever, achieved the technocratic goals of high modernity promised in donor-drafted RFPs. "Why is that?" they ask. They then suggest a new solution, and perhaps propose a dissertation project that identifies another overlooked technocratic key, validated perhaps by commendable (but narrow) goals of the Western-centric United Nations' Sustainable Development Goals (SDGs). But, during their coursework, the PhD students start asking deeper questions about the relationships between peace and the historical stories they imbibed in Karen and Myanmar school systems, and what they learned about from their parents and grandparents. The stories start with British colonialism, Second World War, the Burmese Civil War, and the Ne Win coup of 1962. It is at this point when the search for that technocratic "key" and the SDGs become more complicated. In addition to Lederach and Galtung, they then read Alasdair MacIntyre, and find out that "Justice" is a product of a larger society, and not modern technocratic law books, or even courts, which are the creation of that society. They also find out from Max Weber (1919/2015) that politics inherently involves violence and tempts the baser instincts of political leaders. Karen and Burmese students also quickly saw echoes of Ne Win's harsh Burmanization policies in Benedict Anderson's (1993) book *Imagined Communities*. From Anderson they recognize the difficulties associated with imagining shared history in a historically diverse place.

After years working for faceless, and seemingly emotionless bureaucracies, whether those of the Burmese military government, foreign INGOs, or Ethnic Armed Groups, the PhD students find that human affairs are rooted in values and emotions. Answers become more complicated as they propose their dissertation research, and the certainties set by the technocratic "frames" prevalent in donor research agendas, maybe dissipate. They begin questioning the foundations of society with their own independent questions and see the complexities of the issues. This is the opposite of donor-driven research, where results are simplified and rationalized to meet donor objectives specified in the RFP. The research conclusions then narrowly answer the donor's policy-focused questions, no more and no less.

Policy-Driven Research, Evidence, and Donors

Enrique Mendizabal (2010) at the "On Think Tanks" website recently described three types of research. He classifies research as independent research, contract research, and influencing/advocacy research. In independent research, researchers

Table 9.1 Selected Independent and Contract/Advocacy Research in Myanmar

Independent research		Contract/advocacy research
Alwyn (2021)	Maung (1983)	CESD (2020)
Aung Hla (1939/2004)	Myat (2019)	FHI 360 (2020)
James Scott (2009)	Suu Kyi (1991)	International Alert (2019)
Lall and South (2018)	Thant (2019)	Joint Peace Fund (2020)
Leach (1973)	Thwe (2002)	Siegner (2020)
Lintner (1996/2012)	Walton (2012)	South and Lall (2016)

have the liberty to choose their research questions and methods to focus on long-term issues or "big ideas" with perhaps no immediate policy relevance. Contract researchers on the other hand attempt to address one or two key questions requested by specific clients, typically in response to a pre-existing agenda or problem. Influencing/Advocacy researchers may use evidence emerging from independent or contracted research work, and typically advocate for policy preferences through communications, capacity development, networking, campaigns, lobbying, etc.

The research funded in Myanmar today is, as CESD (2020) noted, about contracts, and influencing/advocacy (see Table 9.1), and is done with donor goals in mind. Contract research may be done via a university, but is still funded by donors who have a policy or business goal that addresses donor questions. As for advocacy research, it typically starts with a policy preference, and then seeks data to verify the pre-existing view. Often advocacy and contract research are similar to each other, which is why I have grouped them together. The point being that the moral cosmology donors bring to Myanmar underpin contract and advocacy research. Compliance with the desired advocacy goal is ensured via carefully worded RFPs, which includes careful language limiting the conditions of research by time, methods, location, conclusions, etc. Finally, there is typically a requirement that the donor be permitted to review and critique results before publication. The research becomes a contracted "deliverable" to be used for advocacy (see, e.g., FHI360 2020).

Evidence-Driven Research and Theory

Independent research is typically found in universities and undertaken by professors and graduate students without subsidy or with open-ended subsidies via scholarships and fellowships. There are few of these in Myanmar, with the net result that stakeholder-generated "research" in Myanmar is heavily weighted toward contracts and advocacy, neglecting the capacity to investigate independent of the donor's pre-baked policies and the funder's "deliverable."[2] "Evidence driven

2. See also Dick, Rich, and Waters (2016), which discusses applied research in California prisons where the dependent variable was assumed to be prisoner recidivism, and the independent variable was vocation education classes.

policy" is the jargon framing contract and advocacy research for peace in Myanmar, and elsewhere. By its very nature such research promises to identify the magic key to a pragmatic positive peace. The key is usually assumed to be found in a specific *program* developed as best practice imported from abroad. Research is focused by workshops, meetings, infrastructure purchases, government regulations, etc. All will be undertaken and assume measurable goals for the dependent variable, which is "peace," or maybe "peace dividend" (see International Alert, 2019; Asia Foundation, 2020; FHI 360 2020; Siegner, 2020).

In such evidence-based research, my students were told data equals evidence, and evidence equals research, even though evidence is at best half of "research." The problem is that the collection of data (evidence) in donor minds supports their own pre-determined measurable policies moving Myanmar toward the vaguely defined dependent variable, "peace." In this way, Myanmar researchers are co-opted by donors from investigating the half of the research question, which is "theory," that is, the taken-for-granted generalizations that inform every research question, and which tell the researcher which kind of evidence will be collected and privileged, and which kind will not. In a basic research methods course, the relationship between the theory and data is considered to be an iterative dialectical one, meaning as more data is collected, the "theory" changes, and as theories are developed new relationships are found, and as a result, data collection also changes (see Layder 2020 in press for a discussion of this problem). But in the Yangon consultancy report, the process is separated. Theory in the form of "the question" (i.e., assumptions) is embedded in the RFP, developed by the donor even before the researcher is hired. To the credit of CESD (2020), this propensity to rely on donor assumptions is noted throughout their report about research in Myanmar.

However, this raises a philosophical question about the nature of donor-funded contract and advocacy research. What comes first, the evidence or the policy? The more I have talked to my students, it is apparent that social research in Myanmar is often policy chasing after evidence to justify the pre-conceptions of donors regarding what is best for Myanmar. Someone with tongue in cheek called this "policy driven evidence," and this is in fact what was requested of my students by donors posing pre-determined "questions" that need to be "answered." Data collection driven by policy demands is a major limitation of Myanmar's researchscape. Most importantly it chases Myanmar researchers away from seeking Lederach's *moral imagination*, which emphasizes that peace thinking is inherently outside the box. Donor insistence on sticking to "the question" as a contracted deliverable limits the capacity of Myanmar researchers to ask their own provocative questions about "soul of place," sagacity, and risk-taking as they emerge. Serendipity in a war-torn society like Myanmar is particularly important because Myanmar attitudes are almost all outside the box of the pre-baked moral universe brought by donors from abroad.

Pre-Baking the Research Results: Three Examples

Here are three examples of how pre-baked assumptions/questions are presented to potential researchers in Myanmar. In each, there is a close connection between policy goals and the lessons/evidence collected. In a philosophical sense, donors are starting with a "positivistic assumption" that a research question is describable before the research is done. In this positivistic universe, the research is undertaken with the utilitarian goal of informing policy. A contract is then provided to collect "the data," which addresses that policy goal. An unwritten assumption in such contracts is that research conclusions cannot conflict with the embedded policy goal from a pre-existing agenda (see CESD 2020, p. 37). Nor can researchers' bidding on the research contract question how the questions are framed and the stakeholders defined. To do so is to waste valuable time on the bid.

For example, The Hanns Seidel Foundation of the German Federal Democratic Party granted money to investigate the role of federalism in Myanmar's "state-building process and peace initiatives." In the first pages of the contracted report which the Foundation commissioned, the author lists very systematically the questions to be answered: (1) What role has federalism played in Myanmar's state-building process and previous peace initiatives? (2) What factors have hindered the development of federalism in Myanmar? (3) What lessons can be drawn from the past to break the deadlock of the current peace process? (Siegner 2019). The Hanns Seidel Foundation is perhaps actually asking a utilitarian question focused by a policy interest: "How can Myanmar create a federal republic like Germany?" Or more to the point, "please do not recommend that Myanmar have a centralized government like France, Thailand, or the current regime in Naypyidaw." The Hanns Seidel Foundation pushes alternative options off the table by the way that it asks its questions.

Another example is from the Joint Peace Fund (JPF), which controls a large pot of money contributed by different embassies in Yangon to administer the Ceasefire of 2015. Looking at what it seeks to fund tells you about the shared values of the embassies. Thus, they fund the reporting system which collects data about violent incidents which become measures for a dependent variable "peace/violence." JPF Projects (research and other reports) also explicitly reflect a Western focus on intersectionality and inclusivity, and puts these values at the center of their request for proposals. This is defined very precisely in terms borrowed from American and European social science jargon focused on a particular view of human rights. Thus, funded projects must be "inclusive," which means the proposal must do the following:

> Address inclusivity by considering how different groups might be affected differently depending on their gender, ethnicity, location, religion, age, language and indicating how the proposal will respond to those differences to be inclusive; and address gender by articulating how the proposal understands and responds to the differing experiences and needs of women and men. In line with the JPF's overall goal of allocating at least 15% of funding to gender related activities, project budgets should aim for this allocation as a minimum or explain in detail why this is not feasible or desirable.

(JPF, 2020. website)

JPF's research goals are deeply rooted in donor values reflecting the need for inclusivity along the lines of gender, ethnicity, location, religion, age, and language. There is an unverifiable assumption that such intersectionality is at the root of why the ceasefire might fail. But left out are other questions my Myanmar students raise about destabilizing foreign investment from China, Europe, and North America; and the nature of military government, all favorite questions of Myanmar people. Also left out are theories regarding foreign occupation; the consequences of Burmanization (Eh Htoo 2021); the nature of nationalism and militarism (Alwyn 2021; Eh Htoo 2021); Aung San Suu Kyi's peace philosophy (see Myat, 2019), or Saw Aung Hla's peace philosophy (Alwyn, 2021), all issues proposed by my students as dissertation subjects. Such research subjects are not a good fit for JPF's criteria, and according to informal contacts I made with JPF, studies that address these questions are unlikely to be funded.

The Asia Foundation is known for favoring projects emphasizing the quantitative research techniques taught in international social science programs, particularly economics and political science. Asia Foundation-funded research typically involves collection of government statistics and social surveys. Questions often emphasize market economics, both because such issues are central to development studies, and also because the discipline of economics takes advantage of the power of statistical analysis.

Such quantitative research usually requires researchers to frame a question by identifying dependent and independent variables. Statistical relationships are then interpreted via tools such as regression equations which positivistically identify precise relationships between various factors (i.e., independent variables) and a single dependent variable. This is a powerful tool in business where the dependent variable is easily defined as financial profits. However, it is more problematic for a ceasefire where the elusive dependent variable of "peace" is not easily measured with numbers. A deep unanswerable philosophical question rooted in moral dilemmas regarding such things as positive peace, negative peace, and that ever-elusive "moral imagination" requires more than what quantitative research can measure.

Variables also chosen for quantitative studies reflect the values that donors bring. For example, an Asia Foundation study recently identified economic, physical, and interpersonal well-being as being the "dependent variables" which have utility for policymakers. "The 2018 CLS [City Life Survey] is an initiative to understand the well-being of urban residents living in five cities across Myanmar: Yangon, Mandalay, Mawlamyine, Monywa, and Taunggyi" (Asia Foundation 2020 website). The Asia Foundation's CLS explicitly has three key goals: (1) providing policymakers with the information they need to make informed decisions; (2) helping policymakers understand the priorities of their communities; and (3) facilitating lesson learning and healthy competition between cities (Asia Foundation, 2020).

The survey itself includes 135 questions, ambitiously covering "all aspects of urban life." Questions are divided into the categories of economic, physical, and inter-personal well-being. Questions were selected, the Asia Foundation wrote, to either capture holistic determinants of well-being or to meet the specific needs of municipal authorities. The survey itself was conducted in 2018 in collaboration with the Yangon University School of Political Science, and is intended to be repeated every two years alongside parallel programs such as according to the plan, city-level briefings, the development of a public data portal, data analysis training workshops, and thematic discussion papers (Asia Foundation, 2020).

Admittedly all three examples (i.e., The Hanns Seidel Foundation, JPF, and Asia Foundation) competently reflect the utility of what the donors call "international best research practice." Good governance means for the Germans, federalism; for the JPF, inclusivity for six specific intersectionalities; and for the Asia Foundation, economic, physical, and interpersonal well-being, which are all measurable using quantitative techniques and 135 questions covering "all aspects of urban life." These are all grounded in what the funding agencies commissioning the research already believe is morally right and good. In this way, moral dilemmas of war and peace are oddly reduced to technocratic problems. The question underpinning each of these programs is an assumption that Myanmar should become what Heinrich et al. (2010) reminds us are "WEIRD," that is, Western, educated, industrial, rich, and democratic.

The Soul of Myanmar's Research Terrain

The inherent conflicts of interest found in contract and advocacy research are a moral hazard for peace researchers. As Lederach (2005, p. xv) emphasized, peacebuilding assumes a "moral imagination" requiring leaps in logic, an aesthetic appreciation for social change, a search for "the soul of place," serendipity, accidental sagacity, and acknowledging the mystery of risk. Such an ethic is at the heart of what Mendizabal might call "independent research"; but such mysteries are not possible to explore in contract or advocacy research.

Indeed, subjects like serendipity and soul of place are anathema to lawyerly RFPs, framed questions, and advocacy research in Myanmar which, so far as I can tell, does not acknowledge the soul of Myanmar (or anyone else). As for risk, the research contract is inherently about avoiding financial risks for the donor, and protecting the reputation of the funding agency. Serendipity, or accidental sagacity, particularly the type that turns up in *The Irrawaddy*, and other independent media outlets, is to be avoided. More to the point, the donor does not want a lawsuit, to be accused of mismanagement of funds, associated with generals coordinating clearance actions in Rakhine, or even with Daw Aung San Suu Kyi who fell out of international political favor following the Rohingya crisis of 2017.

This brings me to the odd sub-thesis for this chapter. My sub-thesis is that what research for peace needs is an iterative dialectical process capable of developing that "moral imagination" that emerges from the "soul of place." What is "soul of the place" in a diverse place like Myanmar with such a diverse range of narrative histories? The answer is: I don't know, but I also know that this is an important subject for the peace researcher to explore. The soul of Myanmar of course is not the same as that of North America, Europe, or China. It is also probably not the soul of the donor bureaucracies, which makes contracts with Western pragmatism and utilitarianism.

But before returning to the issue of the "soul of place" and soul of bureaucracy in the conclusion of this paper, I would like to write a bit about why "Seeing Like a State," which is about how bureaucratic actors see themselves and their tasks (see Scott, 1999).[3] As Scott describes, bureaucratic "eyesight" requires the simplification of complex phenomenon into bite-sized chunks which can be digested from a height of "30,000 feet," which metaphorically speaking is the altitude from which a bureaucrat sitting in Yangon, Bangkok, Geneva, Naypyidaw, or New York sees the contracts over which they rule. Bureaucrats see the dominion they rule as tiny boxes, connected by roads and rivers, just like you see from an airplane. They cannot see into the souls of peoples from such an altitude, and so simplify matters of the soul to what can be "seen" via the Excel spreadsheets of today's modern Yangon INGO and government bureaucrats. Such account books inevitably squeeze out the peacebuilders interest in sagacity, serendipity, soul of place, and risk. The questions behind peace become technocratic musings of chair-bound bureaucrats in New York, Geneva, Bangkok, Yangon, or even Moung Lo in Wa State, sitting in their offices studying spread sheets from the JPF, sitrep summaries of Burmese newspapers, and the reports of the bureaucratic stakeholders who are also soulless bureaucrats. There is no dependent variable "peace" which fits in a spreadsheet. You cannot see peace from 30,000 feet. To know the soul of peace, it is best to listen deeply to those who know what it means to have lost peace. Myanmar is full of people like this.

Peacebuilding and the Moral Imagination

The Moral Imagination and the Two Hundred-Year Present

Peace researchers John Paul Lederach and Elise Boulding emphasized that the present is always a product of habits of thinking and memory making. Lederach (2005, pp. 135–47), for example, explains that humans walk backwards into the future, and cites a Kikuyu parable from Kenya to illustrate this point: "People look backwards to history when deciding about walking into the future." The memories, emotions, sense of belonging, and our sense of moral righteousness are inherited from a shared past. Which is why, the Kikuyu parable notes, humans only walk backwards into the future. That past, Lederach (2005, p. x) writes, is fourfold.

- a narrative history told in the textbooks of our schooling,
- the remembered past of our grandparents,
- our own experienced past of private and public events, and
- an immediate past which disproportionately shapes our daily conversations.

---

3. See also Ferguson 1993 with respect to the "Anti-politics Machine."

This typology is reflected in Table 9.2 as a hypothetical forty-year-old Burmese adult raised in Ne Win's schools, and in Table 9.3 as a forty-year-old adult from Kawthoolei raised in Karen National Union schools.

Standards of grievance and righteousness frame how conflict and unity are credibly remembered. History itself is narrated in a credible, creditable, and plausible manner, and in the context of remembered "grandparent" knowledge, that is, that remembered history, which is related formally and informally (see Waters, 2005). The emotional content of such history contains the soul of the people, and it cannot fit into spreadsheets of the bureaucrats. This is what books like Thwe's (2002) memoir, Lintner's story (1996/2012) of his travels through northern Burma in the 1980s, and Alwyn's (2021) description of Karen historian Saw Aung Hla share. For that matter, it is also found in histories and literature.

Lederach's point of course is that ultimately grandparents' remembered history is more important than the policies developed at the United Nations asserting a new sense of technocratic best practice. In other words, a grandparent's account carries with it the righteous moral sense that technocratic JFP reports lack. Technocratic best practice emerges from rationalized evaluations of scientists, through the political filter of the United Nations (UN). The sense of righteousness expressed by grandparents and righteousness expressed by the JPF bureaucrats differ. Grandparent history does not necessarily reflect "recognized best practices" as defined by the UN, or SDGs. Nor does such a "soul of place" reflect a consensus from large international meetings where righteousness comes mainly from the immediate past, as narrated perhaps by CNN, or another favorite English-language news source.

Elise Boulding (2000) makes a similar point as Lederach about history and writes of a "two hundred-year present," which reflects the taken-for-granteds such

Table 9.2 Burma's History (See Taylor 2009 and Myint U 2019)

Narrative history	Remembered history (100 year present)	Experienced history	Current history
The Three Great Burmese Kingdoms (Pagan, Taungoo, Konbaung)	British Colonialism, particularly Saya San Rebellion	Ne Win and Military Authoritarianism, prisons, Burmanization campaigns. Expulsions of Chinese, Indians, and civil war (1962–2012).	2015 elections
Brutal British Occupation, exile of King, persecution of monks	Japanese Occupation, British Withdrawal, and 250,000–1,000,000 war dead	Anti-military demonstrations in 1988, 1996, and 2007.	Expulsion of Rohingya in 2017 and international response
Expropriation of lands and businesses by British, Indians, and Chinese	Assassination of Aung San, Independence, and Burmese Civil War	Emergence of NLD and Aung San Suu Kyi (1988–now).	Chinese expansion into Myanmar, and February 1, 2021, coup

Table 9.3 Karen Nationalist History (See Saw Aung Hla 1939/2004, Alwyn 2021)

Narrative history	Remembered history (100 year present)	Experienced history	Current history
Arrival from Mongolia, indigeneity, establishment of Pyu States, and invention of writing. Arrival of Buddhism.	Golden age of Karen advancement in alliance with the British colonial authorities.	Burmanization, and four cuts attacks. Closure of Karen schools. Harsh military rule, and banning of Karen language and culture.	2015 Ceasefire. UNHCR voluntary repatriation plans, attacks by Tatmadaw. Uneasy relationship with Thai government.
Betrayal by the Burmese, enslavement, and persecution.	Second World War, Japanese and Burma Independence Army invasion of Karen territory,	Establishment of Karen resistance groups in alliance with other opposition groups. Defeat at Manerplaw.	Erection of Chinese "New City" in Myawaddy, dam construction. With and without KNU cooperation.
Arrival of British and liberation. Arrival of Christianity, and the advent of Karen schooling.	Rally of 400,000 Karen demanding independence (1948). Betrayal by the British, assassination of Saw Bao Gyi, Karen defeat in the Battle of Insein.	Withdrawal of KNU to Thailand, establishment of large refugee camps, IDP camps, and diaspora in USA, Canada, Australia, etc. More assassination. Establishment of Dr. Cynthia's Mae Tao Clinic in Mae Sot.	2020 KNU elections, Covid, sealing of Thai-Myanmar border. February 1, 2021 coup, National Unity Government, Civil Disobedience Movement, etc.

as personal stories from our elders, which include reflection on morality-infused events which may have happened 100 years ago. She goes on to make the point that how we remember and recreate these stories today affects our own grandchildren 100 years in the future, whether we are literally grandparents or not.

Different groups in Myanmar have different "grandparent stories" to frame today's political views. For Bamar families, it perhaps starts with uncles, grandfathers, and elders hanged by the British following the Saya San rebellion (1930–1). Aung San and the Japanese invasion of Burma is still current for children and grandchildren who themselves were present in the 1930s and 1940s, including Daw Aung San Suu Kyi who spent much time as a girl with her grandfather who was born in the late nineteenth century, and to whom she read *The Bible*. The Battle of Insein in which Burma's government forces beat back advancing armies of Karen from the east in 1950, is front and center for the children and grandchildren of the men who fought and died there, and for the children raised on a diet of Ne Win inspired dramas played endlessly in remote villages and on Burmese television for the last fifty or sixty years.[4]

4. See Chapter 2 of *The Land of Green Ghosts* by Pascal Khoo Thwe (2002), "Grandfather's Dream."

Ethnic minorities have different narrative pasts; and in the case of Myanmar memories are often oppositional. For example, the Karen-remembered history focuses on the protection the British extended the Karen from Burmese exploitation, the Karen alliance with the British before and during the Second World War, betrayal by the British at the independence talks in 1946–7, expropriation of Karen rights following the Battle of Insein in the Burmese Civil War, and decades of attacks on Karen villages by Burmese military (see Alwyn, 2021; Aung Hla, 1939/2004). Kachin, Arakan, Shan, Mon, Chin, Chinese, Indian, and other grandparents tell similar stories of alliances, betrayal, and exploitation of their people (see, e.g., Craig, 2018; Ghosh, 2002).

The souls of Westerners working in Burma and passing judgment on grant proposals are not immune to the stories of their own grandparents, either. They are typically heirs to stories rooted in memories of righteousness from the Second World War, Nuremberg Trials, the post-War Marshall Plan to rebuild Europe, and interpretations of the events underpinning the post-Second World War architecture for the International Humanitarian Relief Regime (see Waters, 2001). Specifically British memories are of a recent time when Empire was central, and indeed there are many popular films and literature drawing on a nostalgia that both glorifies Empire, and more recently, critiques it, but always with the British role at the center.[5] Memories of victories in the Second World War, and for aid workers, a humanitarianism rooted in memories of the Jewish Holocaust, and the emergence of the post-Second World War world humanitarian order are also central (see Power, 2002). Indeed, this narrative history is probably one reason why Myanmar Nobel Peace Prize winner Daw Aung San Suu Kyi is accused of betrayal by the international community—her ambivalence toward the expulsion of the Rohingya in 2017 implicitly challenged values from the West's remembered history, that is, the values transmitted by actual European grandparents about expulsion and genocide in Europe and elsewhere.

Notably, Burmese-remembered history of Second World War and after is very different from the remembered history of Europeans or Americans (compare Tables 9.2 and 9.3 to Tables 9.4 and 9.5). Burmese memory is of the extreme brutality of the Japanese occupation, the British retreat to India, and a war in Burma in which 250,000–1,000,000 died as Japanese, British, Burmese, Chinese, Thai, and American militaries used the country as a battlefield. This manipulation is at the center of Myanmar's memories, not The European Holocaust, German occupation of Europe, Rape of Nanking, or bombings of the UK, Pearl Harbor, Germany, and Japan. The post-War independence movement which erupted into the Burmese Civil War by 1949 is also remembered by my PhD students' parents

---

5. The literary traditions of Somerset Maugham, Rudyard Kipling, George Orwell all emerged out of the need to remember the British Empire in Burma and India. American Hollywood gave a try at remembering Empire through, among other devices, movies like *African Queen* (World War I), *Casablanca* (World War II), and *Mutiny on the Bounty* (Captain Cook's era in the late 1700s).

Table 9.4 British National History

Narrative history	Remembered history (100 year present)	Experienced history	Current history
Roman Britain, King Arthur, Queen Elizabeth I, and Sir Walter Raleigh. Lord Nelson, Waterloo, Indian Empire.	Second World War, Establishment of the British Commonwealth, Peaceful Decolonization.	End of the British Empire, establishment of European Union. Spice Girls, Elton John, James Bond, and Punk Rock.	Brexit and Boris Johnson
Great Literature, and the English language. Oxford and Cambridge.	Establishment of the NHS and the modern welfare state.	Popular Culture, The Beatles, Rolling Stones Football.	International travel in Europe and abroad
Democratic rule, naval prowess, benevolent empire.	Service in the colonial empire. The Beatles, Rolling Stones.	Margaret Thatcher, and the re-emergence of Brittania.	Covid

Table 9.5 UN "National" History (after Waters 2001)

Narrative history	Remembered history (100 year present)	Experienced history (forty years)	Current history
Armenian Genocide League of Nations, and Birth of Red Cross (see Power 2002)	Second World War, Holocaust, Nazism, Biafra, Cold War, Vietnam War (see Power 2002)	Indochinese Refugee Crisis, "We are the World" concert for Africa, "Black Hawk Down" in Somalia, Former Yugoslavia and Srebrenica, Rwanda Genocide, East Timor, Congo, Syria (see, e.g., Autesserre 2014)	Rohingya and Aung San Suu Khi, Syria, Afghanistan, 2015 Ceasefire and election, 2020 election, February 1, 2021, coup and aftermath

and grandparents. My students themselves experienced the "negative peace" of the authoritarian Ne Win regime, and the military government, in which police, soldiers, spies, government informers, and the threat of prison created a pervasive sense of fear.[6] The Holocaust and the Nuremberg Trials gave birth to international tribunals and are central to the remembered history of the international community, but only tangential for the Burmese who remember with emotional clarity the suffering of their own grandparents. There is though little emotional connection to German crimes in Europe, or even Japanese war crimes in China, Korea, or the Philippines.

6. See, e.g., Burma Story Book (2017), Thwe (2002), and Myat (in preparation) for English writings by Burmese about the period of repression. There is much more written in Burmese and ethnic languages.

Philosophy and Peacebuilding Research in Burma/Myanmar: Restorying the Unaskable Questions

Restorying by peacebuilders is rooted in the "sphere of communication action" (see, e.g., Habermas, 1983) unique to each culture group, and that is where the stories from the narrative, remembered, and experienced history emerge. Language use often demarcates social boundaries in Myanmar whether between the foreigners bearing gifts who speak English (and Chinese), the shared desire for a national language like Burmese, as well as the simultaneous desire by some for mother tongue instruction in the many regions where Karen, Shan, Kachin, Mon, Arakan, and Rohingya languages of the grandparents and parents are spoken and cultivated.

That is why language-in-education policies are contentious in Myanmar, and the reason so many Karen, Kachin, and Shan schools became targets for *Tatmadaw* (military) campaigns, bullets, mines, and torches. The narratives taught in these schools are a challenge to the hegemony of the Myanmar State with its appeals to nationalism and group identity inherited from Bamar ancestors. They are also the point at which restorying must begin, whether as the Myanmar Nation or autonomous ethnic regions.

Restorying in a multi-lingual society is difficult. Each group has narratives inherited from grandparents who defined themselves relative to "enemies." A good example for Myanmar is the different ways that the Burmese Civil War is remembered. Karen remember it as a battle where the Karen National Defense Organization (KNDO) rescued the Rangoon (now Yangon) government from an advance by the Communist forces from the north, but then were betrayed with the assassination of their leader Saw Bao Gyi (see Alwyn, 2021). On the other hand, government forces remember it as a time when the country almost fell to treacherous Communist and Karen forces, who were beaten back to the mountains through the martial abilities of the *Tatmadaw*. The government view of course prevails in the narrative storytelling of textbooks from the Myanmar Ministry of Education—but the Karen view is still deeply held in the remembered history of today's Karen National Union, which retells the Karen account in an enduring school curriculum taught in Kawthoolei.

The Moral Imagination and Languages in Myanmar

English is the dominant language of research in Myanmar's donor world and was for many years the language of higher education (see CESD, 2020, p. 41).[7] Research is framed in professional English, as are contract negotiations and international advocacy. As a result, English frames how research questions are asked and how reports are written. When foreigners are involved, little negotiation is done in

---

7. English was the language of university instruction until 1964 when General Ne Win switched it to Burmese. The language of the university officially reverted to English in the 1980s, but in practice still remains Burmese (CESD, 2020, p. 41).

Burmese, a language that most Myanmar people prefer. Westerners and Burmese with a high proficiency in English, often acquired at Western universities, are at an advantage in negotiations with Myanmar people, not only because they control the money, but the built-in socio-linguistic advantage.

The same linguistic advantage though is found in negotiations within Myanmar between ethnic groups, typically done in Burmese, rather than Shan, Karen, or Jing-Paw Kachin, and many other languages. Burmese has long been the lingua franca in most parts of Myanmar where it is widely used in trading situations and negotiations. Burmese popular culture is well-developed and seeps into ethnic-controlled areas along with its Burmanized context. But just as English puts westerners at a linguistic advantage, native Burmese speakers are at an advantage, particularly those educated to a high level of fluency via secondary and tertiary education. This puts ethnic negotiators at the same disadvantage vis-a-vis the Burmese negotiators, as Burma negotiators are in English-language contract negotiations.[8]

Several ethnic languages are taught in ethnic-based school systems, including university-level education conducted in Karen, Kachin, Mon, Karenni, and Shan with Burmese, Chinese, and/or English as an additional language.[9] Just as few Westerners are capable of negotiating in Burmese, few Burmese are capable of conducting business in ethnic languages.

English, Burmese, Ethnic Languages, and Power

Language use is at the heart of peacebuilding research in Burma or at least it should be. Language choice is an expression of power. At the nineteenth century Konbaung court, the "Central Burmese" that is today's national language, emerged with the arrival of printing in the mid-nineteenth century. English then supplanted this language to the extent that General Aung San did most of his writing in English, and the Burmese government was conducted in English until Ne Win replaced it with Burmese again in the 1960s. English again became important with the return of the international community after 2010, and especially after 2015 when

---

8. *The Irrawaddy* recently described this issue at the 2020 National Peace Conference, where it was noted that Shan lead negotiator RCSS Chairman Yawd Serk was required to speak Burmese, and not permitted to speak Shan. https://www.irrawaddy.com/news/burma/military-chief-blames-ethnic-armies-govt-myanmars-protracted-peace-process.html.

9. Secondary and tertiary education systems are being developed by a number of Ethnic Armed Organizations using ethnic languages first, and then English and Burmese. These degrees are not recognized by the Burmese system, so credit cannot be transferred and degrees cannot be used to qualify for further study in Myanmar. The credentials issued though are used as qualifications to teach in primary and secondary schools administered by the EAOs. See South and Lall (2016) and Yeo, Gagnon, and Thako (2020).

it became clear that English skills gave access to international jobs and patronage. Ironically, at the same time skills in ethnic languages improved, as institutions of learning were established by Karen, Kachin, Karenni, Shan, and Mon.[10] But ethnic-language education was largely ignored by the central government, which only reluctantly permits limited use of ethnic-language texts, which typically are translations of Burmese texts reflecting a Burma-centric narrative, remembered, and experienced history (Eh Htoo, 2021). Burmese nationalism is thereby inserted into ethnic schools. In much the same way that the Burmese translations of donor documents reflect foreign donor goals, ethnic-language translations of Burmese texts still reflect Burmese goals.

In the context of ethnic-based education in Myanmar, primary, secondary, and higher education institutions make trade-offs. For example, in the case of some Karen schools, English and the ethnic languages became important, while Burmese-language instruction is lacking, resulting in graduates unable to matriculate to universities in Myanmar. This may not be the case in Mon ethnic-based schools, where Burmese is taught alongside Mon, starting after grade three. To summarize, both the dominant language, Burmese, and the international language, English, threaten ethnic languages, but all three languages are valuable for different reasons. How might a moral imagination for peace reconcile this linguistic diversity in a sagacious fashion (see Wong, 2019)?

The language issue is often pushed aside in the pragmatic world of Yangon's peace research, which accepts quick translations of questionnaires, protocols, and the report itself. Such practices mean that the taken-for-granteds of moral righteousness reflect Western traditions, and not those of Myanmar. What is missing? Perhaps they are the unspoken and emotionally generated theories of culture and righteousness inherited from Burmese and ethnic grandparents. That serendipity, sagacity, and the "soul of place" Lederach wrote about are effectively replaced in such translations by ethics that are WEIRD.

The Importance of Social Theory

Social theories, whether received from our grandparents or books, reflect beliefs regarding how the social world works. This social world makes assumptions about morality, and as Durkheim (1973) points out, is embedded in religious narratives. Different cultures have different estimations of what is moral, including who belongs to the group; what is good, bad, and beautiful; what acts are righteous or to be condemned; and what is the appropriate role for the state, particularly in the administration of justice. Such traditions are readily defined by sociologists and philosophers for many centuries, and are widely taught in university sociology, anthropology, philosophy, and religious studies departments.

---

10. See South and Lall (2016).

The Hegemony of Western Theory in Research: Utilitarianism, Materialism, and Pragmatism

Western sociological theory is rooted in a logic which assumes that utilitarianism, materialism, and pragmatism are right and appropriate (see Layder, 2018). Social science is valued for "what it is good for" in a materialistic fashion and assessed by how well it can be used to solve an identified social problem. Such an approach identifies a problem, and then zeroes in on "the solution," which is reduced to a program with definable material inputs that can be measured and audited. This is an effective way to do engineering, run a large capitalist organization, and maintain a government bureaucracy. The ethos of this philosophical approach permeates the agencies like the JPF, and other investors in peace, which Severine Autesserre (2014) calls *Peaceland*. Peace in this context is a positivistic independent variable waiting to be explained and fixed with financial and physical inputs, that is, "programs, programs, programs" (see Dick, Rich, and Waters, 2016, p. 16). Measuring the inputs and outputs of such programs for pre-identified stakeholders is at the heart of the modern accountability movement in public administration.

This theory of action emerges from moral assumptions regarding Western political, economic, and social experiences. Such theories emphasize the centrality of market activity, materialism, utilitarianism, individualism, human rights, and particularly property rights. These theories are the inheritance of Hobbes, Locke, Adam Smith, and Jefferson who emphasized that government is a "contract" around which people organize to protect life, liberty, property, and happiness. Modern versions of this are found in the behaviorist traditions of psychology and economics, which assume that there is a cause and effect relationship between incentives, punishments, and particular results.

Such materialist theories are embedded in the JPF's description of itself described above, and summed up in an ideology of "good governance" and democracy. But JPF did not invent these theories, which in fact are older, and even underpinned British colonialism with its emphasis on mercantile profitability and the rule of British Common Law. Today the same goals underpin the "development discourse," which defines peacebuilding as a series of social problems awaiting a solution, as specified in documents like the SDGs which themselves are embedded in the language of utilitarian accountability. Such goals prescribe a morality rooted in rationalism, materialism, utilitarianism, and a particular view of good governance. Peace from this view is rooted in issues highlighted by the Hans Seidel Foundation, JPF, and the Asia Foundation quoted above. But prescribing such rational presuppositions is particularly problematic in the case of peace research, because it means that thinking outside the box—that is, in other forms of rationality—is off the table. But what Lederach and the other peacebuilders teach us is that violence is not about the calculation of a regression equation with a dependent variable, but the values, emotions, and habits behind enmities and identity which ultimately are cultural inheritances from our grandparents.

What Is the Habitus of Burmese Social Thought?

The metaphor of the Excel spreadsheet is a good representation of the Western bureaucratic cosmological view with its pragmatic independent and dependent variables. But does it summarize the Burmese worldview? To a certain extent it surely does—the Myanmar government like all others is indeed bureaucratic. But does this mean that it shares an emphasis on individualism and utilitarianism in the same way that Western governments implementing programs in Myanmar do? Do Burmese grandparents transmit the values about individualism and utilitarianism in the same fashion that grandparents from the United States or UK do? I do not have a definitive answer to this question—but the cosmology of Burmese political discourse is different from that of the West.

Burmese I talk to often start by lamenting the authoritarian nature of the Burmese hierarchy which Maung (1983) very explicitly wrote about in his book *Burmese Political Values: The Socio-Political Roots of Authoritarianism.* Maung and others point out that Burmese are ever-ready to obey those in authority without question, be they Konbaung Kings, British police officers, Japanese military, or Burmese military. The point being that *habitus* of obedience and fear interferes with democratic modernization they dream of. The democratic responses in 1988, 2007, and now 2021 are challenges to this ingrained habitus. Myanmar's people may have habitus of obedience and acquiescence, but whatever the source, there are also reservoirs of rebellion.

This habitus of authoritarianism and obedience, whether found in Myanmar, the Soviet Union, the United States, or elsewhere, comes from somewhere (see Waters, 2018). I will describe some better-known elements of Burmese culture shape worldviews in manners not typically noticed by modern, pragmatic utilitarian WEIRD Westerners. Here I will highlight four such issues: the Buddhist focus on the inner self, the harshness of British colonial rule, and what inter-cultural studies scholars call group orientation. Fourth, there is the cosmological focus in Buddhism on the pursuit of dharma, which can be translated roughly as "virtue" or the "teachings," which emerged first from Hinduism. The cosmology is not as neat as an Excel spreadsheet, or even a course in "Western Social Thought: Plato to Bourdieu," but it does provide enough context to begin a conversation about the clashing cosmologies that confront social science research in Myanmar.

Buddhism and Inner Peace

In Buddhism, a strong connection is seen between the inner peace of the individual and the harmony of society and meditation is at the center of both Buddhist theory and practice. Meditation addresses calming the mind to achieve a sense of inner peace, which harmonizes relationships. This emphasis is weaker in Western traditions which equate peace as something that reflects "security" from personal violence, and protection of property. This security is so important that it is often at the center of what the United States in particular exported since the

Second World War, and emphasizes the peace guaranteed by police and militaries, in what might be called "outer peace," in the tradition of the authoritarian *Pax Romana*. Such a view of peace justifies "foreign security assistance packages" to Myanmar, the *Tatmadaw* itself, and assistance to armed ethnic group militaries by more surreptitious means.[11] Such security assistance to the Tatmadaw is viewed skeptically by a Myanmar population conditioned by the terror of the Ne Win years.

The Burmese Buddhist search for this inner-self starts with purification. This is perhaps why there are deep traditions of holy men in Myanmar leading revolts against the colonial powers, including the revolt of the monks after the occupation by the British in 1885, the Saya San rebellion in the 1930s, the "Saffron Revolt" of 2007, and most recently the central role that monks played in mobilizing sometimes violent responses to the presence of Rohingya and others in Rakhine. Among the ethnic minorities there are also strong traditions of holy men leading revolts against civil authority. James C. Scott (2009) dedicated an entire chapter of his book *The Art of Not Being Governed* to the role that often ephemeral charismatic leaders have played among the hills peoples, be they animists, Christian, or Buddhist.

But the bulk of the Western peace studies literature is about outer peace with its WEIRD values for outer peace and the need for mediation, diplomacy, economic development, and human rights. Restorying, and reimagining a society in which fighting is replaced with the broad liberal peace of the global nation-state system. Such liberal peace perhaps serves the West and the world well. However, two centuries of experience in Myanmar, beginning with its arrival via Indo-British colonial power in 1823 when the British introduced the modern nation-state system, raise questions about the wisdom of such a liberal peace for Myanmar. Missing though from reports is that a liberal peace in the context of the international political system may not be the only way to seek peace in Myanmar, a place where peace starts from within, and not from the diplomats' green baize tables in Geneva, New York, or even Chiangmai.

Nationalism and Identity

Nationalism and group identity in Myanmar are key values challenging Western theories of materialism, pragmatism, and utilitarianism in ways best understood as a remembered history of British colonialism, Japanese occupation, and decades-long dictatorships. Nationalism for Burma's ethnic groups is clan writ large—as it is in most nations (see Anderson, 1993). But nationalism is also viewed in Myanmar (and many former colonies) as a series of wrongs perpetrated by colonizers. In the case of Burma, there is a particularly rich crop of such outsiders, starting first with

11. An American who highlighted the need for inner peace in peacebuilding and nonviolence was Martin Luther King, Jr., who discussed the importance of "self-purification" before undertaking nonviolent actions (see King, 1963).

the British and their Indian/Bengali clients, but also including Chinese occupiers from after the Second World War (both Kuomintang and Communist), Thai military meddlers in Shan, Karen, and Karenni States; American CIA and DEA agents in northern Burma; and at times agents from Arab countries aligning with Muslim forces.

The British ruled Burma harshly when they were there (1823–1948), typically through divide and rule techniques favoring ethnic minorities over the Bamar-speaking majority whose identity was aligned with the disgraced and deported Konbaung dynasty. Prisons and the hangman's noose were used liberally by the British to subdue the Burmese population in particular. Indians were often favored with civil service appointments, business advantages, and were assigned land in the lowlands to produce rice. Karen, Kachin, Shan also aligned with the British after generations of exploitation by the Burmese-speaking courts.

Adding to the colonial mix was the delegitimation of the Buddhist Sangha by the British, at the same time that British and American Christian missionaries were encouraged to establish schools among the Karen, Kachin, Chin, and others. Hinduism and Islam were also permitted to expand, particularly in Rakhine where land was granted to Bengali peasants between 1825 and the 1930s.

The net result is a modern Burmese nationalism suspicious of outside meddling that seeks isolation from powerful interlopers. This tradition goes back to the independence days when Burma was one of the few former British colonies to refuse Commonwealth membership. Wariness of Chinese, British, and the CIA during the Burmese Civil War (1949–50); the isolation of the country during Ne Win's rule; and the resistance to Western involvement in the Rohingya crisis after 2017. The long-term closure of airports during the recent Covid crisis, and the run up to the November 2020 elections, is consistent with these habits. Simplistic Western calls for nonviolence following the February 1, 2021, coup are contributing factors.

Group-Centered Identity: Whose Rights, and Whose Justice?

In the well-known Hofstede "Cultural Compass," there is a variable "individualism vs. collectivism." This is defined in the following fashion:

> The high side of this dimension, called Individualism, can be defined as a preference for a loosely-knit social framework in which individuals are expected to take care of only themselves and their immediate families. Its opposite, Collectivism, represents a preference for a tightly-knit framework in society in which individuals can expect their relatives or members of a particular ingroup to look after them in exchange for unquestioning loyalty. A society's position on this dimension is reflected in whether people's self-image is defined in terms of "I" or "we."
>
> (Hofstede, 2020 website)

Myanmar is not rated directly by Hofstede, but many of the Myanmar groups are probably high on "collectivism." Individuals are part of extended families, ethnic groups, rebel groups, religious groups, and the nation. This is in contrast to the NGO and donor community with the Western "individualism" embedded in the Anglo-centric cosmology. Collectivist societies in Myanmar (and elsewhere) tolerate more hiring and organization along kin lines, while more individualist cosmologies focus on individual achievement, often at the expense of group loyalty. The clash between the two is found in Asia, Latin America, and other countries where people from more individualistic societies seek to do business, and in Myanmar where Western NGOs seek to implement programs.

Virtue (Dharma) for Its Own Sake

Buddhism uses as its organizing principle the pursuit of virtue (Dharma) in the context of the cause and effect of cosmic karma. Embedded in this are assumptions about the moral nature of politics (see Walton, 2012). Myanmar's politicians reason about politics from a "Buddhist Theravadian point of view," which reflects a *habitus* of thoughts regarding the exercise of power, and definitions of government. Aung San, a secularist, wrote about this while seeking independence, but still emphasizing Buddhist ideas of moral cause and effect. He wrote, "As a matter of fact, politics knows no end, it is *samasara* in effect before our eyes, the *samasara* of cause and effect, and past and present and future which goes around and around and never ends" (Aung San quoted in Walton, 2012, p. 76).

As for human nature, there is an acknowledgement in Burmese Buddhism of the centrality of "desire" corrupting the individual, and by extension the state. Overt desire for power is suspect, while also acknowledging that acts of goodness in past lives can result in the karmic call to wield power in the everyday world. In this karmic world, power holders are assumed to be the beneficiaries of karma accumulated in previous lives. Such an ideology of course is easily used by those in power to justify existing inequalities, and justify the authoritarianism Maung (1983) wrote about. It also leaves little role for social mobility. In a functional fashion, it is assumed that the low status, poor, and peasants are also in their positions due to the fruits of karma, and previous immorality. And while Myanmar never had the extreme form of the caste system like Hindu India, there are similarities.

What is also apparent is the role of dialectics in Buddhist reasoning—there are tensions between individual and society, which are not resolvable. Rather there are unending cycles created by the immorality of sin in the context of karmic cycles. Governments and societies are assumed to be subject to such tensions too. This is notably different from the rationalist thought emerging from Anglo-American pragmatism in which progress toward an ever more perfect society is assumed.

The Hegemony of Western Thinking and the Habitus of Burmese Social Thought

The Western view of course is hegemonic in Yangon's "Peaceland" (the international funding agencies), which reserves to itself the right to judge the appropriateness of program implementation. This has resulted in the funding of any number of rigidified ideas regarding governance, property, economics, gender, ethnicity, religion, and other subjects that Peaceland sees as being at the heart of Myanmar's problems. In this world, Buddhist views about inner peace, nationalism, the dialectics of karma, and the importance of ethnic identity are assumed away in RFP prepared by JPF, and other donors.

But this leaves the classic question of the pragmatic modern administrator "What should we do?" without an answer. Policymaking without positivistic pragmatic goals is at the heart of traditional peacebuilding bureaucracies. But precisely defined goals and objectives are also at the heart of the bureaucratic institutions which perform only specialized tasks designed with inputs and outputs in mind. That is why the research contracts in Yangon routinely specify tangible "deliverables." The deliverables are contract specific, and while they refer to an abstraction like peace, this is operationalized as attendance at a workshop, completion of a survey, or production of a research report. Ceasefire is measured via incident reports. Such approaches have yet to work in Myanmar since 2012, or for that since British administration first arrived in 1823. Counting workshop participants, completing surveys, and counting incidents is not peace research, at least not as Galtung and Lederach defined it because there is little room for emotion, feelings, dharma, and karmic cycles, much less the "soul of place" inherited from the stories told by grandparents, and the nation. Inner peace, nationalistic emotions, and collective identity are also missing. There is no mention of positive and negative peace, cultural violence, or structural violence in Myanmar's peacebuilding research. Instead there are counts of incidents, students funded, Likert-level attitudinal measurements about the delivery of services, and so forth. And this is the frustrating point at which policy meets peace research. A moral imagination is what brings them together.

Conclusion

This chapter has reviewed the relationship between first the nature of "framing the research question" and secondly "the moral imagination." The two do not match in Myanmar's Peaceland—which is perhaps why the research enterprise of today's Yangon remains so narrowly focused on "policy" as defined by the donors. For Myanmar-based peace research to mature, it needs to develop a base broader than just policy workshops. It needs to begin exploring how Myanmar people see their problems, and issues. There needs to be a way to connect the tensions embedded in diverse "grandparent wisdom" of Burmese, Karen, Shan, Kachin, Rakhine, Chinese, Rohingya, Chin, and others.

In glimmers, this is beginning to be expressed in Myanmar, mainly in the Myanmar, and ethnic languages which I do not have ready access to, but millions of Myanmar's peoples do. I hear glimmers of what they are concerned about by talking with my PhD students, and asking what they see as the root of Burma's problems. Their answers are no longer in terms that are fundable by the English-speaking research regime coming from Europe and North America with their research methods classes, good governance assumptions, and policy imperatives. Rather they focus on what they view as being "wrong" with their country. There is a focus on what they perceive as authoritarianism, which they believe the army has taken advantage of, and the NLD is seeking to preserve. They dream of a new Myanmar, Kawthoolei, or other political entity which is at the soul of what they consider a nation. Thus, proposed dissertation topics address the nature of Karen nationalism, peace philosophies of people like Daw Aung Suu Kyi, the impacts of Ne Win's Burmanization policies (Eh Htoo, 2021), the role of Karen education (Hayso in press), the consequences of press restrictions, and the role of economics and education in local development (Lwin, 2020).

Behind these concerns there are personal memories of what it meant to stay scared and quiet, during the oppressive decades of harsh military dictatorship. These are all compelling issues which the peoples of Burma talk about and seek to explore. I hope in a small way that the writings my students produce in Burmese, Karen, and English will transcend the narrow pragmatic agendas of applied and advocacy research they are solicited by foreign donors. Finally, I should note that underpinning their comments are understandings of Burmese and Karen philosophy that I only come to understand by reading and coaching them to express themselves in English, a foreign language for all.

As for the Yangon consultancy report, the memories of imprisonment are rarely expressed in what is published as "research." This is particularly odd, because the prison and exile is so widespread in the literary expressions written about Burma, such as Pascal Khoo Thwe's *The Land of Green Ghosts*, Kyaw Zwa Moe's *The Cell, Exile, and the New Burma*. Or the novels *Miss Burma* by Charmaine Craig and *Have Fun in Burma* by Rosalie Metro have a firmer grasp on the nature of exile and imprisonment in the Burmese imagination. As does *The Glass Palace* by Amitai Ghosh, which starts with the exile of King Thibaw in 1885. For that matter, the type of oppression is even found in Georg Orwell's *Burmese Days*. There is of course much more undoubtedly written in Burmese, Karen, Kachin, Shan, and other languages, which reveals the soul of Burma in ways that the Yangon consultancy reports do not.

In pointing to such tensions, I do not have a new formula for seeking peace in Myanmar beyond the fact that donors should fund the development of introspective social theory, philosophy, and literature, and do so in a fashion that respects the souls created by the cosmologies already found in Southeast Asia. The bureaucratic mercantile utilitarianism of Peaceland has perhaps reached its limit via misbegotten wars, colonial excess, military authoritarianism, and utopian socialism, in which the costs and benefits are calculated in a state-centric fashion. Which is why, perhaps, a new approach acknowledging Burmese cosmologies is needed.

How do we frame a research question which also acknowledges a moral imagination? To know what peace and the "soul of place" is you must listen to those who know what it is that have lost that sense of peace. And often that means listening to that which is not said; it is the pauses and silences in which the soul of peace is found.

Works Cited

Alwyn, Saw. (In Press). *The imagined Karen community of Kawthoolei as a nation-state.* [Unpublished doctoral dissertation]. Payap University.

Alwyn, Saw. (2021). The historiography of Saw Aung Hla and its influence on the modern Karen history curriculum. *Journal of Burma Studies 25*(1), 1–28.

Anderson, B. (1993). *Imagined communities.* London: Verso Books.

Asia Foundation. (2020). Public finances and the social contract in Myanmar: Reflections from the City Life Survey. https://asiafoundation.org/wp-content/uploads/2020/03/Public-Finances-and-the-Social-Contract-in-Myanmar-Reflections-from-the-City-Life-Survey_EN.pdf

Aung Hla, Saw. (1939/2004). *The Karen history.* Trans. Pu Tamla Htoo. Mae Sot, Thailand: Pu Kweh Ka Baw.

Autesserre, S. (2014). *Peaceland: Conflict resolution and the everyday politics of international intervention.* Cambridge: University Press.

Boulding, E. (2000). *Cultures of peace: The hidden side of history.* Syracuse: Syracuse University Press.

Burma Story Book. (2017). ZINDoc Amsterdam.

CESD Report. (2020). Doing research in Myanmar. https://cesdwebsitefiles.s3-ap-southeast-1.amazonaws.com/PDF/DRA/Doing±Research±Mayanmar±Country±Report_withISBN.PDF

Craig, C. (2018). *Miss Burma.* New York: Grove Books.

Dick, A. J., Rich, W., & Waters, T. (2016). *Prison vocational education and policy in the United States.* New York: Palgrave MacMillan.

Durkheim, E. (1973). *On morality and society.* Chicago, IL: University of Chicago Press.

Eh Htoo, Saw (2021). "Ne Win's Echoes: Burmanization and Peacebuilding in Myanmar Today," In Perry Schmidt-Leukel, Hans-Peter Groshans, & Madlen Krueger (Eds.), *Ethnic and Religious Diversity in Myanmar.* Bloomsbury. In press.

FHI360 (2020). Request for proposal "networks for peace" for Thailand, Myanmar, Sri Lanka. https://www.fhi360.org/projects/networks-peace

Galtung, J. (1964). An editorial: What is peace research? *Journal of Peace Research,* 1(1), 1–4.

Ghosh, A. (2002). *The glass palace.* New York: Random House.

Habermas, J. (1987) [1981]. *Theory of communicative action, volume two: Lifeworld and system: A critique of functionalist reason (book).* Trans. Thomas A. McCarthy. Boston, MA: Beacon Press. ISBN 0-8070-1401-X.

Hayso, Saw. (in press). *A comparison of four Karen education systems.* [Unpublished doctoral dissertation]. Payap University.

Heinrich, J., Heine, S. J., & Norenzayan, A. (2010). The weirdest people in the world? *Brain and Behavioral Sciences,* 33(2–3), 61–83. DOI: 10.1017/S0140525X0999152X.

Hofstede. (2020). The Dimensions of National Culture. https://hi.hofstede-insights.com/national-culture#:~:text=INDIVIDUALISM%20VERSUS%20COLLECTIVISM%20(IDV),themselves%20and%20their%20immediate%20families.

International Alert. (2019). *Forest management and peacebuilding in Karen areas in Myanmar*. Yangon: International Alert.https://www.international-alert.org/sites/default/files/Myanmar_ForestryManagement_ENG_2019.pdfJointPeaceFund.(2020). https://www.jointpeacefund.org/en/what-we-fund.

JPF (2020). Joint Peace Fund Web-Site. Retrieved August 2020. https://www.jointpeacefund.org/en

King, M. L. (1963). Letter from a Birmingham Jail. https://www.africa.upenn.edu/Articles_Gen/Letter_Birmingham.html

Lall, M., & South, A. (2018). Power dynamics of language and education policy in Myanmar's contested transition. *Comparative Education Review, 62*(4), 482–502.

Larkin, E. (2017). *Burma storybook*. Amsterdam: ZINDoc.

Layder, D. (2018) *Investigative research: Theory and practice*. London: Sage.

Leach, E. (1973). *Political systems of highland Burma*. Boston: Beacon Press.

Lederach, J. (2005). *The moral imagination: The art and soul of peacebuilding*. Oxford, England: Oxford University Press.

Lintner, B. (1996/2012). *Land of jade*. Bangkok: Orchid Press.

Lwin, Moe Thida. (2020). The Labour market in Mae Sot 1990–2017 and Thailand's new special economic zone policy. *Hue University Journal of Science, Economics and Development, 128*(58), 95–109.

Maung, Maung Gyi. (1983). *Burmese political values: The socio-political roots of authoritarianism*. New York: Praeger.

MacIntyre, A. (1988/2017). *Whose justice? Which rationality?* Notre Dame, IN: University of Notre Dame Press.

Mendizabal, E. (2010). On the business model and how this affects what think tanks do. In *On Think Tanks* website. https://onthinktanks.org/articles/on-the-business-model-and-how-this-affects-what-think-tanks-do

Metro, R. (2018). *Have fun in Burma: A novel*. Illinois: Northern Illinois University.

Moe, Kyaw Zaw (2018). *The cell, exile, and the new Burma*. Yangon: New Myanmar Publishing House.

Myat, M. M. (2019). Is politics Aung San Suu Kyi's vocation? *Palgrave Communications, 5*(50). https://doi.org/10.1057/s41599-019-0258-1

Myat, M. M. (in press). *The peace philosophy of Aung San Suu Kyi*. [Unpublished doctoral dissertation]. Payap University.

Orwell, G. (1934) *Burmese days*. New York: Harper Brothers

Power, S. (2002). *A Problem from hell: America and the age of genocide*. New York: BasicBooks.

Scott, J. C. (1999). *Seeing like a state*. New Haven: Yale University Press.

Scott, J. C. (2009). *The art of not being governed*. New Haven: Yale University Press.

Siegner, M. (2019). *In search of the Panglong spirit: The role of federalism in Myanmar's peace discourse*. Yangon: Hanns Seidel Foundation. https://view.publitas.com/hanns-seidel-foundation-myanmar/in-search-of-the-panglong-spirit-the-role-of-federalism-in-myanmars-peace-discourse/page/2–3

South, A., & Lall. M. (2016). Schooling and conflict: Ethnic education and mother tongue-based teaching in Myanmar. Policy Dialog Brief No. 15. Asia Foundation, Yangon Myanmar and United States Agency for International Development (USAID). Retrieved 19 January 2022 from https://asiafoundation.org/wp-content/uploads/2016/12/Policy-Brief_Schooling-and-Conflict-Ethnic-Education-and-Mother-Tongue-Based-Teaching-in-Myanmar_ENG.pdf.

Kyi, Aung San Suu (1991/2010). *Freedom from Fear and Other Writings*. Ed. Michael Aris. New York: Penguin Books.

Taylor, R. H. (2009). *The state in Myanmar.* Singapore: NUS Press.

Thant, Myint U. (2019). *The hidden history of Burma: Race, capitalism, and the crisis of democracy in the 21st Century.* New York: W. W. Norton.

Thwe, P. K. (2002). From *the land of green ghosts.* London: Harper Perennial.

Walton, M. (2012). *Politics in the Moral Universe: Burmese Buddhist Political Thought.* PhD. Dissertation in Political Science. Seattle: University of Washington.

Waters, T. (2001). *Bureaucratizing the good Samaritan.* New York: Routledge.

Waters, T. (2005). Why students think there are two kinds of American history taught. *The History Teacher, 39*(1), 11–21.

Waters, T. (2018). *Max Weber and the Modern Problem of Discipline.* Lanham: Hamilton Books.

Weber, M. (1919/2015). Politics as vocation. In *Weber's Rationalism and Modern Society: NewTranslations on Politics, Bureaucracy, and Social Stratification.* Edited and Translated by Tony Waters and Dagmar Waters. New York: Palgrave MacMillan.

Wong, M. (2019). The peace dividend of valuing non-dominant languages in language-in-Education policies in Myanmar. *FIRE: Forum for International Research in Education, 5*(3), 49–68.

Yeo, Sara, Terese Gagnon, & Hayso Thako (2020). Schooling for a stateless nation: The predicament of education without consensus for Karen refugees on the Thailand-Myanmar border. *Asian Journal of Peacebuilding. 8*(1), 29–55.

Conclusion

RAISING THE STAKES: RE-ENVISIONING SOCIALLY JUST EDUCATION FOR MYANMAR

Mary Shepard Wong

> When my teaching becomes challenging, I motivate myself by remembering
> my vision of peace for Rakhine State.
>
> (Soe Khine, p. 99, this volume)

This book addressed the question "How are various actors [in Myanmar] designing and implementing peace education endeavors [and] how are educators and learners making meaning of such peace education efforts?" (Bajaj & Hantzopoulos, 2016, p. 6). Authors from outside and inside Myanmar collaborated to draw from their identities, evoke their agency, and apply critical pedagogy in a common struggle for social justice to advance peace. The foreword provided the personal journey of a prolific scholar, who experienced and now writes about the political and economic plight of the peoples of Burma/Myanmar, and their ongoing struggle for social justice and peace. The Introduction chapter described why this book about teaching for peace and social justice in Myanmar is so necessary by highlighting what is at stake, especially with escalating tensions and conflicts both in the world and within Myanmar. The nine main chapters provided specific examples and compelling stories of educators who pursue peace in their classrooms and communities, from the major cities of Yangon and Mandalay, to the outer regions of Kachin, Shan, and Rakhine States. The topics discussed included addressing structural violence, peace curriculum development, identity-based conflict, teaching the history of the country, promoting inclusion, civic education, critical pedagogy, teacher agency, and agendas of research funding for peacebuilding.

Compiling this volume in 2020 during a global pandemic felt like trying to build a plane while flying it. Then in 2021 in the aftermath of the military coup, it felt like trying to build a plane while flying it during a dogfight with only one engine. It became apparent more than ever of the importance of our work. The stakes had been raised. Although some of us were forced to "parachute" to safety (leave Myanmar), we are still united in the struggle to envision peace and a more socially just Myanmar. What was and is still happening in Myanmar is beyond words. So much has been stripped away (educational systems, basic human services) and lost (lives, jobs, well-being). Yet we stand amazed at what is emerging from the ashes, a vision for an alternative education, one that is socially just and in its collaborative formation and inclusive purpose, has the potential to promote peace.

A theme found across the chapters of this volume is that of envisioning peace. Lederach (2003) notes that "envision is active, a verb. It requires an intentional perspective and attitude, a willingness to create and nurture a horizon that provides direction and purpose" (p. 15). Vision can be powerful as it can inspire us to do the seemingly impossible. It is used by Olympic coaches as they lead their athletes through exercises to anticipate every aspect of their dive off a high platform so that they can perform it with precision and confidence. It was used by Dr. Martin Luther King, Jr. in his famous "I have a dream" speech, calling forth images of "little black boys and black girls joining hands with little white boys and white girls as sisters and brothers [...] when all of God's children, black and white, Jews and Gentiles, Protestants and Catholics, will be able to join hands and sing in the words of the old Negro spiritual, 'Free at last! free at last! thank God Almighty, we are free at last!'"

Vision is also used in several religious texts to inspire and to instruct, including the Qur'an, the Bible, and Buddhist texts (Dörnyei & Kubanyiova 2014). Below, I explore Buddhist texts for the use of vision for inspiration for peace. However, first it must be acknowledged that religion, religious leaders, and sacred texts have been misused to evoke violence, supporting acts of terrorism on individuals, groups, institutions, and nations. There is no denying that acts of genocide have taken place in the name of religion. The Crusades, 9/11, and the Burmese Ma Ba Tha/969 movements are Christian, Muslim, and Buddhist examples of religion being used to promote violence. Religion is powerful, and so are religious leaders. Wade (2017) writes about his interactions with the Organization for the Protection of Race and Religion in Myanmar, or Ma Ba Tha. He learned that this group of Buddhists would defend their race and religion by "building a fence with our bones" (p. 1). They believe that Buddhism stands for truth and peace, and if Buddhist culture vanishes, so would peace, and "Yangon would become like Saudi and Mecca" (p. 5). The notorious Buddhist leader, Ashin Wirathu, has been called a "Burmese Bin Laden" (BBC News Asia, 2021). He was banned from preaching for a year in 2017, had his Facebook account wiped in 2018, was charged with inciting hate and contempt against the civilian government in 2019, turned himself in in 2020, and was released by the military junta with all charges of sedition dropped in 2021. This is an extreme case and reminds us not to essentialize religions and actions of religious leaders as always benevolent. Yet to claim that religion, religious leaders, and religious texts cannot be used for good because extremists have used them for ill is shortsighted. We need to draw upon all our resources, be they religious or otherwise, to promote peace and combat xenophobia.

Appleby's "ambivalence of the sacred" premise contends that internal pluralities are found in the holy and in any religious tradition (Appleby, 2000, pp. 30–1). There is potential in exploring the religious views of peacebuilding, and seeking to address the need for more research in this area as Appleby (2000) eloquently states:

> I refute the notion that religion, having so often inspired, legitimated, and
> exacerbated deadly conflicts, cannot be expected to contribute consistently to

their peaceful resolution. I argue that to the contrary that a new form of conflict transformation—"religious peacebuilding"—is taking shape on the ground, in and across local communities plagued by violence. This is a promising development, but it remains inchoate and fragile, uncoordinated and in need of greater numbers of adequately trained practitioners, more study and testing, and theoretical elaboration.

(p. 7)

It is with this caution that I explore Buddhist teachings for the potential they may have to support peace in Myanmar. I must add that I am not Buddhist and apologize for my incomplete understanding of it. I am eager to learn about Buddhism, as well as from all religions, to explore how they can support peace and how to mitigate the ways in which some religious leaders and interpretations of religious texts impede peace.

In *The Teaching of Buddha* (Bukkyo Dendo Kyokai, 1966), the use of imagery is found in numerous places. Buddha's compassion is referred to as "a fire that, once kindled, never dies until the fuel is exhausted," and the "wind that blows away the dust" (p. 28). Buddha is also "exactly like the moon: He neither appears or disappears; he only seems to do so out of love for the people that He may teach them" (p. 30). And just as the moon appears to change, waxing and waning, in fact "is always perfectly round" and never changes, just like Buddha (p. 30). Followers of Buddha are compared to a calf who will not leave its mother (p. 30), and the Buddha like both a father and mother to the people of the world (p. 33). Buddha is referred to as a river with great depth, and his teaching "flowing on pure and undisturbed" (pp. 34–5). In an appropriate analogy at the time this is being written, Buddha is said to appear "as a healing physician in an epidemic" (p. 35).

Imagery of equality, peace, tolerance, and respect are also found in Buddhist texts. This excerpt compares Buddha's compassion to rain, "Just as rain falls on all vegetation, so Buddha's compassion extends equally to all people. Just as different plants receive particular benefits from the same rain, so people of different natures and circumstances are blessed in different ways" (p. 21). The following excerpt extends Buddha's compassion and lack of prejudice and equal treatment to the sun, "The sun rises in the eastern sky and clears away the darkness of the world without prejudice of favoritism toward any particular region. So Buddha's compassion encompasses all people, encouraging them to do right and guides them against evil" (p. 22). Other texts that speak to peacebuilding include, "In a time of war, [Buddha] preaches forbearance and mercy for the suffering people" (p. 35). This text provides an example of both imagery and a call for peaceful coexistence from the Buddha, "You should respect each other, follow my teachings, and refrain from disputes; you should not, like water and oil, repel each other, but should like milk and water, mingle together" (p. 12). Finally, Buddha states, "You should follow my teachings. If you neglect them, it means that you have never really met me" (p. 12). For more nuanced ways that Buddhism can support the process of peace, see Arnold Kotler's 1996 edited volume *Engaged Buddhist Reader*.

Vision, and more specifically envisioning peace and socially just systems, can help people in conflict find common ground and consider new ways to achieve more peaceful communities. Conflict is natural, and will always exist. It occurs when people or groups want different things. A common view of conflict is that in order for one side to win, the other must lose. However, when both sides come to see that they may be after a similar end result, solutions can sometimes be found that do not pit people as winners or losers. Envisioning peace and socially just systems can help communities in conflict find this common ground. However, sustainable peace cannot be realized at just the local level. Larger, systemic issues need to be addressed, as sustainable peace cannot be achieved in the midst of social injustice, poverty, and inequality. A question to consider is how vision can be used to help actors see and address these larger issues.

To illustrate the power of vision and mental imagery to promote peace at both the local and global levels, consider the following example of a mental image or vision of an analytical framework of peace education. While working on this book, I read Higgins and Novelli's (2020) critique of the dominant approach to peace education that seeks attitudinal and behavior changes in conflict-affected societies. Higgins and Novelli (2020) argue that local educational initiatives seeking behavioral changes are not enough. They contend that a more comprehensive Cultural Political Economy (CPE) approach is needed that engages more deeply with structural and geopolitical drivers of conflict. They ask, "How may the analytical and conceptual tools of CPE enhance critical explanation and interpretation of the aims, goals, development, and implementation of peace education [...]?" (p. 8). They demonstrate in the case of Sierra Leone that the peace curriculum privileged one type of peace education, and in so doing narrowed down the potential of possibilities of their work. Some possible factors that are "deselected" by a behavioral change approach include an awareness and strategy to confront social injustices linked to conflict, be they local, national, or global. Also missing in a strictly behavioral approach is an informed response to systemic and structural violence, ineffective governmental policies that threaten peace, and the many economic inequalities that result in conflicts. Higgins and Novelli (2020) make a strong case for careful conflict analysis prior to peace education that avoids applying a generic "best practices approach" and instead creates a bespoke peace curriculum that addresses the drivers of the particular grievances of each context. They warn readers not to assume drivers of conflict are all internal to the country or a problem of the people who need to be "enlightened" or changed, and that the contribution of local actors needs to be substantial, and more than just symbolic.

After reading this article, I woke up the next morning having dreamt about it, which left me with a moving image in my head of how I was making sense of the article as applied to our work of peace education in Myanmar. I pictured a bright and vibrant Myanmar, rich in cultural, linguistic, and religious diversity and distinctiveness, reminding me of the huge overly idealized mural of foklorized minorities on the wall at the Yangon Airport in the 1990s. I saw our team facilitating workshops among teacher educators in schools and universities in this vibrant and diverse context. A moving spotlight was shining down on us, like a search light of a helicopter at night searching for someone lost at sea. As the spotlight darted around, it looked at first as if we were just exchanging valentines' cards with candy hearts, with people smiling and joining hands in a circle, while a dark storm was looming overhead. This seemed like a stinging critique of our work, as if we were oblivious to the larger forces at work all around us, as described by Higgins and Novelli (2020).

However, something else was starting to happen as if I was trying to respond to Higgins and Novelli's critique of this type of myopic approach to peacebuilding and essentialized versions of the ethnic groups, like the eight sets of male and female figurines sold to tourists. When the valentine cards were opened, a flat pair of paper spectacles dropped out, like the kind one gets at a 3D movie, with a red lens and a blue lens. When we put them on, they morphed into night vision binoculars, allowing us to see through the darkness to shapes, which became animals above us in the dark clouds: a large Bengal tiger, a pack of wild monkeys, and a huge black bear. I understood the tiger to be cultural practices that hindered peace such as gender inequality, nationalism, or unfair and unjust social policies. The monkeys were the political impediments to peace both national and international, wreaking havoc through backroom deals, corruption, and interference. The bear was the economic factors that prevented peace to flourish, such as poverty, income gaps, low wages for teachers, and the suppression of workers' rights. This moving image was so vivid I could not shake it or forget it like one does with most dreams. I started to think more about it and write it down, embellishing it so it could be a reminder to me not to limit our work in peace education to handing out valentines and seeking only local attitudinal and behavioral changes. We must provide critical lenses, like night vision binoculars, so we are aware of the larger forces that impede peace. Then we need to create opportunities for local actors to strategize how to address those cultural, political, and economic factors that drive conflicts and impede peace.

This "evolving graphic novel in my head," as I now call it, has grown in intensity, especially the monkeys. Some older readers may recall a scene for the 1939 film *The Wizard of Oz*, when the witch sent out flying monkeys to capture Dorothy and her friends. As a young child, that scene terrified me. It is telling that I imagine the military junta as these flying monkeys. (If you Google "Wizard of Oz flying monkeys GIFs" you can see how scary this would seem to a child.) In the film, the story turns out to be a dream Dorothy had in oder to make sense of a tornado that destroyed her community. It was through the collaboration of a very diverse group (herself as an alien to OZ, a tinman, a lion, and a scarecrow) that they survived their ordeal.

I believe this type of envisioning of what impedes peace and what can promote it holds great potential. Hantzopoulos and Bajaj (2021) use this type of envisioning in a collaborative artistic creation described as a possibility tree. They provide an example of first a problem tree that in their words "is a heuristic or visual device that allows people to explore the root causes of a particular issue that affects their daily lives by mapping these causes [in terms of] experiences, policies, and practices" (p. 2). The leaves are the symptoms, or the daily experiences, the branches are what feeds these experiences, while the roots are larger causes. I found this problem tree akin to what Lederach (2003) refers to as the descriptive level, attempting to understand how cultural groups are impacted by conflict.

Hantzopoulos and Bajaj (2021) then re-position this to a more positive version, called the possibility tree. This is what Lerderach (2003) would identify as prescriptive. While the goal of a problem tree is descriptive, to seek to identify the consequences, symptoms, and drivers of conflict, the possibility tree involves transformation, not just looking, but seeing (understanding), with a longer-range lens. It helps us see beyond a specific episode to the epicenter, as Lederach puts it, to "identify, promote and build on the resources and mechanisms within that culture for constructively responding to and handing conflict" (p. 26). In the possibility tree, the leaves are specific examples of what a more equitable, peace-sustaining society would look like, such as a living wage for teachers that is growing off the branch of educational reform. Another leaf might be defunding the military, growing off the branch of military reform. The larger branches are fed by the roots, such as positive peace, human rights, demilitarization, etc. (Hantzopoulos and Bajaj, 2021, pp. 8–9).

I include this description of envisioning peace as it supports many of the activities that were described in the book. It provides a means to contextualize what peace means to local communities, for the people to name what it would look like to them in a myriad of small ways (the leaves), determine what is needed to support it (the branches), and what needs to be in place for peace to grow and develop (the roots). This visual project provides a means for groups to collaboratively envision peace and articulate what is needed to achieve it. It could be conducted independently at first, with the trees shared in small groups, that could be formed into a more robust tree, and then trees from different groups shared with other groups to create a forest, and ecosystem.

In the aftermath of the coup in the spring of 2021, many sectors of Myanmar society united in protest, including teachers, the medical community, factory workers, clerks, store keepers, common citizens, and others. Grandmothers banging on pots joined others to stand up to challenge current injustices, even at the risk of their own lives. Burmans and ethnic minorities joined in solidarity. For many Bamar people, the injustices they faced at the hands of the military on their city streets brought an enhanced sensitivity to what ethnic groups have been experiencing in remote regions of Myanmar for decades. In the foreword, Thawnghmung describes this growing sensitivity:

> Numerous community leaders and members of non-government organizations, including authors in this volume, have joined the civil disobedience movement opposing the coup, and supported in varying capacities or participated in a parallel government now known as the National Unity Government (NUG). Despite many challenges and limitations, the NUG has quickly adopted policies that are more inclusive and sensitive to the needs of minorities.
>
> (this volume, p. xix–xx)

In the months following the coup, while witnessing the ensuing violence and brutality against the common people, some of us asked ourselves if all our work to promote peace and social justice these past years was for nothing. Have all the gains been lost and left the people in Myanmar worse off, with now even more people living in terror and uncertainty? Why, as Thawnghmung (2021) asks in another publication, has Myanmar gone "back to the future"? In this volume, she reminds us that the work of peace advocates, such as the authors of these chapters, was not in vain. She states:

> There is no doubt that increased awareness of and exposure to human rights, federalism and tolerance for differences, through a series of workshops, pilot projects and media coverage during Myanmar's brief democratic era, have prepared civil society groups to push for more drastic reforms in the aftermath of the coup. This edited volume sheds light on some aspects of those grassroots efforts to promote peace, justice, and equality that have been incubated over the past decade and will help guide the nature and direction of opposition to authoritarian rule in the future.
>
> (this volume, p. xx)

With great risk comes great reward and the stakes have been raised for many of the authors inside Myanmar. Those who we were teaching about social justice and peace are now teaching us about what it means to struggle for it daily and the sacrifices needed to bring it about. From February 2021-2022, AAPP (2022) claims that over 12,000 Myanmar citizens were detained and over 1,500 killed by the military. The impact of the February 1, 2021, military coup on education in Myanmar is substantial. In June 2021, over 139,000 K-12 and higher education educators who took part in the Civil Disobedience Movement (CDM) were dismissed from their teaching positions, with many in hiding to evade being arrested (Frontier Myanmar, June 8, 2021). This includes over 19,000 university professors, many who were forced to leave their homes in campus housing and work from undisclosed locations seeking to support their students however they could. In the summer of 2021, dismissed university faculty would be arrested if they tried to teach online due to their participation in CDM. As few as 10 percent of students returned to schools in June (Metro, 2021), many hoping their boycott would demonstrate their resolve in seeking democracy and social justice in Myanmar.

The future of Myanmar is not clear, but the struggle to work toward peace and social justice is. Not only have the people of Myanmar sought to create a parallel government, they are also seeking to establish alternative education systems. Their education possibility trees are growing before our eyes, creating a forest and eco system. The educational re-designers are several: teachers' and students' unions, The National Unity Government, ethnic nationalities' education departments, non-profit organizations, civil society groups, international organizations, and "overseas scholars" invited to participate in the educational transformation by the emerging parallel government. The content of these reimagined education systems is both inclusive and critical, in sharp contrast to the military-backed nationalism promoted in government schools. The hope of transformation of the educational landscape of Myanmar is real, and is taking place in many forms including Spring University Myanmar (SUM), Virtual Federal University (VFU), and other schools that plan to have both a virtual presence and physical campus. Collaborations between different groups are taking place, as they come together to imagine what education can and should be. The Ministry of Education of the NUG is soliciting help from university professors both inside and outside the country to establish homeschooling for basic education, as well as university-level lectures and courses for college students. These emerging innovative and collaborative educational systems bode well for Myanmar, for, as Metro (2021) states, if this succeeds, education in Myanmar can "become not only a response to change, but a driver of it." This collaborative vision of a new alternative more socially just educational system is a prime example of peacebuilding in demonstrating how people in Myanmar can come together across generational, ethnic, religious, regional, and economic differences to accomplish a common goal for the greater good. They have, in Lederach's (2003) words, honed the ability to "recognize an opportunity and design responses processes with innovation and creativity" (p. 59). It is these activists, educators, and peace workers this book is meant to celebrate.

Questions for Reflection

Here is a list of questions readers can consider reflecting on:

1. How has your life journey shaped you and how has that led you to be interested in this book and in social justice and peacebuilding?
2. What activities described in the book did you find most engaging and which will you apply in your own context? How will you adapt them to be more appropriate for your context and students?
3. What theories of peace and conflict mentioned in this volume did you find most relevant and helpful? How will you find out more about them?
4. The introduction asked what is at stake if peace is not made a priority. Make a list of what is lost when both positive and negative peace are not sought out in your community.
5. What peace-related resources have you found to be most helpful? Where can you find more resources and connect with others who are engaging in peace education in your context?
6. This chapter talks about raising the stakes of peace education. What might that look like for you? How could you be more involved in teaching for peace and social justice or in promoting peace in your community or in sharing what you learned from this book?
7. What challenges do you find in seeking peace where you are? How can you and others find ways to address those challenges?

8. Several chapters discuss envisioning peace. What would peace in your context look like to you? What specifically would be different? You can journal about it, discuss it with someone, or work with others to create a possibility tree.
9. If you could create an alternative educational system, what would be its mission statement? What key values would it support? How would it differ from what is currently offered by private and governmental systems?

Works Cited

AAPP (2022). The Assistance Association for Political Prisoners (Burma), retrieved from https://aappb.org/.

Appleby, S. (2000). *The ambivalence of the sacred: Religion, violence, and reconciliation.* Lanham: Rowman and Littlefield.

Bajaj, M., & Hantzopoulos, M. (Eds.). (2016). *Peace education: International perspectives.* London: Bloomsbury Academic.

BBC News Asia. (2021, September 7). Wirathu: Myanmar military releases firebrand Buddhist monk. https://www.bbc.com/news/world-asia-58471535

Bukkyo Dendo, Kyokai. (1966). *The teaching of Buddha.* Tokyo, Japan: Kosaido Printing Co., Ltd.

Dörnyei, Z., & Kubanyiova, M. (2014). *Motivating learners, motivating teachers: Building vision in the language classroom.* Cambridge: Cambridge University Press.

Frontier Myanmar. (June 8, 2021). Junta plan to replace striking staff will wreck education, say teachers.https://www.frontiermyanmar.net/en/junta-plan-to-replace-striking-staff-will-wreck-education-say-teachers/?fbclid=IwAR10H0aQyxGy-zFhEErkRYa_ZcGpLRAi_z2RQhUiE01zsTSYIVMiTD-A8qo

Hantzopoulos, M., & Bajaj, M. (2021). *Educating for peace and human rights: An introduction.* Bloomsbury, UK: Bloomsbury Academic.

Higgins, S., & Novelli, M. (2020). Rethinking peace education: A cultural political economy approach. *Comparative Education Review* 64(1), 1–20.

Kotler, A. (Ed.) (1996). *Engaged Buddhist reader.* Berkely, California: Parallax Press.

Lederach, J. P. (2003). *The little book of conflict transformation.* New York, NY: Good Books, Skyhorse Publishing.

Metro, R. (2021, June 24). The emerging alternatives to "military slave education". *Frontier.* https://www.frontiermyanmar.net/en/the-emerging-alternatives-to-military-slave-education/

Thawnghmung, A. M. (2021). Back to the future? Possible scenarios for Myanmar. ISEAS Yusof Ishak Institute. Perspective. 2021 30, ISSN 2335-6677. Retrieved from https://www.iseas.edu.sg/articles-commentaries/iseas-perspective/2021-30-back-to-the-future-possible-scenarios-for-myanmar-by-ardeth-maung-thawnghmung/

Wade, F. (2017). *Myanmar's enemy within: Buddhist violence and the making of a Muslim other.* London, UK: Zed Books.

Wong, M. S., Matthews, Z., & Kyawt, Thuzar (under contract). Embers of hope: Teacher agency in English education in promoting social justice and peacebuilding Myanmar. In C. S. Duran & S. Boun (Eds.), *English education in Southeast Asian contexts: Policy, practice, and identity.* Lexington Books (Rowman & Littlefield).

AFTERWORD

Ashley South

What an extraordinary and important book—which speaks both to the past and the future.

Reading the rich and varied chapters, one cannot avoid a sense of poignancy and loss. Several of the authors reference the February 1, 2021, military coup in Myanmar. The research and experiences reported here occurred before the illegitimate and illegal takeover of power by the Myanmar Army. They remind us of the relatively safe political and social "spaces" which opened up in the decade after 2011—only to be brutally curtailed a decade later.

Myanmar's contested and tragically incomplete transition was very much a work in progress. The previous government, led by Daw Aung San Suu Kyi and the National League for Democracy (NLD), did little to address the deep-rooted grievances and aspirations of Burma's ethnic nationality communities; other attempted reforms were also incomplete or otherwise disappointing. Furthermore, for many communities in armed conflict-affected areas, the situation under the previous government remained dire, with extensive and ongoing rights violations and immense humanitarian and developmental needs. Nevertheless, there were some positive changes too (many initiated by the previous U Thein Sein regime), including greatly improved freedom of speech and association. Above all, there was widespread hope that Myanmar was heading toward a better future. The Tatmadaw crushed these green shoots of peace and democracy, with the military coup and subsequent deadly suppression of widespread opposition to the military takeover.

The essays contained in this book remind us of the possibilities which existed before the coup, and the opportunities for personal and societal growth which have been dashed by the generals. However, hope lives on. A new wave of brave and dedicated activists is struggling for justice and democracy in Myanmar. Therefore, this book also points to the future, and the transformative experiences which are possible and necessary—the dreams of a country suffering, but with visions for a peaceful and just future.

Now more than ever, there is a need for equitable and sustainable conflict resolution in Myanmar. This book is therefore all the more relevant, despite the deep crisis in Burma.

My own perspective is that of an independent author, researcher, and consultant. I have worked in and on Burma for most of the past quarter-century, with a focus on ethnic politics, conflict, and peace processes (and the politics of language and education, and climate change). For a while about ten years ago, I was quite closely involved with the peace process in Myanmar as a Senior Adviser to the Norwegian government-sponsored Myanmar Peace Support Initiative. At the time, elite-level negotiations seemed to me the epitome of peacebuilding, with lots of backroom intrigue, and attendant drama. Working particularly with a small group of Ethnic Armed Organizations (EAOs) and ethnic nationality politicians, we arguably made some progress—at least until the peace process stagnated under the NLD government. During this period, I also had some opportunities to visit Mindanao in the southern Philippines, and research probably the most well-known and celebrated peace process in Southeast Asia—between the government of the Philippines and the Moro Islamic Liberation Front.

The comparative perspective of analyzing the Philippines peace process helped me to understand that elite-level political negotiations are probably necessary, but not sufficient to achieve deep and sustainable peace. The 2014 Comprehensive Agreement on the Bangsamoro—(arguably) like the 2015 Nationwide Ceasefire Agreement in Myanmar—is an impressive achievement, including many of the political demands of the Moro community, which has long been suppressed and subject to multifaceted armed conflicts. However, following a major clash the following year (the Mamasapano incident, which resulted in at least sixty-two deaths), the peace process almost fell apart, with hardline politicians (particularly from the Filipino majority community) denouncing this agreement with the rebels. I saw how easy it was for populist politicians to draw on deep-seated prejudice and cultural stereotypes regarding the Moro "other," demonizing the minority community in order to score cheap political points. This comparative experience helped me to realize that, without a peace process which addresses underlying attitudes and values ("hearts and minds"), elite-level negotiations are of limited value (although probably still necessary). This is also the case in Myanmar, where decades of military rule have led to distorted narratives and sometimes hateful images of key stakeholders—including ethnic nationality communities and EAOs, which have long struggled for self-determination against a military-dominated state bent on forceful assimilation.

I have been fortunate over the years (at least until Covid, and the coup) to visit many remote and conflict-affected parts of Myanmar. Again and again, communities have told me how much they yearn for peace—but peace with justice, which addresses the underlying issues driving decades of conflict in Burma. At the same time, there is a need to address hurtful and unhelpful stereotypes regarding ethnic communities, often reproduced under the military-controlled media in Myanmar. Without a shift in underlying attitudes and identities, values and positions, it is difficult to imagine peace emerging in Myanmar in a deep and sustainable manner.

At the time of writing, elite-level peace negotiations seem further away than any time in the past decade-plus. However, this doesn't mean the work of peacebuilding should be put on hold. The chapters in this book describe manifold ways in which communities, CSOs, and peace educators can work together, to address some of the underlying barriers to achieving just and sustainable peace.

The pairing of international and national authors in most of the chapters is a particularly valuable contribution. This kind of partnership will be essential in moving beyond the "outsider as expert" mentality which is widespread in so many conflict contexts (and relates to the "banking" view of education, described by several authors).

Editor Mary Wong's opening chapter admirably sets the scene, exploring the connections between critical education and peacebuilding. She introduces the following chapters with a deft combination of personal reflection and policy-relevant academic analysis. Mary highlights the importance of "intersectionality"— the interconnectedness of social realities and actors—and the importance of the political. The aid industry has a tendency to re-frame sites of political struggle as technical problems, amenable to the application of foreign aid. While aid donors and their diplomatic masters seek to reduce risk, this "Anti-politics Machine" (James Ferguson 1994) fails to address underlying issues and can easily become part of the problem—obscuring and marginalizing fundamental struggles, issues, and concerns. Thus the importance of the fine-grained and well-informed peacebuilding approaches described in this book, which engage with (rather than ignoring or trying to marginalize) the social, economic, cultural, and political drivers of conflict.

Kyawt Thuzar and Zoe Matthews explore the relationships between teaching and social change. They provide a useful framework for understanding education reforms in Myanmar prior to the coup, and the parallel ethnic-language education systems delivered by a number of Ethnic-Based Education Providers (EBEPs), mostly associated with some of the country's EAOs. (A topic which other authors also address.) Thuzar and Matthews' chapter is particularly useful for its in-depth exposition and examples of peace education methodologies, which will be valuable for many peace-educators reading this volume.

Kaung Zan and Joanne Lauterjung explore the use of creative dialogue as a learning tool, again with concrete examples and illustrations. Their two chapters include important critiques of standardized aid agency approaches to conflict resolution, which are often limited by donor-imposed timelines and reporting demands. Zan and Lauterjung rightly identify a multifaceted lack of trust as a key obstacle to conflict transformation in Myanmar, and provide a number of case studies, exercises, and reflections to address this complex issue.

Reference to concept of "social cohesion" is mentioned in some of the chapters. I must admit to finding this concept problematic, in the Myanmar context. For many years, under successive military (and until, 1988 state-socialist) regimes, the central government has sought to impose social cohesion, often at gunpoint. Too often in Myanmar, a hoped-for "cohesive" society has been promoted through standardizing and homogenizing differences, generally in terms of a template based on the *Bamar* majority language, culture, and historical experiences. Although "social cohesion" is an unhelpful term, the analysis and practices described in this and other chapters, exploring and celebrating Myanmar's diverse cultures and societies, are of great value.

Melanie Walker, Soe Khine, and Ko Thant explore how narratives of identity and conflict emerged historically, and can be transformed, in the particularly difficult context of Rakhine State. This chapter explores experiences and perspectives of the Rakhine Buddhist community, as well as Myanmar's Rohingyas, who have suffered so much prejudice and violence over many decades. The authors analyze the politicization of citizenship in Myanmar, and the alienation of many youth groups (including from the Rakhine community), which has led to a polarization of narratives and identities. As with the other chapters, the personal, political, and analytical are skillfully woven together—with some inspiring stories of transformation, and suggestions for how to develop a more inclusive curriculum in Myanmar schools.

Also effectively combining the personal and analytical, Jasmine Tintut Williams and Erina Iwasaki provide a useful overview of ethnic-language education issues in Myanmar. Pointing out that some 10 million people (20 percent of the population) do not speak Burmese fluently, they focus on the importance of providing appropriate early childhood education in local languages (mother tongue based-multilingual education: MTB-MLE). As well as the pedagogic arguments for supporting MTB-MLE in order for children from minority communities to get the most out of school, the teaching of ethnic languages and cultures are key demands of ethnic nationality stakeholders, which have long been a driver of conflict in Burma.

Grace Michel, Arkar Phyo Thant, and Katie Zanoni describe an innovative peace education project in Karen State. Despite the emphasis on social cohesion, the project clearly contributed toward transformative outcomes for many of those involved. This chapter also describes the limitations of short-term NGO and donor project cycles, which are often ill-suited to the long-term processes of transformative peacebuilding. As Arkar observes, "Peace is a process, not a project."

Kinsa San Yi, Naw Sah Blute, and Radka Antalíková explore how narratives and images of a rights-based and just peace are included in the government's middle school curriculum—or not. Like several other chapters, this one includes detailed methodological notes, which will be useful to practitioners. Noting the discrimination and structural violence in the existing curriculum, the authors make recommendations for transformation and improvement. They note that in the meantime many teachers are in practice adopting more inclusive and respectful methods, despite the limitations of the curriculum.

Rosalie Metro and Aung Khine described the origins, development, and implementation of their influential 2013 *Histories of Burma* source/textbook. This chapter describes how the Burmese proverb, "Pick up your weapon when you talk about history," can be transformed through skillful guidance and practice into "Putting Down Our Weapons When We Talk about History." Exploring primary historical documents (rather than secondary narratives) allows Metro and Aung Khine's students to adopt the *other's* perspective, and explore different understandings of history and politics. Again, the chapter is rich with methodological and pedagogic insights and advice. U Aung Khine's personal experiences and reflections are particularly instructive, including the disturbing account of his interrogation by the Myanmar military.

The final chapter addresses many of the issues explored by other authors, in Tony Waters' inimitable style. He makes the important opening point that peace is a contested concept, meaning different things to different actors. Waters analyzes the problems inherent in assuming that peace can be produced through aid programming, and the ways in which commissioned research is often used to justify donors' geopolitical preferences and (sometimes unconscious) ideological assumptions and positions. Like other contributors to the book, Waters critiques the donor-centric and Western-oriented approach of many peace-support initiatives, reserving particular criticism for the Joint Peace Fund and other examples of the complacent and self-regarding "peace Raj" (my phrase). These include German political foundations and the Asia Foundation, which together with other aid agencies occupied many of the most pleasant (and expensive) accommodations in Yangon, at least until the coup.

Which brings us full circle. Myanmar today (at the time of writing, but quite likely also at the time of reading) is in a period of deep crisis. First and foremost, this has been inflicted by the military, whose domination of Burmese society has been a blight on the country's peaceful development for over half a century. This important collection of essays helps us to better understand some of the underlying drivers of conflict, and how these can be addressed and transformed through the techniques and values of peace education.

INDEX

www.ingramcontent.com/pod-product-compliance
Lightning Source LLC
Chambersburg PA
CBHW050417280326
41932CB00013BA/1898